"This essential two-volume collection maps the shared roots between abolitionist life-making and feminist resistance, showing us how rebellious organizing and radical care is always at the heart of real change. Brimming with dispatches across borders and prison walls, archives of movement building, and striking creative work, *Abolition Feminisms* describes a breathtaking body of freedom practices, galvanizing us to do everything we can to help forge the liberatory future that we urgently need. Anyone who engages this collection is guaranteed to learn something new."

—**MARIAME KABA**, author of *We Do This 'Til We Free Us*

"This beautiful two-volume collection of essays, poems, and artwork brings a refreshing vibrancy to the radical work of abolition feminism. Inspiring, accessible and far-reaching, the books are precisely what is needed right now: clear demands for radical change, reflections on the power of radical organizing, and radical statements of hope. Readers will be lifted up as they turn the pages, where each entry is a reminder of how abolition feminism is critical to freedom struggles, and our movement will therefore be challenged and changed."

—**BETH E. RICHIE**, coauthor of *Abolition. Feminism. Now.*

"Contrary to popular belief, revolutions don't come with handbooks or blueprints. They do carry histories, memories, manifestos, maps, moments of clarity and deep contradictions, dreams, principles, and real people who endure the oppressions they are seeking to overturn. This extraordinary collective of activists, artists, and scholars understand that this is what revolutions are made of, and that through study and struggle we see abolition feminism not as a variant or a tendency within some larger liberatory movement but the revolution we need to genuinely overturn things."

—**ROBIN D. G. KELLEY**, author of *Freedom Dreams: The Black Radical Imagination*

"*Abolition Feminisms: Organizing, Survival, and Transformative Practice* upends feminism's relegation to an afterthought or appendage of abolition and urges us toward social arrangements defined by caring collectively. One of the most exquisite volumes on abolition feminism to date, this gathering of essays, dispatches, art, and poetry features a constellation of vibrant theorists, including those who have been criminalized and imprisoned. *Abolition Feminisms* offers original insights into the everyday terror and annihilating deprivation facing people inside women's prisons, the work of imprisoned people to challenge gender and sexual oppression, the structuring role of gender violence to the logic and technologies of the carceral state, the nexus of imperial and domestic modes of repression, the carceral production of gender and sexual normativity, settler-colonial and anti-Black carceral violence, and more. Bierria, Caruthers, and Lober effectively establish abolition's feminist provenance in an utterly brilliant account of abolition feminism's decolonial heart, intimate practice, and radical momentum. This collection will be an instant classic in feminist and queer of color critique."

—SARAH HALEY, author of *No Mercy Here:*
Gender, Punishment, and the Making of Jim Crow Modernity

"The creative, political, intellectual interventions in this book, with their deeply intersectional locations of study and methods of analysis, fuel our ongoing work to understand what we are taking apart and to tear it down fully, once and for all. These articles, poems, and images also provide the warm, inviting entry points we need to imagine how bold, risky, ordinary work done by brave, ordinary people is the only path for building a world in which it is impossible for anyone to put anyone in a cage."

—DEAN SPADE, from the foreword

ABOLITION FEMINISMS

ORGANIZING, SURVIVAL, AND TRANSFORMATIVE PRACTICE

Volume 1 of *Abolition Feminisms*

Edited by
Alisa Bierria, Jakeya Caruthers, and Brooke Lober

Art edited by
Amanda Priebe

Foreword by
Dean Spade

Haymarket Books
Chicago, Illinois

Published in 2022 by
Haymarket Books
P.O. Box 180165
Chicago, IL 60618
773-583-7884
www.haymarketbooks.org
info@haymarketbooks.org

ISBN: 978-1-64259-694-6

Distributed to the trade in the US through Consortium Book Sales and
Distribution (www.cbsd.com) and internationally through Ingram Publisher
Services International (www.ingramcontent.com).

This book was published with the generous support of Lannan Foundation
and Wallace Action Fund.

Special discounts are available for bulk purchases by organizations and institutions. Please email orders@haymarketbooks.org for more information.

Cover artwork by Eileen Jimenez, www.eileenjimenez.com,
@maese.art.by.eileen.jimenez.
Cover design by Amanda Priebe, www.amandapriebe.com.

Printed in Canada by union labor.

Library of Congress Cataloging-in-Publication data is available.

CONTENTS

PART THREE: OTHERWORLDS

FOREWORD

Dean Spade

It's August 2021, and I am filled with gratitude, taking in the essays, poems, stories, and visual artwork in this collection. We are waist-deep in what is unabashedly a new moment in the centuries-long movement for abolition. A year ago, our opponents were overwhelmed by the disruptive spontaneous militant actions happening in the streets, scrambling to respond in ways that would restore their legitimacy. New promises were emerging from city councils to defund the police, from universities and other institutions to take up reparations pledges and bring the study of Black struggle and liberation to the center of core curricula, from various extractive formations to stop anti-Black police terror and make Black life livable. We have had a year to see (yet again) what tired, old, familiar backpedaling and lip service looks like, to chart the vast distances between what is promised and what is delivered, and to dive into new fronts of the work to force implementation in hostile council chambers, court rooms, and board rooms. Everything is up in the air, as it has always been, but with new players and new plays at hand. The very idea of abolition went mainstream in a way that could not have been predicted, even if long awaited and anticipated. And the powers that be relentlessly work to right the ship, with all their money and their guns. As usual, all we have on our side is the well-being of all the people on the planet and the utter fragility of their pyramid schemes. We celebrate our victories—prison expansion projects we've forced them to cancel, prisoners our movements have forced them to release, dollars carved out of police budgets and reallocated to human needs—but we also track the betrayals and co-optations with care, learning every countermove and sharing every lesson learned across our states, countries, cities, and counties, circulating abolitionist wisdom and backing up each other's campaigns.

What is more useful at a time like this (and at every time I can recall) than to deepen our study of abolition feminism? Abolitionism is inconceivable without feminist, queer, trans and femme practices of resistance. Millions of new people are learning about abolition right now for the first time, and many are getting mobilized to actively participate in local collective action strategies to dismantle police and prisons of all kinds. One of the threats to this mobilization is the prevalence of masculinist, statist theories of social change. Our opponents would like nothing more than to have newly mobilizable people believe that the conditions they are angry and scared about are going to be taken care of by legislatures, nonprofits, elected officials, experts, courts, corporate leaders, and corporate media. The idea that solutions come top-down through policy, and that ordinary people should limit our activities to voting, donating, being unpaid writers of woke content for social media corporations, and volunteering at a nonprofit or going to a permitted march once or twice a year is a perfect fit for keeping us in our places and preventing the disruptions that actually cause change.

The accounts of abolition feminism in this book are the antidote to the elitist demobilization spell that is feverishly cast and recast to sustain the brutal status quo. This book is full of vibrant stories about how people actually make change that breaks people out of cages and burns those cages to the ground. Tina Shull's exploration of the leadership of queer and trans Mariel Cubans in resistance to detention in the 1980s, which included prison uprisings alongside drag, provides immense inspiration and profound insight into the ways that disposable people refuse death, choose connection, and cultivate capacity for bold and risky resistance together. Gloria A. Negrete-Lopez analyzes the abolitionist femme Instagram accounts that mobilize bodysuits, nail art, and other femme adornment practices to sustain bail funds, to promote feminist, fat-positive, femme-centered abolitionist messages that refuse and disrupt problematic advocacy strategies. Minh-Ha T. Pham's argument that abolition is incomplete without the abolition of sweatshops demonstrates the necessity of internationalist, feminist, anti-capitalist commitments and praxis to all our struggles for justice, making plain that there is no way of remaking a world without prisons and borders without destroying extractive global economic arrangements that require the brutal exploitation of Black and brown women and their captivity in deadly workplaces. Other pieces in this anthology document the grassroots unpaid organizing of thousands of people who have been part of INCITE! and California Coalition for Women Prisoners. This work teaches us how to directly support prisoners and other survivors of violence, beat back carceral expansion done in the name of saving women, and build community practices that actually increase the well-being of women and everyone. Learning from this work is particularly important right now as funders "discover" transformative justice and community accountability while threatening to evacuate its radical politics through institutionalization. Brooke Lober's review of Emily Thuma's *All Our Trials* lifts up the centrality of feminist defense campaigns for imprisoned survivors of sexual, gender, and medical violence in developing the abolitionist strategies and tactics that are still in use today. These accounts of mutual aid work—work that addresses direct survival needs of individuals from a perspective that indicts brutal systems and uses strategies that mobilize for collective action—lets us see exactly how transformation occurs when unpaid people do work to attack and tear apart systems and to save each other's lives. This is transformation that cannot and will not occur through "inside" or elite strategies by people climbing career ladders in nonprofits or government, so it is not surprising that it is work led and developed by BIPOC femmes, queers, trans people, people with disabilities, migrants, prisoners, and women.

This book shows us how feminist abolitionism has always provided a better, more accurate understanding of what we are fighting against than any abolitionism not grounded in feminism possibly could. As so many abolitionist luminaries, like Mariame Kaba, Andrea Ritchie, and Kimberlé Crenshaw have argued, if we do not center the experiences of Black women in our assessment of what is wrong, and in our efforts towards solutions, any attempted abolitionist work will be woefully inadequate and likely reproduce what it seeks to dismantle. The creative, political, intellectual interventions in this book, with their deeply intersectional locations of study and methods of analysis, fuel our ongoing work to understand what we are taking apart and to tear it down fully, once and for all. These articles, poems, and images also provide the warm, inviting entry points we need to imagine how bold, risky, ordinary work done by brave, ordinary people is the only path for building a world in which it is impossible for anyone to put anyone in a cage. Feminist abolitionists look where we are told not to look, ask the questions we are told do not matter, and surface the resistance strategies that our opponents would prefer go unnoticed. We imagine billions of people mobilized for collective self-determination in their own communities, mobilized to change diapers, provide each other with health care, grow and cook food, build local energy grids without fossil fuels, respond to climate disasters, unarrest people, break each other out of prison, help people cross borders and escape law enforcement, redistribute wealth and land, restore balance to poisoned ecosystems, prevent and respond to violence, and end wealth and poverty. The seeds of these new social relations have already been growing, carefully cultivated, carried between communities and across generations, all along. If they weren't, none of us would have survived till now (and we have lost so many), much less passed along this powerful thirst for justice, beauty, glamour, magic, healing, and creativity. This book is a study of those sustaining practices, a vital tool for our next tactical moves in the fight for freedom.

INTRODUCTION

ABOLITION FEMINISMS IN TRANSFORMATIVE TIMES

Alisa Bierria, Jakeya Caruthers, and Brooke Lober

> *The tension builds behind these walls like a wild fire.*
> —Charisse Shumate, cofounder, California
> Coalition for Women Prisoners

This volume was forged during a flux of carceral crisis and feminist insurgency. The call for contributions was released in late 2019, and the project paused, unfolded, and was reinvented as the following months were occupied by the ongoing devastation of a global pandemic; wildfires that wrecked communities and turned western skies a dystopic orange; accelerating crises of racialized gender violence and imposed economic scarcity; another unbearable bombing of Palestine; an attempted white supremacist coup of the colonizing Capitol . . . all of it escalated and often enabled by a relentless system of punishment, policing, and cages.

As much as the violence was breathtaking, the defiance was life-giving. We witnessed and participated in brilliant mutual aid strategies that saved lives and strengthened networks in local communities and around the world; Black uprisings and unprecedented efforts to defund and overthrow the police, the heart of it led by anti-violence feminists and trans/queer activists; refusals by Black, Indigenous, women of color, and disabled feminists to comply with disposability, rebelling within homes, hospitals, prisons, and schools; and the rise of new coalitions forged within dynamic intersections that cross borders, detention/prison walls, and public and private spheres.

1

It has been a *time*.

Revealed in this time (and out of it, as the contributions to this volume explore) is that abolition is inherently a feminist, queer praxis of burning down, shaking off, and building up. Abolitionist politics demand a *literal* end to all punitive systems, including militarism, prisons, policing, the punishment of migration, the entry of state regulation into the social institution of the family, and more. Indeed, abolitionist politics aim to realize a further vision to end all of the social and economic conditions that produce, and are enabled by, state systems of violent control, such as racial capitalism, sexual violence, and genocide. Abolition, as Ruth Wilson Gilmore teaches us, simultaneously calls for *radical presence*, inventions of new (and recovery of submerged) knowledge systems, relationalities, social practices, and shared governance systems that reject racist/sexist punitivity as a foundational principle. As feminist scholars and activists, we find abolition to be foundationally feminist, as it calls for the recognition and conscious enactment of the entwined personal and political. After all, what is more feminist than the everyday practice of willing an impossible future while resisting the deadly chaos of the present?

Eileen Jimenez, the artist who created the cover image for this volume, declares: Revolution is not abstract. Abolition feminism emerges at the fulcrum of many dissident, radical feminisms that are not relegated to theoretical realms but trek between the specific and the speculative. These feminist currents are embodied and activated daily within precarious zones such as the rent, the police car, the safety plan, and sometimes—as this volume shows—they stretch remarkably, forming a transnational and transtemporal reach. Trans/queer/women's revolts inside, outside, and across prison walls; survivor knowledge production; Indigenous feminist refusal of colonial/carceral relationalities; Black feminist fugitive resistance throughout public and private space; feminist of color anti-colonial and anti-imperialist coalitions that cross and contest borders; radical collectivized economies led by poor and working-class women, trans, and nonbinary people; and sex worker and reproductive politics grounded in self-determination and radical care are all examples of abolition feminisms that provide essential blueprints for conceptualizing and materializing the world after the end of the world.

Abolition feminism has sometimes been defined as merely an intervention, an alternative to carceral feminism's paradoxical insistence that safety from gendered violence can only be achieved through the gendered violence of carceral control. Abolition feminism has also been read reductively as a rebuke to masculinist anti-carceral ideologies and attitudes that can't quite shake the premise that feminist and queer analytics are late-stage add-ons to abolition (if that). Although indispensable in their capacity to challenge limited and liberal politics and masculinist norms, abolition feminisms represent a long arc of ethical life-making and everyday practice that has always been at the root of abolitionist possibility, the heart of abolition itself.

Sarah Haley, Beth Richie, Mimi Kim, Luana Ross, Mariame Kaba, and many others have mapped diverse and fluid genealogies of transformative feminist resistance to carceral regimes. Featuring contributors from a broad spectrum of abolitionist critique, *Abolition Feminisms, Volume 1: Organizing, Survival, and Transformative Practice* builds on this rich legacy of deliberate feminist rebellion and reflective analysis. This collection asserts abolition *feminisms* as a pluralist rather than homogeneous politics, recognizing the wide spans of formations of carceral gender violence as well as the deep roots of feminist abolition across contexts of time and space. After we circulated the call for submissions, we received so many strong essays and art pieces that we produced two manuscripts; the companion to this volume is entitled *Abolition Feminisms, Volume 2: Feminist Ruptures against the Carceral State*, also published by Haymarket Books. Together, these volumes provide a chorus of dialogues, political analysis, visual art and poetry, research, and vivid chronicles, all echoing worlds of prescient meaning and action that will radical freedom and expansive possibility into being.

Abolition Feminisms, Volume 1 is organized into three themes: "Genealogies," "The View from Here," and "Otherworlds." Legacies of abolition feminisms have created insurgent possibilities that dismantle heteropatriarchal, white supremacist carceral systems and invent new forms of being and being with each other. In "Genealogies," the

volume revisits these legacies while emphasizing their visions for transforming social relations. Offering a reflective account of the neoliberal
era, it begins upon the precipice of 9/11 and the inauguration of the
"forever war of terror," when INCITE! Women of Color Against Violence, then a newly constituted feminist collective, traveled to Durban,
South Africa, for the World Conference Against Racism. In "Genocide
and 'US' Domination ≠ Liberation, Only We Can Liberate Ourselves:
Toward an Anti-Imperialist Abolition Feminism," Nadine Naber
and Ana Clarissa Rojas Durazo, two INCITE! members, expose the
architecture that bridges feminist of color activism against prisons and
activism against war. This "bridge" formed the ground for INCITE!'s
anti-imperialist abolition feminism, counteracting the policing of the
world and the world of police in and from the home base of empire.
This feminist/queer past is further documented and reconsidered in
"Caring Collectively: Twenty-Five Years of Abolition Feminism in
California," the history of the California Coalition for Women Prisoners, an archival portfolio of political analysis, much of it radiating from
inside California women's prisons. This section closes with Brooke
Lober's "The Presence and Reach of Abolition Feminisms: A Review
of Emily L. Thuma's *All Our Trials*," a review of Thuma's historical
excavation of anti-carceral feminist activism from the late 1960s to the
early 1980s.

In the second section, "The View from Here," the volume continues
to bring attention to the raced and gendered space of the prison and
other sites of gendered carceral violence. Opening this section, "Coronavirus Chronicles," by incarcerated survivor April Harris offers readers a searing visit to the coronavirus ward in the prison, the California
Institution for Women. Adding to the tradition of Black radical prison
letters catalyzing abolition politics, Harris's series of live journal entries
bears witness and analyzes the deathly logics of carcerality, panic, and
confinement as evidenced through pandemic practices within the space
of prison walls. Harris also recounts daring efforts of those trapped in
the punitive quarantine to speak back and take care of each other as
acts of survival and urgent defiance. In "A World Without Sweatshops:
Abolition Not Reform," Minh-Ha T. Pham explores the forgotten

places of sweatshops both *in* prisons and *as* prisons, not only clarifying the specifically racialized, gendered, and (trans)national exploitation of carceral and sweatshop labor and punishment but also enacting an apt read of the material and conceptual co-construction of sweatshops and prisons. Pham also critiques the ways in which "free market feminism" crosses discursive and material paths with carceral feminism to reconfigure sweatshop wage work as "empowered," contributing to the social terra nullius and abstraction of workers "offshore" in both the production of commercial garments and masks for use within the COVID-19 socio-medical crisis that amplified the abandonment of workers and the incarcerated to a realm outside of the social. Tina Shull uses narratives to understand the forms of resistance that arise in carceral space in "QTGNC Stories from US Immigration Detention and Abolitionist Imaginaries, 1980–Present." Through an analysis of government documents, media sources, and the cultural production and acts of resistance by detained migrants, Shull explores the stories of queer, trans, gender nonconforming (QTGNC) migrants in detention and their collaborators since the 1980s. Shull considers how stories, in various forms, serve either to fuel or counter state violence, and how QTGNC migrants and collaborators wield them to forge "abolitionist imaginaries." This section closes with continued attention to anticarceral feminist praxis that moves transnationally and militates against empire, recognizing the role of imprisonment and women's everyday forms of resistance and *sumud* (صمود), or steadfastness, in the struggle for freedom. The concept of sumud is foundational to Palestinian resistance and, in "The Politics of Everyday Life: Palestinian Women Inside Israeli Colonial Prisons," Samah Saleh traces the management of political conflicts and explores the cultural practices that form the pedagogy and the social fabric of incarcerated Palestinian women held in Israeli colonial prisons.

Finally, "Otherworlds" engages the space of anti-carceral feminist activism to muse on its capacities for making worlds and otherworlds. Through rigorous engagement with social media posts that "think for themselves," Gloria A. Negrete-Lopez's "'I'ma Make it Look Fly!': Abolitionist Feminist Aesthetic Coding in Fashion and Adornment" investigates the work of the #DefendTheCriminalized Collective, a group of militant femmes who take to Instagram, occupying the space of capitalist white supremacy for a subversive project. Negrete-Lopez's reconceptualization of movement aesthetics offers the notion of embodied difference as the crux of abolitionist praxis; she examines the aesthetic logics, politics, and outcomes of sartorial and embodied expressions of abolitionist, Xicana femme, feminist ideology, turning against given forms of abolitionist aesthetics to offer a new "comrade"-ship. Christine Finley contributes to the volume's thinking otherworlds and other*wise* by highlighting the role of relationality and "care" as a decolonial, abolitionist tool in "Ghostly Care: Boarding Schools, Prisons, and Debt in *Rhymes for Young Ghouls*." In particular, Finley critiques the carceral and settler colonial institutionalization of care—specifically punitive mental health care among Native communities. More, she critiques the ways in which such regimes of "care" are designed, like carceral institutions, to isolate, individuate, and castigate. To undermine these regimes, she proposes a formulation of *ghostly care* built on relations and sociality with ancestors, ghosts, and kin beyond the temporal, terrestrial, and "species"-level realm to which we are assumed to belong. Closely reading the 2013 film *Rhymes for Young Ghouls*, Finley finds a model for ghostly care among the characters and expounds on the capacity for this model to work toward feminist abolitionist ends.

Edited and introduced by Melanie Brazzell and Erica R. Meiners, this final section continues with "Mapping the Networks: An Opening Roundtable on Transnational Transformative Justice," a critical roundtable conversation first convened at the National Women's Studies Association (NWSA) meeting in 2018. In the conversation, feminist abolitionist thinkers and organizers not only grapple with varied ideas and definitions of the principle-practice of transformative justice but also seek to decenter the United States as the overwhelming origin and practice site of transformative justice as a methodology and analytic. The conversation traces the ways the brilliant and inventive transformative justice formations, especially among immigrants and communities of color in Germany, the UK, Australia, Canada, and the US, give contour to the methodology, and indeed, how these formations critically changed and challenged prevailing ideas of transformative justice. Attending to the local/transnational political and material contexts that give necessary nuance to the meaning and power of transformative justice, the conversation also unearths the ways power can be built not only toward an otherworld but also as a function of "crossworlds" that surpass space and borders to achieve abolitionist ends. We close this section with Ash Stephens's "How Much Do My Black Life Matter?," a revelatory dialogue with Black trans abolitionists, CeCe McDonald and Ky Peterson, that begins with an assertion that Black trans subjectivities and experiences of criminalization and resistance must be centered in abolitionist praxis. Both McDonald and Peterson were targeted by racialized/gendered/sexualized attacks and criminalized for defending their lives from those attacks. Their experiences of *ongoing* political and personal self-defense and participatory defense invites us to engage the principle of self- and collective-defense as a Black trans methodology of abolition. While the conversation provides a fierce critique of the anti-trans/anti-Black violence that constitutes jails, prisons, and parole, it also challenges us to transform Black feminist and freedom organizing, recognizing that Black trans radicals have always been at the foreground of Black survival, and trans visions for liberation map the landscape for Black abolitionist futures.

Art and print culture have also been a central epistemic-emotional political practice in abolition feminist organizing and knowledge production. In line with that tradition, both volumes incorporate evocative poetry, photography, and graphic art that offer another bold dimension of abolition feminist critique and possibilities. In addition to the photo documentation, social media images, and other artworks engaged with and shared by several essays, this first volume of *Abolition Feminisms* features visual art and poetry by Asantewaa Boykin, Esmat Elhalaby, Maria Gaspar, Whess Harman, Tori Hong, Lacey Johnson, Tabitha Lean, Cristy C. Road, Favianna Rodriguez, and Jana Traboulsi. This collection of creative work provides visceral pathways to consider what has been made unknowable or unspeakable, inviting us to engage Audre Lorde's provocation: "What are the words you do not yet have?"

We thank the authors and artists whose incisive and captivating contributions lay bare the political stakes of abolition feminism. We also thank the Abolition Collective for catalyzing this publication as well as the companion anthology, *Abolition Feminisms, Volume 2: Feminist Ruptures against the Carceral State*. The collective has produced a critical body of abolitionist writing and art on their blog and within *Abolition Journal* issues, creating a vital compilation of abolitionist discourse that helped make these volumes possible. We particularly appreciate Amanda Priebe and Mary Jo Klinker of the Abolition Collective, who have offered their commitment to this project as well as their labor and care throughout the process of its creation. We extend our sincere appreciation to the volume's reviewers for their invaluable feedback. We have also been honored to partner with Haymarket Books and their generous and thoughtful editorial team. Their author-centered approach to publishing made it possible to produce these volumes with gratitude, trust, and genuine joy. We are so thankful for our friends, family, and collaborators whose support and feedback were essential throughout the development of this project, including Kinneret Azaria Alexander, Wanda Bierria, Xandra Ibarra, Mariame Kaba, Colby Lenz, Dean Spade, Emily L. Thuma, Lee Ann S. Wang, Craig Willse, and Satya Zamudio.

Finally, we are deeply grateful to our enduring lineage of freedom fighters—social movements, communities of resistance, grassroots organizations, and infinite networks of activists, artists, and theorists—for creating a world where this collection could be imagined and produced. As this volume suggests, many of those moments and people who are crucial to our struggles will never be named in its official archives. May these words honor them. We hope this offering will help inspire future ongoing cycles of conjuring and manifesting freedom.

PART ONE:

GENEALOGIES

GENOCIDE AND "US"* DOMINATION ≠ LIBERATION, ONLY WE CAN LIBERATE OURSELVES

TOWARD AN ANTI-IMPERIALIST ABOLITION FEMINISM**

Clarissa Rojas and Nadine Naber

> *We seek to build movements that not only end violence, but that create a society based on radical freedom, mutual accountability, and passionate reciprocity. In this society, safety and security will not be premised on violence or the threat of violence; it will be based on a collective commitment to guaranteeing the survival and care of all peoples.*
>
> —Critical Resistance-INCITE! Statement on Gender Violence and the Prison Industrial Complex

> *I want to emphasize the importance of approaching both our theoretical explorations and our movement activism in ways that enlarge and expand and complicate and deepen our theories and practices of freedom.*
>
> —Angela Davis, *Freedom is a Constant Struggle: Ferguson, Palestine, and the Foundations of a Movement*

> *[W]e must dream in this moment about what can grow in the absence of empire.*
>
> —Nick Estes and Roxanne Dunbar-Ortiz, "Examining the Wreckage"

---

*   The literary device of placing quotation marks surrounding the "US" references a long tradition of Indigenous decolonial resistance that questions the legitimacy of the "US" nation-state. Since this writing focuses on the "US" empire, we use quotation marks, but we could extend that interrogation to question the colonial afterlife formations of other nation-states or the nation-state itself.

**   The title combines language from INCITE!'s anti-war poster campaigns made possible with the visionary artistic leadership of artists Favianna Rodriguez and Cristy C. Road, whose coalitional praxis was key to INCITE!'s anti-imperialist movement.

In August and September of 2001, just before 9/11, tens of thousands of people of color gathered at the World Conference Against Racism (WCAR) in postapartheid South Africa. It was there that our paths first crossed, as did those of the feminist of color movements with which we walked.* We came from the Bay Area to join a global convergence of freedom movements against empire, racism, and heteropatriarchal violence, and to uplift and learn from the South African struggle against apartheid. In the air were the sounds of sufferers' truth telling alongside the beats of indefatigable resistance and cultural roots unwilling to yield. We joined Brazil's landless people's movements in the streets of Durban, galvanized for migrant and refugee justice for the millions displaced from ancestral lands, and mobilized movements to end militarized borders. INCITE! Women of Color Against Violence was there to build on a global scale with Indigenous, Black, and people of color movements around the world.

We worked on what would eventually be adopted as the United Nations Declaration on the Rights of Indigenous Peoples, participated in global movements for Black reparations and migrant justice, and joined the global struggle for Palestinian self-determination.** We were there to join organizers across the world, building conjoined transnational movements against all forms of racist state violence.[1] The "United States" refused to participate in the WCAR, citing the discussion of slavery/reparations and a refusal to allow the Palestinian perspective to be heard. The "US" made it clear that both the struggle for Black reparations and the struggle of Indigenous peoples, in this case Palestinians, were a threat to its imperial power. At WCAR, INCITE! practiced organizing at the interstice of inherently conjoined movements for liberation. Both the movements for Palestinian liberation and Black reparations emerge, in part, in contestation to the violence

---

*   Clarissa Rojas attended the conference with INCITE! and Committee on Women, Population, and the Environment; and Nadine Naber, who joined INCITE!'s mothership leadership in 2002, went with the Women of Color Resource Center's delegation.

**   INCITE! joined the global Palestinian struggle to define Zionism as a form of racism and the international launch of the "Divestment from Israel" campaign on the streets of Durban.

of the "US" state. Yet the "US" empire works hard to separate inherently conjoined struggles that, when considered together, reveal the different, intertwined strands of its imperial project, for it understands the threat to the "US" empire catapults when these movements converge. The empire benefits when our social movements reify imperial distinctions such as "domestic" versus "global" that both stem from and further the logic that nation-states are natural, bounded entities; or that struggles like Palestinian liberation are about Indigenous people far away, entirely disconnected from the struggles for justice we take up in places like Oakland or Chicago. The "US" issued two seemingly disparate reasons for its refusal to participate, but the global peoples' movements on the ground at WCAR were galvanized at the *convergence* of these movements. We understood that living out our full destinies on this earth, in dignity with, and in honor of, land and life, necessitates conjoined movements that will free us *all* from empire.

INCITE!, the movement of radical feminists of color dedicated to ending state and intimate violence against women of color and our communities, had just formed the prior year. INCITE!'s work was centrally informed by a long arc of Indigenous, Black, and women of color's resistance to colonial and imperial invasions. Since its inception, INCITE!'s analysis posited that any solution to end state violence against our communities must tackle the violent nature of the "US" colonialist state and commit to a politics of decolonization and anti-imperialism that structure and inform all forms of heteropatriarchal "US" state violence—from slavery to the prison industrial complex to anti-immigrant violence, support for the Israeli colonization of Palestine, and war. The founding vision illustrating INCITE!'s global approach to ending violence against women of color states, "Through the efforts of INCITE!, women of color, and our communities will move closer to global peace, justice, and liberation!"

The gathering of movements we attended in Durban took place just days before 9/11 and exposed the global networks of imperialist, colonial, and neoliberal capitalist violence at the turn of the twenty-first century. We did not yet know that we were preparing ourselves on the global stage of the peoples' movements, to commit our energies to fending off the intensified violence the "war *of* terror"* would deploy in the decades that followed. As the "US" expanded its imperial reach, INCITE! pressed on, forging a women of color, queer and trans people of color movement rooted in the praxis of collective coalitional multi-issue decolonial/anti-imperialist/anti-racist feminist of color organizing.

As we write in 2020, the forever war of terror has expanded the architecture of violence the world over. The earth continues to burn as communities targeted by state violence across the globe face even harsher realities from the proliferation of police violence and killings, an ever-expanding military-industrial complex, violent repression of social movements, catastrophic climate crisis alongside continued environmental degradation, unprecedented numbers of peoples displaced from ancestral lands, a global pandemic and the massive siphoning of wealth at the expense of economically devastating the masses. Yet in the "US," social movement coalitions connecting these phenomena, as we saw in the years following 9/11, have dwindled. We see fewer political formations organized by and for radical feminists of color that, for example, connect the struggle against police violence in the "US" to struggles against "US" military invasions around the world and their mutually constitutive capitalist, colonial underpinnings.

We are writing in the politically transformative abolitionist year of 2021, twenty-one years after INCITE!'s founding, on our own movement experiences as coleaders of INCITE!'s anti-war strategy between 2000 and 2005. We write to uplift the theories and methods that emerged out of INCITE!'s formative praxis of coalitional feminist of color organizing to render lessons we learned about the inseparability of abolitionist and anti-imperialist struggles. We write as Arab/Arab-American and Méxican/Xicanx sisters in struggle. Our Indigenous roots emerge in diaspora from lands that are presently known by western epistemology as "Jordan" and "México." Our relations to kin/land inform how we approach our activist scholarship. Our lives

---

*   We called it the "war *of* terror" instead of the "War on Terror" to focus our attention on the global scale of violence it deployed and to center the perspectives and experiences of the many peoples who would become its target.

and ancestors' lives are deeply shaped by the ravages of colonial and imperial wars, by policing, border-making, carcerality, and neoliberal economic restructuring. As migrants and the children and grandchildren of migrants, we have lived through and witnessed the fending off of Border Patrol harassment when crossing the "US"-México border, (militarized) policing attacks on protesters, "US"-made automatic rifles at Israeli checkpoints, the criminalization of our communities, colonialist illness, and impossible bail hikes; and we learned that the predicaments we face in the "US," just as in our lands of origin, are organized on a global scale. Our consciousness and commitments deepened through our participation in the many local and global struggles that informed our organizing with INCITE! then and our scholarly reflection on INCITE!'s work in the pages that follow. The embodied knowledges that emerge through movement participation and generational lessons of survivance are never individualized. We wield a collectively held pen as we walk and write in the company of those we struggle(d) and learn(ed) alongside, with the legacies of the many ancestral kinship networks that continue to teach us.*

In this essay we trace a particular set of pertinent genealogies to what Black and women of color feminists are urgently naming and theorizing as abolition feminism. We reflect on INCITE!'s anti-war and anti-militarist campaigns alongside some of the early roots of what is now known as transformative justice and community accountability strategies aimed at generating practices to counter the carceral and colonial heteropatriarchal patterns of violence playing out within and against our relations and communities. INCITE!'s organizing aimed to end the imperial reach of the "US" carceral state *with* its attendant colonial and militarized police violence within "US"-based Indigenous communities and communities of color. As we reflect on lessons gleaned from INCITE!'s coalitional organizing, we seek to uplift the possibilities of an anti-imperialist abolition feminism that recognizes

---

*   We lift up the countless contributions that forged INCITE!'s movement
      including many generations of mothership leadership, chapter and affiliate
      members, and the efforts of the thousands of movement makers who
      participated in campaigns, events, activist institutes, and conferences.

that our visions for abolition will be as capacious and potent as our framework for understanding the scope of the violence we set out to abolish.

INCITE!'s praxis of what we call a "coalitional feminist of color movement of many movements" articulated a politics that conceptualized the "US"-led prison industrial complex and "US"-led militarism as mutually constitutive. This coalitional approach was not simply theoretical; it emerged out of shared lived and ancestral memories of survivance and struggle. INCITE! forged a collective of feminist of color–embodied knowledges whereby activists embedded in struggles for immigration justice, decolonization of Indigenous lands, Palestinian liberation, anti-war movements, movements seeking to end sexual and intimate violence, and the prison industrial complex conjoined in one organizing space.

INCITE!'s praxis of building a "movement of many movements" also engendered coalitional convergence in joint struggle with other movement formations. Because INCITE! self-identified more as a movement than an organization, its more boundless ends made for frequent coalitional partnering with relevant movements and organizations like Critical Resistance and organizations like the Women of Color Resource Center (WCRC) and the Arab Women's Solidarity Association, San Francisco Chapter (AWSA SF), and many more. Some became formal INCITE! affiliates, such as Sista II Sista in Brooklyn, AWSA SF, and Young Women United in Albuquerque. Up to thirteen local INCITE! chapters across the "US" added to this network of affiliates and partners, fomenting myriad local struggles and catalyzing the politics and strategies of INCITE! as a coalitional "movement of many movements." INCITE!'s movement of many movements brought about an organic convergence between, or a conjoined struggle constituted by, feminist struggles for prison abolition and anti-imperialist feminisms. These convergences led to a shared understanding that "US"-based prisons and policing *and* "US"-led militarism mutually constitute each other through domestic *and* international structures of power. Therefore, INCITE!'s strategy for dismantling prisons, policing, and militarism necessitated a transnational coalitional approach.

As we argue in this essay, by bridging movements that many of us had been forging separately throughout the 1990s (e.g., women of color organizing against prisons on the one hand and against war on the other) within a shared collective movement space at the turn of the twenty-first century, INCITE! was articulating a theory and practice of "anti-imperialist abolition feminism." While INCITE! activists did not formally articulate our "anti-militarism" and "anti-prison" work in these terms, when analyzed together more than a decade later, the INCITE! movement offers an archive for theorizing prison abolition through a transnational feminist, anti-imperialist, and decolonial lens. INCITE!'s political framework and set of movement methodologies have urgent implications today.

INCITE!'s feminist activism to end the prison industrial complex *and* to end militarism and war were driven by an overall anti-imperialist vision and struggle. INCITE! activists understood that while the violence of *prisons and police* on the one hand and *militarism* on the other impact different communities in specific ways, the structures that sustain them—such as global economic neoliberalism, the development of policing technologies, and war—are intertwined. Moreover, while both gravely constrain, violate, and entrap the lives of working-class people of color living in the "US," the structures that sustain them extend from the "US" to the rest of the world and operate through power structures that are global in scope.

In this essay, we frame anti-imperialism as the political vision and struggle seeking to end "US" colonialism and expansion that sets out to dominate the global political economy by controlling land, resources, and labor through military force and/or political, economic, and cultural control. European and "US" imperialism have structure(d) racial capitalism and heteropatriarchy through colonialism and slavery which employed both militarism and carceral strategies. Throughout this essay, our decolonial and freedom seeking aspirations lean on anti-imperialism as a framework and strategy to capaciously hold the convergence of the complexity and variance of colonial and racial capitalist conditions through which Indigenous peoples and people of color have historically been, and still are, targeted by a deluge of state violence—from land, wealth and wage theft to containment, expulsion, illness and genocide. In particular, our commitment to the critical inquiry and activist undertaking of dismantling empire seeks to expose the structural technologies of military and carceral strategies (inclusive of the gamut of policing, prisons, and the detention and deportation regime) that co-constitute the always incomplete project of "US" dominance through the decimation, containment, separation, and disappearance of peoples.[2]

We draw inspiration and guidance from the work of Black feminist abolitionist visionaries such as Angela Davis and Julia C. Oparah as they interrogate the structural and technological symbiotic relationship between the prison industrial complex and the military-industrial complex.[3] They posit that this symbiosis can be understood as productive of the "US" political economy, and we argue it is productive of the "US" settler colonial and imperial state. We situate our analysis of INCITE!'s twenty-first-century approach within histories of anti-imperialist abolitionist visions in the Black radical imagination which together compel an anti-imperialist, abolition feminism. We walk, and write, with deep commitments to ending anti-Black racism, which must necessarily undergird the goal of ending racial capitalism by mapping and analyzing the global structures that sustain it through prisons, policing, border enforcement and detainment, and the "US" war machine.[4] Our contribution joins the growing conversation on abolition in the current era by uplifting the integrity of Black anti-imperialist, abolitionist, and radical Black feminist visions for liberation as we both build on and further illustrate the significance of ending war and militarism to abolitionist politics.

We posit that engaging in the work of undoing carcerality necessarily beckons the work of undoing a social landscape productive of empire, for carcerality is derivative of and co-constituted by empire. This analysis has the potential to grow possibilities of coalitional abolition feminisms that defy the disarticulation of abolition feminisms/struggles from anti-colonial feminisms/struggles, and leading us toward methods, movements, and visionary practices that build a present and future where prisons/policing and militarism are *incomprehensible*. The turn toward coalitional consciousness and praxis, or conjoined struggles, is distinct from the practice of solidarity politics. The latter can hinge on, and reify, ideological frameworks based on separate structures of violence, which enables the bifurcation of social movements that counter structural violence and limits the potential of our political contestation and survival. The coalitional praxis of movements of many movements is the terrain on which we believe the practice and social organization of violence free futures rests.[5]

TU LUCHA ES MI LUCHA/YOUR STRUGGLE IS MY STRUGGLE: LEGACIES OF RESISTANCE ANIMATING THE ANTI-IMPERIALIST ABOLITION FEMINIST IMAGINATION

> *My ancestors knew something more; they knew, tasted, smelled, and felt the edges of multiple deaths. They knew more than just their own death. To share the hemisphere with Indigenous people also experiencing the day-to-day terror of conquest molds the form of your own experience with conquest as slavery . . . I do not believe that genocide and slavery can be contained. Neither has edges, yet each is distinct. Each form of violence has its own way of contaminating, haunting, touching, caressing, and whispering to the other. Their force is particular yet like liquid, as they can spill and seep into the spaces that we carve out as bound off and untouched by the other.*
>
> —Tiffany Lethabo King, *The Black Shoals*

> *Decolonization, as we know, is a historical process . . . it cannot become intelligible nor clear to itself except in the exact measure that we can discern the movements which give it historical form and content.*
>
> —Frantz Fanon, *The Wretched of the Earth*

The condition for the existence of the "US" nation-state is colonialism, empire building, war making, and slavery. To quote INCITE! sister Sora Han, "[T]he 'US' is not at war, it is war." Its character is expansionist—obsessively concerned with the extractivist accumulation of land, resources, cultures, and peoples it commodifies into power and capital. It devours the life of Indigenous peoples and people of color and the lands on which it feeds through the structural violence of heteropatriarchal racial capitalism on which it relies and which in turn imbues its colonial imaginary.* Our peoples have always known this. We come from a long line of ancestors who understood this and wielded a continuous and powerful resistance.

Our framing of anti-imperialist abolition feminism emerges from our conjoined ancestral genealogies, which inform our epistemological commitments to mobilize insurgent anti-colonial knowledges. We continually learn and walk in the footsteps of our ancestors who taught us how to understand, enliven, and sustain the struggle against empire. Nadine's ancestors fought against British colonizers from their land in Al Salt, Jordan, land currently entrapped by "US"-led imperial domination. Partnerships between the "US" and countries like Jordan and Egypt helped normalize the Israeli colonization of Palestine across the Arab region as well as "US"-led wars of counterinsurgency that repress resistance through militarized policing and its sexualized violence, emergency law, incarceration of activists, and the sexualized torture of prisoners. Today, leftist activism across the Arab region, including those that culminated in 2011's Arab Spring, approaches these imperial collaborations by resisting both the authoritarian policing of working-class people and/or activists and various Arab regimes' investments in the global prison and military-industrial complex.

Clarissa's ancestors resisted the continuous deployment of the "US" and México nation-building projects following the Spanish colonial invasions of Yoeme/Yaqui homelands in what, in the colonial vernacular, is known as the states of Sonora and Arizona in the "US"/México borderlands. The first Spanish settlers to arrive in these lands were trained to capture North African Muslims for enslavement during and after la Reconquista. In Sonora, they sought to capture Indigenous peoples for chattel. The Spanish missions and later "US" military forts that followed were institutional structures of captivity built for the practices of torture and disappearing Indians. The policing and containment practices of the Spanish empire since the sixteenth century

---

* José Martí, the anti-imperialist Cuban liberator, and Harriet Tubman both used the same metaphor to name "US" empire and slavery: "the beast."

and the "US" empire since the nineteenth century, which included "US" military and extralegal vigilante violence, targeted Indians in these lands in the period leading up to and following the "US" imperial invasion of México. The institutional inheritance of vigilante settlers and a genealogy of colonial violence formalized into "la migra": the Border Patrol, Immigration and Customs Enforcement (ICE), Customs and Border Protection (CBP), and the Detention and Deportation Regime.[6] The Texas Rangers, which hails itself as the oldest law enforcement group in the "US," is la migra's predecessor. According to Kelly Lytle Hernández's historical account, the Texas Rangers's principal strategy "in defense of the colonists" was to chase and capture people escaping slavery (sometimes to México), to terrorize Méxicans, and to kill Indians. In her place-based perspective of the rise of carcerality in Los Angeles, Hernandez references the Méxican-American War as the historic shift from early incarceration during the Spanish empire to the "boom" that grew incarceration into a "thick pillar in the structure of US conquest."[7] Formal institutions of containment emerge historically in periods of land settlement that condition imperial tactics of nation-building, thereby engendering empire by "securing the nation."[8] This is why policing and the militarization of the border, for example, emerge and escalate with every declaration of war. Punishment and containment/disappearance on the one hand, and invasion and expansion on the other, are two sides of the same coin. They are conjoined and inseparable strategies of empire building that are structured and made material through the technologies of policing and militarization. Indigenous peoples and their descendants are still waging a constant and unrelenting struggle against the violence of policing and militarization on the bordered lands of the "US"-México border. As always they fight to protect Indigenous lands and life.

In *Inventing the Savage: The Social Construction of Native American Criminality*, Luana Ross testifies that since European contact, Indigenous peoples in the Americas have always been imprisoned; they have been "confined to forts, boarding schools, orphanages, jails and prisons, and on reservations."[9] She says, growing up, "I imagined that all families had relatives who went away." Policing and containing difference was, since inception, a tactic of European, "US," and the Spanish empire. In the Americas, we can trace the colonial histories of policing and punishment to the earliest points of contact with Indigenous peoples in the early 1500s. In *Queer (In)Justice: The Criminalization of LGBT People in the United States*, Joey L. Mogul, Andrea J. Ritchie, and Kay Whitlock argue that systematic policing and punishment of gender and sexual variance were integral to colonization in the Americas.[10] This text alongside INCITE! Binghamton chapter member and philosopher María Lugones's analysis helps to decipher this colonial strategy not as a separate colonial feature targeting the queered subject, but rather colonialism targets the spectrum of Indigeneity, the complex of Indigenous cosmologies.

It is through the violence, through punishment, containment, murder, and disappearance that the categorical dichotomization of gender and sexuality is made material, corporalized; it is through violence that the binaries are made. The punishment industry as a strategy of (corporal) colonial control is integral to and productive of not just the bifurcating technologies of colonial gender and sexuality, but of colonialism itself.[11] In her pivotal essay, "Heterosexualism and the Colonial/Modern Gender System," Lugones counters what is falsely understood in reductive terms as the cultural imposition of European heteropatriarchal values upon a variance of Indigenous sexual and gender ontologies by arguing that structured heteropatriarchy in the Americas is the result of the violent practices of colonization and war. Heteropatriarchy, she posits, is made through the colonial practices of policing, punishment, and attempts at the extermination of Indigenous subjectivities.[12]

The colonial/slavery methods of policing, capture, punishment, containment, and extermination are integral to the ontological ordering of the human, the nonhuman, and the anti-human. The global phenomenon of the transatlantic slavery system emerges amidst colonial conditions; systematic slavery makes the ongoing life of colonialism possible. The technologies of warcraft—innovation in navigation systems and routes, devices for slaughter and torture, structures of confinement, the machinations of heteropatriarchal and racial epistemologies—order the ontological dismemberment of (the continuity of) life disavowing the human from the human, the nonhuman from the human. This separation is the root of the violence through which the colonial/slavery projects forge a capitalist, anti-Black racial cartography of humanness.[13]

The conjoined colonial/slavery analytic frame invokes the many ways these twin projects emerge in tandem and considers their afterlife as the imprint on the terrain of our struggles in the present.[14] Without discounting the particular features and histories, this analysis privileges their convergence so as to highlight their deep entanglements in order to incite joint struggle to eviscerate the aftermath, the conditions of violence in the present. This analytical framing recalls and invokes the coalitional liberation consciousness that led to the first abolition of slavery in the Americas in the early 1500s in then named Hispaniola (Dominican Republic/Haití) in response to the many Indigenous/African joint revolts, among them Enriquillo's Revolt.[15]

Maroon abolitionist struggles continued to be forged throughout the Americas thereafter. Maroon societies consisted of Africans who escaped slavery and gained freedom, often living and struggling in concert with Indigenous peoples. Victorious struggles against colonizers were gained by conjoining African and Indigenous epistemological understandings of the land that facilitated, for example, out-maneuvering colonizers in mountainous regions. Using this strategy in Veracruz, México, in the early seventeenth century, Gaspar Yanga, known as "the first liberator of the Americas," secured the freedom of a maroon society in the town now known as Yanga. Oparah relates that in the twenty-first century maroon abolitionists are connected to earlier manifestations by a "survival imperative" whereby the prison industrial complex is understood by gender-oppressed, anti-prison activists as the colonial war waged against Black people. Oparah argues that the activists' analysis destroys the logic of (prison) reform because in a state of war akin to slavery, only the end of the war, or slavery, will guarantee freedom.[16]

In the nineteenth century's smaller version of the "US," radical abolitionists understood and acted in response to the deep entanglements of colonialism/slavery. For them, abolition was imagined as a multi-issue struggle that engaged in the transnational fight for liberation from slavery, from colonialism, and from the rise of global capitalism. Perhaps recognizing that it is impossible to disentangle colonialism from racial capitalism, radical abolitionists demanded and joined struggles for the humane treatment of Indigenous peoples in the Americas and the ousting of the British empire in India.[17] They conspired with the Haitian revolution and anti-colonial and anti-imperial revolutionary struggles in Africa, the Caribbean, and throughout Latin America. Frederick Douglass lambasted the "US" colonial invasion of México in the abolitionist newspaper *The North Star*:

> Our nation seems resolved to rush on in her wicked career, though the road be ditched with human blood, and paved with human skulls . . . We beseech our countrymen to leave off this horrid conflict, abandon their murderous plans, and forsake the way of blood . . . Let the press, the pulpit, the church, the people at large, unite at once; and let petitions flood the halls of Congress by the million, asking for the instant recall of our forces from Mexico. This may not save us, but it is our only hope.[18]

Douglass understood that the abolitionist struggle and the anti-colonial struggle against the "US" occupation of México were conjoined because the projects of empire and slavery were conjoined. México had already abolished slavery, and southern slave owners set out to colonize México in part to expand slavery while the abolition of slavery was predicated on the constriction rather than the expansion of slave-owning states.[19] This is an example of the many ways slavery and colonialism are co-constituted. And so, the abolitionist fight for the freedom of people enslaved joined the fight for México's freedom from colonial invasion.

The anti-imperialist abolitionist imagination and movement in the twenty-first century is rooted in nineteenth-century abolitionist struggles and the praxis of the Black radical anti-imperialist imagination and Black radical anti-imperialist feminisms. W. E. B. Du Bois's *Black Reconstruction in America* takes on the failure to create an "abolition democracy" as the condition for the possibility of the aftermath of slavery and its concomitant capitalist exploitation of Black workers alongside "yellow" and "brown" workers. Du Bois's abolition democracy calls for the social, political, and economic transformation necessary to realize the yet to be realized potential of emancipation. An emancipation he imagined as necessarily anti-imperialist and internationalist as he understood the conditions that produce capital organization and the degradation of workers are global and imperial.[20]

Angela Davis and Assata Shakur are foundational visionaries of abolition feminism and Black feminisms. Both political prisoners, they remind us that prison abolition is rooted in the consciousness and struggle of people who are or have been imprisoned. They also conceptualize abolition in these terms, as part of the strategic move to accomplish the unfinished work of emancipation.

> We proposed the notion of a prison-industrial-complex to reflect the extent to which the prison is deeply structured in economic, social, and political conditions that themselves will also have to be dismantled . . . Prison abolitionist strategies reflect an understanding of the connections between institutions that we usually think about as disparate and disconnected.[21]

Davis's *Abolition Democracy: Beyond Empire, Prisons, and Torture* builds on Du Bois's abolition democracy to further what she initially invokes in *Are Prisons Obsolete?*—the idea that social transformation is necessary for liberation, or what she envisions as a society without prisons—"the obsolescence of imprisonment." For Davis, the twenty-first century struggle for (prison) abolition is also an anti-imperialist struggle that reckons with the vast web of what she calls the "economy of violence" that is the "United States."[22] Davis contextualizes torture in the war *of* terror, and the specifically sexual violence at Abu Ghraib, as inherent to prison practices. Rather than the imaginary that posits sexual violence and torture as incoherent to "US" democracy, she argues that torture is far from an aberration but an outgrowth of what she terms "the circuits of violence" very much present in the continuum of institutionalized "regimes of punishment" in the "US." Sexual violence and torture, Davis posits, "emanate from the techniques of punishment deeply embedded in the history of the institution of prison."[23] She points out that one of the torturers was appointed by the military to the prison in Abu Ghraib precisely because of his prior experience as a "US" prison guard. Davis asserts that it is precisely the task of radical feminist analysis to "think about disparate categories together, to think across categorical divisions, disciplinary borders."[24] By implication, we affirm that abolition feminism beckons us to think across the fabricated divisions that separate social movements.[25]

Throughout her writing and speeches, Davis explicitly addresses abolition in feminist terms and as necessarily anti-imperialist. The term "feminist abolition" first appears in 2013 in her lecture "Feminism and Abolition: Theories and Practices for the Twenty-First Century."[26] In *Abolition Democracy*, Davis frames imperialism as fundamental to the development of capitalism and prisons: "Linked to the abolition of prisons is the abolition of the instruments of war, the abolition of racism, and of course, the abolition of the social circumstances that lead poor men and women to look toward the military as their only avenue of escape from poverty."[27]

This essay also builds on the expansive foundations of Black radical anti-imperialist thought and movement praxis as is documented in *Black Against Empire: The History and Politics of the Black Panther Party* which traces the Black Panthers' anti-imperialism to the long lineage of Black anti-colonialist imagination all the way back to Du Bois.[28] The text relates how the Black Panthers collaborated with revolutionary movements around the world as well as with Los Siete in San Francisco and the Young Lords in Chicago and New York, movements that practiced anti-colonial anti-imperialist politics. Robin D. G. Kelley's *Freedom Dreams: The Black Radical Imagination* also documents the Black radical anti-imperialist imagination. His approach anchors the Black radical imagination in mass social movement praxis as "a collective imagination engaged in an actual movement for liberation . . . [it is] a product of struggle, of victories and losses, crises and openings, and endless conversations."[29] This framing helps us to consider the intervention we seek to uplift by calling for an anti-imperialist abolition feminism that grows out of radical feminist of color visions to see struggles relationally within the contexts of the many interconnected historical and political conditions out of which they emerge. In this sense, we ground INCITE!'s work within histories of struggles that are rooted in anti-imperialist, decolonial, and Black feminist insurgency toward the potential of social transformation; we invoke a feminist of color anti-imperialist abolition feminism that builds on historic and ancestral legacies as it shifts to address contemporaneous conditions.

Shakur frames revolutionary struggle as necessarily anti-imperialist *and* anti-capitalist, anti-racist, *and* anti-sexist.[30] She historicizes the end of slavery as emergent through northern capitalist investments in saving industrial capitalism by weakening the political and economic power of the plantation economy. Emancipation was never the goal; the goal for a "US" state of permanent war is the persistent ploy to save racial capitalism from its impending obsolescence and untenable fantasy. This is why Reconstruction failed and fails again and again and why, as Ruth Wilson Gilmore attests, "the state-sanctioned exploitation of group-differentiated vulnerability to premature death" via prisons and war and labor conditions and everything in between prevails.[31]

Anti-imperialist scholars note the shift in the 1970s to a new "US" imperial role that strategically populated the world with military bases to protect an ever expansive global commodity line and to threaten the global south into compliance while securing profit-driven, racial capitalism's forever need for unfree labor.[32] And as the world map was dotted with military bases, the prison nation was built, dotting the landscape of California, the "US," and the world over with container structures to imprison and detain unfree labor. Beth Richie understands the political apparatus that builds a prison nation as one that relies on an imaginary of enemies and scapegoats to create fear; this strategy is used to legitimate prisons and policing and is also used as rationale to deploy war and establish military bases.[33]

The "US" empire unleashed an explosion of not just "US" military bases in other countries but also a coordinated expansion of supposed-sovereign nations' military and carcerality structures throughout the world. In the Americas, for example, Plan Colombia, Plan México (also known as the Mérida Initiative), and the Caribbean Basin Security

Initiative mapped and financed the expansion of the criminal justice system, prisons, and policing under the guise of the War on Drugs.[34] This twenty-first century neocolonial imperial strategy weakens sovereign state infrastructure by binding states to a "US" imperial form with deep investments in carcerality. The "US" empire exports criminality as an expression of racial capitalism. The expansion in criminality also emerges through a framework that criminalizes migration on a global level. In the most recent era of the "US" empire's war on migrants, the "US" has contracted, financed, trained, and overseen the expanded securitization/militarization of Latin American national borders, leading to massive rates of detention and incarceration of migrants throughout the Americas.

ROOT WORK KINSHIP/WE ARE RELATIVES IMPLICATED IN EACH OTHER'S SURVIVAL: RADICAL POLITICS IN COALITIONAL FEMINIST OF COLOR ORGANIZING

> *There are women locked in my joints*
> *for refusing to speak to the police*
> *My red blood full of those*
> *arrested, in flight, shot*
>
> ...
>
> *In the scars of my knees you can see children torn from their families*
> *bludgeoned into government school*
>
> ...
>
> *we are prisoners of a long war*
>
> ...
>
> *My knee is wounded*
> *see*
> *How I Am Still Walking*
>
> —Chrystos, "I walk in the history of my people"

There was a deep love energy present at the first Color of Violence conference. It was the birth one, and somehow that vibrational exchange among the more than two thousand people gathered made INCITE! possible. Something about seeing in each other's faces the past of so many lives lived, eyes lit up ready for what was being served, ears wide open, and mouths about to tell all of it. In that willing presence was the deepest honoring and lifting up of each other. The collective sentiment that we were there for each other filled the rooms. We were not the same, lived not the same, yet all our hearts beat to Taiko drums and Maori songs reminding us that our roots, like those of trees, grew interdependently, capable of feeding each other the elements of survival: earth, sun, wind, and water. We were, and had always been, deeply connected. In each other, we recognized the plight of times enduring hardship and droughts, and we gathered that day with the strongest sense that sweet as nectar was our destiny. Two-spirit Menominee poet Chrystos went to the front of the room and read the poem "I walk in the history of my people."[35] The reading was an invitation to dig deep enough to touch the roots of ancestral memories, the generations of suffering endured, and to lift up the wisdom and rebellion and joy embodied in our survival. The conference marked the spirit birthing of INCITE! at the confluence of visionaries, movements, and everyday lesbians of color living their best life in struggle.

Just as when Chrystos spoke, in a room of masses you could hear a pin drop when Davis delivered the conference's keynote. She deplored the continuum of state violence against women of color. She denounced the "militarized violence" of the police and addressed the military and the prison as "agencies of violence" tasked with delivering violence. She remarked that centering Indigenous women within women of color formations posited an analytic that exposed and disavowed "the persisting colonial domination of Indigenous nations and national formations within and outside the presumed territorial boundaries of the 'U.S.'"[36] Haunani-Kay Trask's memorable closing keynote lifted up the indefatigable spirit of resistance of Indigenous peoples across the globe in a mesmerizing poetic cadence that condemned the genocidal violence the "US" empire unleashed in its ongoing attempts to colonize Hawaii, the Pacific, and the world over.[37] Margo Okazawa Rey, Elham Bayour, and Lourdes Lugo denounced the gamut of settler colonialism and militarism on a global scale and the particulars of neocolonial occupations in East Asia, Palestine, Puerto Rico, and Latin America.

Loretta Ross addressed the deleterious effects of "US" interventions in women of color birthing and mothering both domestically and internationally. Luana Ross and Ruth Wilson Gilmore described the prison as violence, calling forth powerful testimonies of incarceration. Immigration justice movement lawyer and organizer Renee Saucedo denounced the carceral violence of immigration surveillance, harassment, jailing, and detention that targeted migrant women and youth. The conference and the scope of the many presentations, their combined voices, stories, and strategies was the inaugural moment through and in response to which, INCITE! came into consciousness.

The initial Color of Violence conference took place on the heels of the Critical Resistance: Beyond the Prison Industrial Complex conference held at UC Berkeley in 1998. Many INCITE! leaders participated in the growing prison abolition movement of the period and organized and attended the Critical Resistance conference. INCITE!'s initial formation in 2000 included folks who organized on multiple fronts. While the founding leadership was principally grounded in movements responding to gender-based intimate violence, folks shared organizing backgrounds in anti-prison, anti-police, anti-racist, anti-colonial, anti-imperialist, queer, and feminist of color movements as well as immigrant justice work. Accordingly, INCITE!'s founding principles of unity named colonialism and the "US" nation-state—and by default "US" imperialism across the globe—as central organizers of violence against women of color and our communities. INCITE! moved forward with a radical solidarity politic of transnational, coalitional, feminist of color organizing understanding that a new space had been forged where our combined stories of struggle, survival, and resistance to "US" empire formed a potent movement antidote to counter, dismantle, and transform the violence that plagued us.

Underlying INCITE!'s coalitional feminist approach was the idea that the various structures that maintained "US" empire and the "US" nation-state (colonization of Native land, the prison industrial complex, militarism/war, and border control/targeting of immigrants) were interconnected and mutually constitutive. Our survivance of these very structures both convened us and galvanized deep kinship.

In other words, INCITE! worked from the idea that if any of us really wanted freedom and liberation, we were going to need to address our seemingly "separate" struggles together.

Rather than naming a fixed politics that INCITE! fostered, we affirm that INCITE! nurtured a politics in motion—dynamic, changing, living, at once local and global, and transnational—that emerged out of specific historical and political conditions, from particular genealogies, and a concert of antecedent imagination and struggles. The idea that struggle is disparate, social movements are separate, and actors are individual and fixed in time and space fails to comprehend the dynamic and ongoing life of resistance. Contestation and resistance to the ongoing violence of colonialism, in all its shades, is in continual iteration, mutation, and transformation, birth and rebirth, growth and regrowth. It is a movement to protect, honor, and dignify life, and as such, is endemic to the movement of natural life. It is steeped in innovation and transformation, as generations and experience teach and remember ongoing strategies for survival, offering the mapscapes of potential futurities. The ongoing life of resistance is never separate, but carries with it the struggles all around, and certainly the struggles of the past. INCITE!'s embeddedness in a constellation of social movements and struggles, its deep-seated coalitional methodology, manifested an anti-imperialist abolitionist praxis that we assess, invoke, and learn from in these pages to think through and urge the most effective strategies to get free from violence.

We focus specifically on INCITE!'s anti-militarism campaigns as a strand of INCITE!'s organizing in the legacy of anti-colonial/women of color/third world feminisms. INCITE!'s goal with the anti-war campaigns was to ignite a Indigenous and women of color–centered and –led joint struggle against the intensification of violence that the war of terror unleashed on all of our communities in 2001. Our analysis shows how INCITE!'s work challenges imperialist notions of the "domestic" and "international" and reveals how the "US" operates on a continuum of settler-colonial and imperial wars waged on a global scale that are localized in the intimacies of our lived dailyness and particular geospatial geographies across intersecting lands and diasporas.

We developed these campaigns based on a shared analysis of "US" imperial policies pre- and post-9/11.

INCITE!'s integration of the conjoined politics of anti-colonialism, anti-militarism, and prison abolition, while specific to the post-9/11 moment, drew upon earlier feminist of color movements, especially those of the 1960s and 1970s—from the work on gender justice among Black women in the Student Nonviolent Coordinating Committee (SNCC) and the Black Women's Liberation Committee (BWLC) to the Third World Women's Alliance (TWWA). This organizing, while centering the intersections of race, class, and gender, had a simultaneous/integrated internationalist analysis influenced by "struggles against colonialism and neo-colonialism in what was then called the Third World that shaped [the] critique of capitalism [and] is rarely recognized in 'US' feminist studies.* This internationalist analysis became more and more central as the BWA transitioned to Third World Women's Alliance (TWWA)."[38]

Anti-war momentum and consciousness had grown in the days of the Vietnam War, which moved "US"-based activism in the latter half of the twentieth century toward a decolonial and anti-imperialist framework. In the 1980s, this strand of feminist of color organizing defined women's liberation in terms of ending Reagan's wars in Central America, apartheid South Africa, and beyond, inspiring international delegations and coalitions across the globe as well as connections with the Union of Palestinian Women's Association. In the 1990s, some strands of radical women of color organizing were making connections between growing global economic neoliberalism (e.g.,

---

*　A common assumption in the field of feminist studies is that transnational feminism was born in the 1990s because this is the period "transnational feminism" was adopted in academia, much like the way the term "intersectionality" was adopted nearly a decade after intersectional feminism was named and practiced on the ground in the social movements of the 1960s and 1970s. See Linda Burnham, *The Wellspring of Black Feminist Theory*, Working Paper Series 1 (Oakland, CA: Women of Color Resource Center, 2001), https://solidarity us.org/pdfs/cadreschool/fws.burnham.pdf; and Nadine Naber, "Arab and Black Feminisms: Joint Struggle and Transnational Anti-imperialist Activism," *Departures in Critical Qualitative Research* 5, no. 3 (2016): 116–25.

privatization) and militarism (e.g., the war on drugs) as key forces that connect "US" domestic struggles and international struggles.

Based on the shared understanding that our struggles are intertwined, and a shared commitment to collapsing the space-time distinctions between "US" empire "abroad" and "domestic" "US" state violence, INCITE! strategically became a coalitional movement of many movements seeking to end violence against women and people of color. Our approach placed women of color at the center of analysis about gender violence, revealing that when those most impacted by a confluence of systemic violence become the center of analysis, the actions and interventions imagined can yield a much more effective outcome because the entirety of the systemic structures of violence need to be challenged.

In order to end the barrage of violence perpetuated against women of color, INCITE! committed to multidimensional cooperative formations. In other words, INCITE!'s approach was that the very prospect of organizing against sexual and intimate violence against women of color necessitated an understanding of the multiple and interconnected sets of conditions that made the violence possible, such that, for example, we recognized sexual violence as a tool of war and empire delivered at the hands of the military, the police, the border patrol, prison guards, and schools. We understood sexual violence as an outgrowth and expression of a network of violence that is constitutive of the heteropatriarchal and racial capitalist "US" state and its global aspirations. This understanding called for a coalitional and a multi-issue approach to organizing that sought to build interconnected struggles and movements to generate social transformation toward an end to all forms of violence.

EARLY MOMENTS IN INCITE!'S ANTI-IMPERIALIST ABOLITION FEMINISM IN PRAXIS

> *We call on social justice movements concerned with ending violence in all its forms to . . . [m]ake connections between interpersonal violence, the violence inflicted by domestic state institutions (such as prisons, detention*

centers, mental hospitals, and child protective services), and international
violence (such as war, military base prostitution, and nuclear testing).
—Critical Resistance-INCITE! Statement on Gender
Violence and the Prison Industrial Complex

INCITE! maintained the position that we cannot end gender violence against women and gender nonconforming people of color unless we end state violence and we cannot end one form of "US" state violence (e.g., prisons/police) without ending them all. As INCITE! puts it, "[We] need to adopt anti-violence strategies that are mindful of the larger structures of violence that shape the world we live in."[39] The conjoined movement praxis between INCITE! and Critical Resistance, which began before the birth of either group, reflects a coalitional approach that led to the "CR/INCITE! Joint Statement on Gender Violence and the Prison Industrial Complex." The CR/INCITE! statement, an early document in the archive of abolition feminisms, articulates INCITE!'s abolition feminisms in anti-imperialist terms, calling on social movements to make the connections between intimate violence and the prison industrial complex, detention centers, and the "international violence" of war.

The CR/INCITE! statement challenges the ways carceral feminisms obscure the structural dimensions of violence by legitimating the individualizing logic of the prison industrial complex.[40] It also situates women of color's life experiences at the center of analysis, revealing a continuum of interconnected forms of sexual and intimate violence imposed upon those enduring military occupation, police violence, and migration.

Much of INCITE!'s first year of work focused on building infrastructure and strategy. We built the movement by connecting to local communities through a series of activist institutes aimed at continuing the Color of Violence conference's politicization of anti-violence movement work while brainstorming and developing strategies and imagination for alternative interventions to system-based responses to intervening in intimate and state violence. Building intracommunity responses to intracommunity violence was a strategy to increase survivor of color safety. Many of us worked directly with or were survivors of color who had experienced carceral revictimization by the police, medical institutions, child protective services, jails, and the courts. Survivors of color were often incarcerated, deported, or separated from their children when they reached out for system-based support with intimate violence. We addressed police violence and imagined interventions, solutions, and possible models for intracommunity practices to intervene in, support, and ultimately end intimate gender-based violence.

INCITE!'s abolitionist strategy aimed to expose the prison industrial complex as a structure of state violence principally targeting women of color and our communities, naming how it is connected to other structures of violence (police, western medicine, militarism, immigration, and border enforcement); delegitimate the carceral logic that the prison industrial complex keeps anyone and certainly survivors of violence safe, and exposing it instead as a site of revictimization for survivors; create alternatives to keep survivors from getting caught up in the system; develop practices for increasing survivor safety and violence intervention; and foster alternative processes of accountability that do not rely on the state and aim instead to end violence by transforming the sets of conditions and relations that make violence possible. This strategy emerged in praxis through on the ground organizing and in coalition. What became INCITE!'s abolitionist strategy emerged organically in concert and coalition with various movement formations. INCITE!'s methods for abolitionist organizing included centering the voices of survivors of incarceration, law, immigration, and enforcement violence as well as survivor advocates. Methods also included moving as a movement of many movements in coalitional form with relevant movements, INCITE! chapters, and affiliates. It also looked like organizing! organizing! organizing! through local activist institutes and a task force dedicated to community accountability/alternatives to responding and intervening in violence.

One of our first activist institutes was held in New Orleans in the spring of 2001. It marked the first time we brought into conversation Indigenous practitioners of restorative justice and local community members interested in ending gender violence. INCITE! cofounder

Janelle White led the local organizing, and the institute marked the first time we organized a large-scale conversation about the practice of alternative interventions in violence and about alternative structures of accountability rooted in the knowledges and practices of Indigenous and Black feminist approaches to addressing gender- and child sexual abuse. While Beth Richie and Barbara Smith addressed the dangers of the carceral response to gender violence and shared historic examples of women of color organizing against state and sexual violence, Tina Beads and Fay Blaney from the Aboriginal Women's Action Network (AWAN) of Vancouver and Barbara Major from the People's Institute for Survival and Beyond shared models of community organizing and accountability to address and intervene in violence. Participants engaged in facilitated small-group discussions to assess models and consider how those models might be useful in their communities.

Prior to 9/11, INCITE! had organized an activist institute in Bushwick, Brooklyn, in partnership with Sista II Sista, a collective of young Black, Latina, and Afro-Latina women. An ominous military/police presence surrounded New York at the time of the institute in early October. Sista II Sista's urgency to organize to address sexual violence and harassment in their communities and at the hands of the police intensified. Davis also joined this important early gathering, which proved to be foundational on many counts, but for the purposes of this essay, we highlight the following: the conjunction of a post-9/11 moment congealed a weaponized military/police heightened surveillance/repression and attack on "suspect" and "targeted" communities of color alongside war-mongering, racial, and heteropatriarchal rhetoric and violence; the creative imagination of the youth present at the activist institute catapulted the realm of what we had previously thought possible in mapping alternatives to violence interventions as young Latina and Afro-Latina activists, inspired by Zapatismo, began imagining turning their communities into liberation zones for women; a strong long-term coalitional movement embrace emerged between Sista II Sista and INCITE! that would deeply shape the terrain of INCITE!'s movement work; and the activist institute became a key moment that strengthened INCITE!'s abolition feminism by deepening its connections and commitments to anti-imperialism.

The roots of INCITE!'s vision and praxis were decolonial and anti-imperialist from its origins. Yet the aftermath of 9/11 combined with our direct participation in the global struggle at WCAR deepened an anti-imperialist abolition feminism in the making that included conjoining the struggles of decolonization and anti-imperialism with struggles against the prison industrial complex with a focus on their heteropatriarchal implications and disproportionate impacts on women of color, and especially queer and transgender people; and focusing on alternatives to the prison industrial complex in connection to colonialism and capitalism as essential to ending violence against our communities and building the world we want beyond the structures of imprisonment, containment, and punishment.

INCITE!'S ANTI-IMPERIALIST FEMINISM IN PRAXIS

Once you understand something about the history of a people, their heroes, their hardships and their sacrifices, it's easier to struggle with them, to support their struggle. For a lot of people in this country, people who live in other places have no faces. And this is the way the U.S. government wants it to be.

—Assata Shakur, *Assata: An Autobiography*

After our return from WCAR in South Africa, days after 9/11, and prompted by the urgency of impending catastrophe, INCITE! mapped out our initial anti-war organizing strategy consisting of a statement that addressed the long history of colonial attacks against Indigenous women and women of color while deploring further colonial invasions and expressing solidarity with the people and women of Afghanistan and the Arab/Muslim regions more generally; an anti-war packet coalescing organizing ideas and feminist of color analysis of colonial invasions and the war of terror; anti-war flyers and posters countering representations of women of color and "Muslim women" as "the enemy" and centering women of color voices against the war; cultural arts organizing; collaboration with anti-war formations; and solidarity

with communities targeted by the war of terror. Our anti-war statement, marking the beginning of a protracted anti-war strategy stated:
"We refute racism against Arab peoples and West Asians within the
United States and throughout the world and support all colonized and
occupied peoples in their struggle for liberation, including Palestinians."

Prior to 9/11, INCITE!'s commitment to local–global coalitional
work emerged, in part, out of INCITE!'s commitment to decolonization and anti-imperialism. Most INCITE! cofounders were themselves
either direct survivors or descended from survivors of "US" colonial
invasion. They shared histories of organizing against "US" imperial
invasions in the "US" and throughout the world. The convergence
of feminist anti-colonial commitments fostered a growing connection between INCITE! and anti-imperialist Arab feminist movement
organized through formations like AWSA SF. In the late 1990s, AWSA
SF was addressing the gendered and sexual effects of the "US" war on
Iraq and the "US"-backed Israeli colonization of Palestine. Although
Palestinian feminists were connected with third world women's organizing in the "US" during the 1970s and 1980s, by 2001, they had been
generally isolated from Indigenous and women of color movement
spaces.[41]

INCITE!'s return from South Africa, where we heard testimony of
the global impact of "US" empire, brought the significance of "US"
imperialism to the fore of our work. The military invasions of Afghanistan began, and Iraq was to follow. Israeli colonialist violence and land
confiscation escalated, and Arab and Muslim immigrants in the "US"
became hyper-visible targets of the "US" war machine through surveillance, immigrant raids, detentions, and deportations. INCITE!'s
analysis affirmed that the "US'" war in the South West Asian and
North African (SWANA) region and against SWANA diasporas in the
"US" were part of the same material apparatus of "US" empire.

Drawing upon our feminist of color methodology, while INCITE!'s
founding leadership included SWANA representation, INCITE! was
in the midst of expanding its Palestinian and Arab leadership when
9/11 happened. Consistent with INCITE!'s survivor-centered methodology, an approach where those most impacted should be central to

forming analysis and strategy, INCITE! moved to increase Palestinian and Arab leadership. The political moment surrounding 9/11 called for Indigenous and women of color organizing to intentionally commit to resisting "US" imperialism in the SWANA region and to work in solidarity with Palestinian liberation and connect anti-colonial/anti-imperialist struggles within and outside the United States.

The title of this essay, "Genocide and 'US' Domination ≠ Liberation, Only We Can Liberate Ourselves," reflects the combined text of INCITE!'s anti-war poster campaigns and its anti-war consciousness. The first posters emerged in coalitional praxis with artist Favianna Rodriguez, and they announced anti-war slogans that were decided through consensus over INCITE! conference calls. The poster of martyred Afghan feminist visionary Meena Alexander read "Genocide ≠ Justice, We are Not the Enemy." The poster led to INCITE!'s National and Bay Area chapter meeting with the Revolutionary Afghan Women's Association (RAWA) based upon our commitment to stand behind the self-determination goals of women in the region facing invasion[42] and center their analyses and organizing. RAWA members implored us to continue our anti-war organizing, sharing their realities of surviving the "US" war machine.

Fig. 1. Favianna Rodriguez, poster, "Genocide ≠ Justice, We Are Not the Enemy."

Fig 2. Cristy C. Road, poster, "Only We Can Liberate Ourselves."

The initial "Not in Our Name: Women of Color Against the War" poster urging an anti-imperialist women of color feminism was later adapted to depict Audre Lorde's call to speak out against violence and injustice, "Our Silence Will Not Protect Us: Women of Color Against the War of Terror." After the invasion of Iraq—alongside threats to invade Syria, Iran, and others—the INCITE! posters developed a more explicit anti-colonial, anti-imperialist framing: "Genocide and U.S. Domination ≠ Liberation, We Resist Colonization," with art design also by Rodriguez, and Cristy C. Road's poster "Invading Armies Have Never Liberated Women of Color and Third World Women, Only We Can Liberate Ourselves." The posters positioned women of color, Afghan and Iraqi women and girls as actively denouncing the war while setting the terms for a self-determined liberation. The posters interrupted the imperial feminist logic that justified the war of terror through the genocidal imperialist feminist rhetoric that "white men heroes would save Muslim women from Muslim men." Instead, the posters named and affirmed an anti-war, anti-colonial women of color, Afghan and Arab feminist–led discourse that came to circulate across the "US." On the streets, under freeways, in office corridors, in university halls, and anywhere and everywhere these posters were seen, they consolidated a feminist of color stance against the war and Afghan and Iraqi feminist led self-determination while fostering a coalitional feminist of color anti-war/anti-colonial consciousness. The anti-war leaflets also decried the war of terror's entrenchment of the rigid binary gender paradigm and the exporting of the "US" long-standing violent colonial practices of white heteropatriarchy abroad that wield devastating effects on the lives of Indigenous, women of color, and queer, trans, and gender nonconforming people of color.[43]

INCITE!'s 2001 anti-war packet frames state violence against "US"-based people of color and people of the global south as ongoing forms of warfare, devastating entire families and communities. It states, "the goal of our campaign is to stop the war on women of color and our communities within and outside the 'U.S.' borders." In the packet, INCITE! affirmed that the "US" was founded on and grows its power through the tactic of genocide including the colonization of Indigenous peoples and lands, slavery, exploitation of migrants, mass incarceration, increasing police violence, economic warfare, and forced/coerced sterilization; and uses the bodies of Indigenous women, immigrant women, and women of color to justify, rationalize, and legitimize itself. Overall, INCITE!'s position was that anti-Arab/anti-Muslim (imperialist) racism that justifies the war of terror through concepts of Arab/Muslim misogyny and homophobia is co-constituted with US anti-Black racism and settler-colonialism that relies upon discourses about savage Black and/or Native masculinity and sexual deviance to justify mass incarceration and genocide. Further, sexual assault is essential to "US" militarism, in the "US" and abroad, and is productive of heteropatriarchy as it is coupled with the destruction of the social and economic resources women and people of color need to survive. INCITE! committed explicitly to solidarity with the Palestinian struggle, focusing on how "US"-backed support for Israeli colonization is an extension and reinforcement of "US" settler-colonialism and how Israeli colonization, like "US" settler-colonialism, relies on sexualized violence, including the repression and incarceration of Palestinian women activists. In 2003 INCITE! leadership visited Palestine and, upon return, INCITE! deepened its position of solidarity as is detailed in INCITE!'s "Palestinian Points of Unity."

INCITE!'s collaboration with the Women of Color Resource Center's (WCRC) Women Raise Our Voices Collective led to the creation of "Ten Reasons Why Women Should Oppose the War" postcards and an article published in the anti-war newspaper *War Times*. The article, "War Hits Home for U.S. Women," like the postcards, deplored the many ways war produces violence against women. In particular, the article documented early spikes in domestic violence–related murders of women married to military men upon their return from invading Afghanistan.

The queer-led Bay Area INCITE! chapter was especially active in anti-war organizing, like many other INCITE! chapters and affiliates, participating in street protests, direct actions, organizing an activist institute, and more. The Bay Area INCITE! chapter created an outdoor art gallery exhibit memorializing "The Dead of All Times;"

detailed histories of "US" invasions and their impact on peoples around the world were posted along the columns at Oakland's Lake Merritt. Poets, artists, and activists told stories of survival and invigorated anti-war movement fervor. Shortly after 9/11, the Bay Area chapter joined AWSA SF to create the herstoric coalitional convergence Sister Rise Up!, a weekly local and transnational public education, art, and culture grassroots anti-war music, performance, dance, and fundraising event held at El Río in San Francisco's Mission District.* Sister Rise Up! Went on to inspire INCITE!'s National Sisterfire Tour, which continued INCITE! national's anti-war strategy.

INCITE! activists were also conjoining struggles for immigrant, racial justice, and anti-colonialism while opposing the Bush administration's use of the "war of terror" to target immigrants and people of color in the "US"—whether through intensified immigration control and border enforcement, recruitment of more working-class people of color to the military, including migrants, or overall growth of "US" militarized policing and prisons. In 2002 INCITE! joined forces with Latinos Contra la Guerra, a San Francisco–based initiative coled by Betita Martinez to foster Latinx leadership to both address and resist the war of terror's impact on Latinxs and the long history of military invasions throughout Latin America. Indigenous movements in the "US" and elsewhere recognized that this was a moment that entailed the strengthening of the "US" nation-state with devastating implications on Indigenous peoples and sovereignty. Activists connected to INCITE! were already engaged in homeland struggles in the diaspora—such as México, the Philippines, Puerto Rico, Hawaii, and Palestine liberation movements as anti-imperialist and anti-policing/prison movements coalesced across the "US" through formations like Racial Justice 09/11. INCITE! was there, integrating a feminist and queer politics into efforts seeking to make connections exposing the

---

* In the days following 9/11, the siphoning of state, corporate, and foundation funds to pay for military expansion and invasion depleted social movement organizations of funding, and many turned to grassroots fundraising such as the Sister Rise Up! strategy, which featured and fundraised for a specific local organization every week in light of the growing realization that the "Revolution Will Not Be Funded."

continuum of the violence of war in places enduring direct and indirect "US" invasion as well as in the "US."

INCITE!'s anti-militarist work was based upon the idea that immigrant, Indigenous, and people of color–based communities in the "US" have been devastated by "US" war abroad, inspiring a commitment to uniting around the ways police, military officers, *and* border patrol *already* unite us by relying upon not only similar but also shared systems of surveillance, containment, and sexual violence to maintain and sustain the power of the "US" nation-state (in different places and to different degrees). We protested the invention of the Department of Homeland Security, ICE, and CBP as an expansion in systematic policing, and we developed a coalition approach to accounting for the complexity of the violence along with the economic and health injustices produced by the war, (e.g., lack of access to clean water and health care, increasing the realities of starvation, cancer, and disabilities) in countries under attack and in the "US," leaving women and caretakers without resources to protect and care for their loved ones and communities.

INCITE! launched an anti-military recruitment campaign as a praxis of transnational coalitional anti-imperial feminist abolition. This campaign addressed the impact of intensified militarism/heightened masculinity on increasing rates of rape and sexual assault in the military, in the communities surviving invasion, and in our communities. The campaign also addressed increased recruitment of people of color to be used as fodder for the war despite the false promises made by military recruiters. This included expanded recruitment to low-income and youth of color through schools and neighborhoods and to migrant communities. By signaling the continuum of suffering produced by "US" empire, we refused the imperialist analytic tendency to spatially and geographically separate the impact of "US"-led empire from the realities of life in the "US." Resisting "US" empire in its local and global forms necessitated reframing time and space—it all happens together—even if in different locations. Those of us living in the "US" are indeed still the subjects of imperial war, but differently so. INCITE!'s anti-militarism campaign was driven by the idea that military violence (e.g., bombs, bulldozers, etc.) and what takes place within the geographic boundaries of the "US" (e.g., the criminalization of migrants, detentions, etc.) magnify each other and are moving parts of the same imperial present.

INCITE!'s work repeatedly focused on creating alternatives, not only resisting state violence. The military recruitment campaign offered a vision of a world where working-class people of color would not have to rely on the military to secure tuition, jobs, immigration status, or resources. We offered a vision of alternatives to joining the military so that working-class immigrants and people of color would not have to die or face the high risk of sexualized violence in the military.

BUILDING COALITIONAL ANTI-IMPERIALIST ABOLITION FEMINISMS

> *If there are any people on earth who understand how new york is feeling right now, they are in the west bank and the gaza strip*
>
> ....
>
> *there is no poetry in this*
>
> ...
>
> *there is death here, and there are promises of more.*
> *there is life here*
>
> ...
>
> *if there is any light to come, it will shine from the eyes of those who look for peace and justice after the rubble and rhetoric are cleared and the phoenix has risen.*
>
> —Suheir Hammad, "First Writing Since"

> *Consciousness emerges through liberatory praxis in struggle.*
>
> —Ruth Wilson Gilmore

Informed by the legacy of INCITE!'s movement, how do we move coalitional anti-imperialist feminisms forward? We are living a moment when the violence of global war, imperialism, and its policing elements is intensified; we write to invigorate the resurgence of anti-imperialist struggle. The reproductive injustice and act of war that took place in Oakland, California, in January 2020 when the

Alameda County Sheriff's department used military-grade tanks and weapons to raid and evict homeless mothers and babies from the home where they were staying urges us to take seriously the ways the prison- and military-industrial complexes have not only expanded but are also more intertwined than ever before.[44] The militarized criminalization of resistance has also intensified, as evidenced by the trumped-up charges, protracted legal battles, and the conflation of resistance to state violence with terrorism that activists from uprisings in Ferguson, North Dakota, and in response to George Floyd's death are facing. The collaboration between immigration control, "US" prisons, and the war of terror, evidenced by the case of Palestinian American Ras-mea Odeh, reinforces the urgency of joint struggle. Incarcerated by the Israeli state in 1967 based on a confession achieved through sexualized torture and later displaced from her land to the "US," 2017 brought about the "US'" targeting of Odeh through deportation. Arrested for "immigration fraud" vis-à-vis a "US" prosecutor who portrayed her as a "terrorist" to the jury using Israeli-produced and fabricated doc-uments, Odeh was incarcerated in a "US" women's prison in Detroit before her deportation to Jordan and continues to be denied access to her homeland, Palestine.

Like generations before us, we are facing the ongoing life of colo-nialism with a determined commitment to eschew its derivatives and mobilize the end of "US" domination. Freedom is a practice that necessitates anti-imperialism. As INCITE!'s anti-war posters testi-fied, Genocide ≠ Justice: Only We Can Liberate Ourselves. Here, we outline a decolonial and anti-imperialist abolition feminism emergent from the collective theories and practices of INCITE! and its con-joined organizing with many interconnected movements.

1. **Abolishing prisons, detention, and policing requires decol-onization.** Foregrounding a critique of the "US" nation-state reveals that the ongoing life of "US" empire depends on the colonial strategy to capture and confine both land and people, in part, to extract the resources of unfree land and labor. The prison industrial complex, the "US"-México border, ICE, CBP, and war are functions of this colonial strategy.

2. **Decolonization and the abolition of prisons, detention, and policing requires a return to Indigenous stewardship of the land.** Movements like LandBack call for the return of (public) lands to decolonizing Indigenous stewardship. Rematriation calls for the return of women's sacred responsibilities to the land, for the return of sacred healing practices and ceremonies, and for the return of right relations with all Indigenous peoples, land, and life. Prisons, detention, policing, and the environmentally catastrophic development of border walls take place on unceded territories.

3. **Decolonization and the abolition of prisons, detention, and policing requires abolishing racial capitalism.** Capitalism and its endemic racial hierarchical structure is the integral logic and imperative that fuels settler-colonial claims of ownership and the accumulation of land and labor in/and during the pursuit of dominance. Prisons, policing, war, and borders both produce and depend on the technologies of racism and white supremacy.

4. **Decolonization and the abolition of prisons, policing, detention, and racial capitalism requires abolishing heteropatriarchy.** Heteropatriarchy is a colonial racial strategy that produces gender/sex(ual) binary hierarchies through violence. Policing, detention, prisons, and war produce and depend on heteropatriarchal racial-sexual violence. Methods of sexualized torture and degradation are shared between "US" prisons, the "US" military, border patrol, and policing, reinforcing the heteropatriarchal "war culture" that permeates "US" law enforcement, schools, hospitals, and civil society.[45]

5. **Decolonization and the abolition of prisons, policing, detention, racial capitalism, and heteropatriarchy requires abolishing the military.**[46] Militarism and policing are inseparable material forces enacting the colonial strategy to confiscate land and life. They produce genocide. They populate prisons and detention centers. They are the force behind the colonial and racial capitalist idea of land and people as property.[47] As Sangeetha Ravichandran explains, with every war "the US empire's surveillance, counterterrorism, and counterinsurgency [are] imported from the global war into policing practices

domestically and have always had an import/export approach to their carceral strategies."*

6. **Decolonization and the abolition of prisons, detention, policing, racial capitalism, and heteropatriarchy requires an end to imperialist war.** Through imperialist wars, the "US" operates as the global police,[48] strengthening the power of the "US" domestically and globally while expanding its settler-colonial project and exporting its practices of enslavement and elimination. "US" imperial wars target countries directly through bombing and invasion or indirectly through support of dictators, supplying military infrastructure, or economic warfare like sanctions and neoliberal restructuring.** In Israel, the "US" supports settler colonialism to expand "US" empire and "US" law enforcement are trained by Israeli soldiers in tactics for combatting activists using military force,[49] reinforcing heteropatriarchal "US" systems of policing/prisons. ***

---

* Ravichandran explains that this is evident through the ways in which DNA gets used as a bio-surveillance tool in the global war and is now becoming a mass-surveillance tool domestically. She says: "The US government has also expanded its forms of surveillance, fusing different units of policing and surveillance such as local police officers, ICE/homeland security and FBI . . . Through my research with the Policing in Chicago Research Group (PCRG) at UIC, we learned that Suspicious Activity Reports undergo a process once they are collected that ties these records to FBI databases." Her work with the Arab American Action Network shows that as a response to 9/11, the "US" established over fifty fusion centers all over the country as deposit points for information exchange across units for targeted surveillance of Black and Brown people, imprisonment through terrorism or racketeering (RICO) charges, and deportation.

** "US"-led global policing entails transferring the incarceration of prisoners to secret prisons (for example, in Guantánamo, Somalia, and Egypt) and funding authoritarian regimes who incarcerate activists resisting "US"-led wars. See Adam Hudson, "Beyond Homan Square: U.S. History is steeped in Torture," in *Who Do You Serve, Who Do You Protect: Police Violence and Resistance in the United States*, ed. Maya Schenwar, Joe Macaré, and Alana Yu-lan Price (Chicago: Haymarket Books, 2016), 47–56, which covers how this also plays out in the "US" with black sites like Homan Square in Chicago.

*** The Black Solidarity Statement with Palestine describes the training accurately: "Israel's widespread use of detention and imprisonment against Palestinians evokes the mass incarceration of Black people in the U.S., including the political imprisonment of our own revolutionaries. Soldiers, police, and courts justify lethal force against us and our children who pose no

7. **Decolonization and the abolition of prisons, policing, detention, racial capitalism, heteropatriarchy, the military, and imperialist war requires abolishing borders, including border walls, ICE, CBP, border patrol, and citizenship hierarchies.**[50] Borders and border wars and walls, sustained through sexual violence, such as the rape and forced hysterectomies of detained migrants, divide Indigenous lands and peoples, and returning the lands to Indigenous stewardship requires bringing down the border walls. Policing and militarism depend on the racial and colonial strategy of citizenship hierarchies. Citizenship hierarchies populate prisons and detention centers, separate children from caretakers, fragment kin structures, and turn survivors of "US" imperial invasions into unfree labor.

8. **Decolonization and the abolition of prisons, policing, detention, racial capitalism, heteropatriarchy, the military, imperialist war, and borders requires abolishing the very idea of a crime and a criminal.** Criminalization is the process whereby "US" empire's white supremacy, capitalism, and heteropatriarchy converge to turn people's everyday living (e.g., cultural practices, ways of being, and surviving in the world) into a crime. What gets called a crime and who gets framed as a criminal is a function of racial and heteropatriarchal colonial strategies to surveil, police, and confine Black, Brown, Indigenous, and Asian peoples, cultures, and resistance through, for example, the technologies of citizenship and gender/sexual hierarchies.

9. **Decolonization and the abolition of prisons, policing, detention, racial capitalism, heteropatriarchy, the military, imperialist war, and borders invites embracing, defending, and uplifting resistance movements.** The "US" state has been repressing resistance through racial and heteropatriachal militarized policing, detention, the incarceration of political prisoners, and the conflation of activists with war criminals, terrorists, or

---

imminent threat. And while the U.S. and Israel would continue to oppress us without collaborating with each other, we have witnessed police and soldiers from the two countries train side-by-side." See "2010 Black Solidarity Statement with Palestine," Black for Palestine, accessed March 2, 2021, http://www.blackforpalestine.com/read-the-statement.html.

enemies of the nation. "US"-backed global policing, as we saw when the "US" backed authoritarian regime in Egypt used virginity testing and denuding of women protesters to shame the women of the Arab Spring revolutions into silence, relies on sexualized violence to contain activists, journalists, lawyers, human rights advocates, and anyone challenging "US" empire.

10. **Decolonization, and the abolition of prisons, policing, detention, racial capitalism, heteropatriarchy, the military, imperialist war, and borders invites building collective consciousness and social organization, nurturing the capacity for creativity, empathy, care, and intimacy.** Colonialism, racial capitalism, and heteropatriarchy rely on systems of policing, prisons, war, and detention to debilitate and incapacitate the masses by separating, individualizing, and killing. They disrupt kin relations and intimacies between people, animals, and the land. Collective social organization and consciousness in defense of our sacred relationships to life, land, the matrilineal, and creative spirit can return balance.

> *"We are practicing emergent strategies*
>
> *…*
>
> *How can we, future ancestors, align ourselves with the most resilient practices of emergence as a species?*
>
> *…*
>
> *We embody. We learn. We release the idea of failure because it's all data. But first we imagine. We are in an imagination battle*
>
> *…*
>
> *What are the ideas that will liberate all of us?"*
>
> —adrienne maree brown, *Emergent Strategy: Shaping Change, Changing Worlds*

The abolition of state violence is potentiated through the building of alternative sets of relations and socialities in the process of dismantling the ways of being the carceral state requires and imagines. For example, relational practices within the praxis of community accountability and transformative justice that guide what can be done instead of calling the police into neighborhoods and apartment buildings have always existed and continue to emerge.[51] Through relationships with women and gender nonconforming health-care workers in New Orleans after Hurricane Katrina and our partnership with Sista II Sista in Brooklyn, INCITE! activists learned how to create violence-free zones and health centers led by women and gender nonconforming people of color. Abolitionist analyses and visions that INCITE! fostered continue today through practices whereby feminist of color organizers are building alternative (not system-based) neighborhoods, communities, health-care centers, schools, and social movement structures.

In the 2020s, we find these discussions in the praxis of building feminist abolitionist futures through community accountability, transformative justice, harm reduction, and mutual aid. The labor and visions of Black feminist abolitionists cited throughout this essay have especially potentiated a set of social conditions where prisons are unfathomable.[52] Here, we are positing that the potential for those same social conditions and practices that make prisons unfathomable also make war, empire, and colonial occupation no longer relevant or even imaginable. Indeed, undoing the work of carcerality in the broadest sense necessitates undoing the work the carceral "US" state does to stitch together structures that strengthen the "US" nation-state and its global heteropatriarchal, racial, capitalist, and colonialist expansion.

Abolition feminism that strives for undoing the colonial-imperial underpinnings of carcerality might, for instance, insist on dismantling militaristic practices that constrain our daily life, socialities, and intimacies, and in doing so, work toward unraveling the inner workings of empire with its attendant divisions and extractivist accumulation, violence, and torture. It might also insist on animating socialities, relationalities, and intimacies that converge countercarceral, decolonial, and anti-imperialist ways of being in the world, beginning with, for example, a refusal to organize movements through an imperial nation-based or a "domestic" versus "global" paradigm; crafting sensibilities that bring symbiotic balance to our relationships with each other and with the land; demanding an end to borders, accountability to Indigenous peoples, and defunding the police and the military. The police, prisons, and detention do not keep us safe nor protect us; neither does the "US" nation-state and its imperialist wars and policing of the border.

Against the capitalist product-oriented approach "Presto! You made an abolitionist society!" INCITE! taught us that movement work is constantly becoming, that we build on legacies and lessons learned through practice. We ask in the most generative sense, what decolonial and anti-imperialist practices can we wield on the daily in our movements, socialities, and intimacies to undo imperialist carcerality and carceral imperialism? What other colonial institutions and techniques of violence grow in irrelevance as we invoke the decolonial and abolitionist imagination and corresponding liberatory practices? Decolonial abolition feminism is so much more than a liberated utopic world without police, prisons, or war; it is a heart struggle and process where over time, we learn/remember the skills for living better, in better and increasingly in right relation with one another and all life, on the path to growing the irrelevance of coloniality and carcerality and ending violence.

In this essay, rather than tracing INCITE!'s history, we posit that INCITE!'s method and praxis (and the many movements through which it emerged) offer up a decolonial, abolitionist feminist vision. Mapping and analyzing this vision necessitated unearthing the histories of the ways policing and prisons are bound to systems of colonization and militarism/imperialism against which INCITE!'s work rose up. Our reflection affirms a decolonial coalitional feminist abolition, including the core belief that if we want to abolish prisons, we must set into motion the dismantling of systems that cage and punish while also interrogating and dismantling the "US" nation-state's systems of genocide and war, displacement, and dispossession. We are going to need to make prisons, policing, and war unfathomable. We write then, to affirm and feed conjoined dreams of reaching the deepest freedoms imaginable and those presently unimaginable. The confluence of anti-imperialist, decolonial feminisms and abolition feminisms coalesce the visionary impulses of generations of struggles against slavery, displacement, genocide, feminicide, carcerality, and imperial invasions. Out of the convergence of shared struggles for liberation, the confluence of anti-imperialist feminisms and abolition feminisms enliven the potentiating ancestor-inspired dreams and practices of nurturing feminist of color socialities of care and healing relations with the land and each other through the wielding of cultural wisdom practices and a commitment to self-determination. And if we were to abolish courts and prisons and cops, border patrol, and ICE and empire, with what would we be left? Everything.

NOTES

1. See Maylei Blackwell and Nadine Naber, "Intersectionality in an Era of Globalization: The Implications of the UN World Conference against Racism for Transnational Feminist Practices—A Conference Report," *Meridians* 2, no. 2 (2002): 237–48.

2. Julia Sudbury, *Global Lockdown: Race, Gender and the Prison Industrial Complex* (London and New York: Routledge, 2005); Angela Y. Davis, *Abolition Democracy: Beyond Empire, Prisons, and Torture* (New York: Seven Stories Press, 2005).

3. Angela Y. Davis, *Are Prisons Obsolete?* (New York: Seven Stories Press, 2003); Sudbury, *Global Lockdown*; Jordan T. Camp and Christina Heatherton, eds., *Policing the Planet: Why the Policing Crisis Led to Black Lives Matter* (London and Brooklyn, NY: Verso Books, 2016); Alex S. Vitale, *The End of Policing* (London and Brooklyn, NY: Verso Books, 2017); Julia C. Oparah, "Challenging Complicity: The Neoliberal University and the Prison-Industrial Complex," in *The Imperial University: Academic Repression and Scholarly Dissent*, ed. Piya Chatterjee and Sunaina Maira (St. Paul: University of Minnesota Press, 2014), 99–122.

4. Harsha Walia, *Undoing Border Imperialism* (Oakland, CA: AK Press, 2013) and *Border & Rule: Global Migration, Capitalism, and the Rise of Racist Nationalism* (Chicago: Haymarket Books, 2021).

5. Davis, *Are Prisons Obsolete?*

6. Justin Akers Chacón and Mike Davis, *No One is Illegal: Fighting Racism and State Violence on the U.S.-Mexico Border* (Chicago: Haymarket Books, 2006); Kelly Lytle Hernández, *Migra! A History of the U.S. Border Patrol* (Berkeley and Los Angeles: University of California Press, 2010).

7. Kelly Lytle Hernández, *City of Inmates: Conquest, Rebellion, and the Rise of Human Caging in Los Angeles, 1771–1965* (Chapel Hill: University of North Carolina Press, 2017).

8. Vicki Chartrand, "Unsettled Times: Indigenous Incarceration and the Links between Colonialism and the Penitentiary in Canada," *Canadian Journal of Criminology and Criminal Justice* 61, no. 3 (July 2019): 67–89.

9. Luana Ross, *Inventing the Savage: The Social Construction of Native American Criminality* (Austin: University of Texas Press, 1998), 53.

10. Joey L. Mogul, Andrea J. Ritchie, and Kay Whitlock, eds., *Queer (In)justice: The Criminalization of LGBT People in the United States* (Boston: Beacon Press, 2011).

11. Maria Lugones, "Toward a Decolonial Feminism," *Hypatia* 25, no. 4 (Fall 2010): 742–59.

12. Maria Lugones, "Heterosexualism and the Colonial/Modern Gender System," *Hypatia* 22, no. 1 (Winter 2007): 186–209.

13. Gloria Anzaldúa, *Borderlands/La Frontera: The New Mestiza* (San Francisco: Aunt Lute Books, 1987); Sylvia Wynter, *On Being Human as Praxis* (Durham, NC: Duke University Press, 2015); kihana miraya ross, "Call It What It Is: Anti-Blackness," *New York Times*, op-ed, June 4, 2020, https://www.nytimes.com/2020/06/04/opinion/george-floyd-anti-blackness.html.

14. Saidiya Hartman, *Lose Your Mother: A Journey Along the Atlantic Slave Route* (New York: Farrar, Straus, and Giroux, 2007).

15. Ida Altman, "The Revolt of Enriquillo and the Historiography of Early Spanish America," *The Americas* 63, no. 4 (2007): 587–614; Bartolome de Las Casas, *Historia de las Indias*, 2nd ed. (México City: Fondo de Cultura Economico, 1965), 260.

16. Julia Sudbury, "Maroon Abolitionists: Gender Oppressed Activists in the U.S. and Canada," *Meridians* 9, no. 1 (2009): 1–29.

17. Manisha Sinha, *The Slave's Cause: A History of Abolition* (New Haven, CT: Yale University Press, 2016).

18. Frederick Douglass, "The War with Mexico," *North Star*, editorial, January 21, 1848.

19. Roxanne Dunbar-Ortiz, *An Indigenous People's History of the United States* (New York: Beacon, 2014); Assata Shakur, *Assata: An Autobiography* (Chicago: Lawrence Hill Books, 1987).

20. W. E. B. Du Bois, *Black Reconstruction in America: An Essay Toward a History of the Part Which Black Folk Played in the Attempt to Reconstruct Democracy in America, 1860–1880* (New York: Harcourt, Brace, and Co., 1935).

21. Davis, *Abolition Democracy*, 50–51.

22. Davis, "Keynote" (Color of Violence 4, Chicago, IL, March 2015).

23. Davis, *Abolition Democracy*, 49.

24. Davis, *Abolition Democracy*, 67.

25. Davis, *Freedom Is a Constant Struggle: Ferguson, Palestine, and the Foundations of a Movement* (Chicago: Haymarket Books, 2016), 104.

26. Davis, "Feminism and Abolition: Theories and Practices for the Twenty-First Century" (lecture, University of Chicago Center for the Study of Gender and Sexuality, Chicago, IL, May 21, 2013), https://archive.org/details/733087.

27. Davis, *Abolition Democracy*, 52.

28. Joshua Bloom and Waldo E. Martin, Jr., *Black Against Empire: The History and Politics of the Black Panther Party* (Berkeley and Los Angeles: University of California Press, 2013).

29. Robin D. G. Kelley, *Freedom Dreams: The Black Radical Imagination* (Boston: Beacon Press, 2002), 150.

30. Shakur, *Assata*.

31. Ruth Wilson Gilmore, *Golden Gulag: Prisons, Surplus, Crisis, and Opposition in Globalizing California* (Berkeley and Los Angeles: University of California Press, 2007).

32. Vijay Prashad, *Washington Bullets: A History of the CIA, Coups, and Assassinations* (New York: Monthly Review Press, 2020).

33. Beth Richie, *Arrested Justice: Black Women, Violence, and America's Prison Nation* (New York: NYU Press, 2012); Gilmore, *Golden Gulag.*

34. Ana Clarissa Rojas Durazo, "For Breath to Return to Love: B/ordering Violence and the War on Drugs," *The Routledge History of Latin American Culture*, ed. Carlos Salomon (New York: Routledge Press, 2018).

35. Chrystos, *Not Vanishing* (Vancouver, BC: Press Gang Publishers, 1988).

36. Angela Y. Davis, "The Color of Violence Against Women," *Colorlines* 3, no. 3 (Fall 2000): 4–8.

37. Haunani-Kay Trask's brilliant talk at the Color of Violence conference was later published in INCITE! Women of Color Against Violence, ed., *Color of Violence: The INCITE! Anthology* (Durham, NC: Duke University Press, 2016).

38. Linda Burnham, "The Wellspring of Black Feminist Theory" (working paper series no. 1, Women of Color Resource Center, Oakland, CA, 2001)

39. INCITE! Women of Color Against Violence, *The 'War Of Terror' Intensifies Violence Against Women of Color, Third World Women and Our Communities* (2001).

40. Mimi Kim, "The Carceral Creep: Gender-Based Violence, Race, and the Expansion of the Punitive State, 1973–1983," *Social Problems* 67, no. 2 (May 2020): 251–69; Ana Clarissa Rojas Durazo, "Medical Violence against People of Color and the Medicalization of Domestic Violence," *Color of Violence: The INCITE! Anthology*, ed. INCITE! Women of Color Against Violence (Durham, NC: Duke University Press, 2016), 179–89.

41. For further Arab and Iranian feminist analysis, see Dena Al-Adeeb, "Reflections in a Time of War: A Letter to My Sisters," in *Color of Violence: The INCITE! Anthology*, ed. INCITE! Women of Color Against Violence (Durham, NC: Duke University Press, 2016), 113–17; Zahra Ali, *Women and Gender in Iraq: Between Nation-Building and Fragmentation* (New York and Cambridge: Cambridge University Press, 2018); Sabrina Alimahomed-Wilson, "The Matrix of Gendered Islamophobia: Muslim Women's Repression and Resistance," *Gender & Society* 34, no. 4 (August 2020): 648–78; Sima Shakhsari and Yousef K. Baker, "Sanctions on Iran," mods. Lara Kiswani and Dena Al-Adeeb (talk, Friday Night Forums, session 4, May 8, 2020), https://politicaleducation.org/resources/sanctions-on-iran/; Lena Meari, "Sumud: A Palestinian Philosophy of Confrontation in Colonial Prisons," *South Atlantic Quarterly* 113, no. 3 (August 2014): 547–78.

42. INCITE!, *The 'War of Terror'*

43. For a more comprehensive analysis on trans justice and policing, see Ash Stephens, "Black Trans Men Face a Constant Threat of Police Violence," *Advocate*, May 28, 2020, https://www.advocate.com/commentary/2020/5/28/black-trans-men-face-constant-threat-police-violence.

44. Jill Cowan and Conor Dougherty, "Homeless Mothers Are Removed From an Oakland House," *New York Times*, January 15, 2020, https://www.nytimes.com/2020/01/15/us/oakland-homeless-eviction.html.

45. Chandra Talpade Mohanty, Minnie Bruce Pratt, and Robin L. Riley, eds., *Feminism and War* (London: Zed Books, 2008).

46. See Nicole Nguyen, *Suspect Communities: Anti-Muslim Racism and the Domestic War on Terror* (St. Paul: University of Minnesota Press, 2019).

47. See also Stuart Schrader, *Badges without Borders: How Global Counterinsurgency Transformed American Policing* (Oakland, CA: University of California Press, 2019).

48. Andrea Ritchie, personal communication, 2019.

49. Danny Biederman and Noel Brinkerhoff, "Jewish Groups Pay to Send U.S. Police to Train in Israel," *AllGov*, September 19, 2014, http://www.allgov.com/news/us-and-the-world/jewish-groups-pay-to-send-us-police-to-train-in-israel?news=854302; "Crowd Control: Israel's Use of Crowd Control Weapons in the West Bank," *B'Tselem*, January 2013, http://www.btselem.org/download/201212_crowd_control_eng.pdf; Ali Winston, "U.S. Police Get Antiterror Training in Israel on Privately Funded Trips," *Reveal*, September 16, 2014, https://www.revealnews.org/article-legacy/us-police-get-antiterror-training-in-israel-on-privately-funded-trips/.

50. Naomi Paik, *Bans, Walls, Raids, Sanctuary: Understanding U.S. Immigration for the Twenty-First Century*, (Oakland: University of California Press, 2020); Cristina Jiménez Moreta and Cynthia Garcia, "The Fight to Melt ICE: Why We're Fighting for a World Without ICE," *Level*, October 12, 2020, https://level.medium.com/why-were-fighting-for-a-world-without-ice-b3b104e95498.

51. INCITE! Women of Color Against Violence, "Community Accountability Working Document," March 5, 2003, https://incite-national.org/community-accountability-working-document/.

52. Mariame Kaba, *We Do This 'til We Free Us: Abolitionist Organizing and Transforming Justice*, (Chicago: Haymarket Books, 2021).

CARING COLLECTIVELY

TWENTY-FIVE YEARS OF ABOLITION FEMINISM IN CALIFORNIA

Edited by Emily L. Thuma and Joseph Hankins

Introduced by Emily L. Thuma,
Romarilyn Ralston, and Joseph Hankins

Afterword by Victoria Law

> It's not a me thing; it's a we thing.
>
> —Charisse "Happy" Shumate, CCWP cofounder

INTRODUCTION

In the mid-1990s, medical neglect in California's state prisons for women hit a crisis point. People at both the Central California Women's Facility in Chowchilla and the California Institution for Women in Chino were dying in startling numbers due to inadequate health care. Treatable conditions were being mismanaged or ignored, collective mental health was suffering, and recourse seemed nonexistent. In this context, Charisse "Happy" Shumate, along with other life-term prisoners, began mounting a campaign to stem this state-sponsored violence. Bringing together the energies of existing collectivities of which they were a part, such as Convicted Women Against Abuse, African American Women Prisoners Association, Mexican American Resource Association, Women's Advisory Council, and the Long-Termers Organization, these activists documented examples of medical abuse and neglect, forged connections with activists and advocates in the "free world," and turned to the courts for justice. Their class action lawsuit *Shumate v. Wilson* (1995) not only resulted in a mandate for the California Department of Corrections and Rehabilitation to improve prison medical care but also fueled further activism by inspiring numerous prisoners to become "proactive about their own healthcare."[1] These actions—caring for each other in the face of prison violence, reaching out across prison walls, and pushing back against narratives of crime and punishment—would become the foundation for the California Coalition for Women Prisoners (CCWP). Now, twenty-five years later, CCWP is a statewide organization that continues to challenge the myriad violences imposed on people in California's women's prisons. And the day-to-day ways in which members behind bars care for one another and help ensure each other's survival continue to be the beacon, and the condition of possibility, for this coalition.

From its inception, CCWP has grounded its abolitionist politics in building relationships and collectivities within prisons and across prison walls, insisting that no one is disposable or forgettable. This feminist relational politics takes shape first and foremost through the community organizing and care work of incarcerated members. Helping each other survive the everyday violences of prison is, in and of itself, political resistance. Another crucial building block of CCWP's relational politics is the organization's long-standing visiting program. Visiting brings members on the outside into California's women's prisons to meet with members on the inside, especially those targeted for heightened forms of state-sanctioned violence on the basis of their racial, gender, or sexual identities; their physical or mental health; or their advocacy and organizing. Members on the outside also maintain a letter writing program that provides resources and referrals to people incarcerated in California and across the United States. Stories, poetry, organizing updates, and other dispatches flow in multiple directions through these communication channels and are then published in CCWP's quarterly inside/outside newsletter, the *Fire Inside*. As numerous contributors note in the next section of this dossier, "Reflections on the California Coalition for Women Prisoners," the *Fire Inside* has served as an immensely important source of life-saving connection, a vehicle for political education, and a means of making the organization's work toward a world without prisons as strategic, relevant, and accessible as possible.

Building from the relationships that organizing inside prison, visiting, letter writing, and the newsletter all foster, over the decades CCWP has fought for policy changes that members inside have identified as critical to their everyday survival. Recent wins include Assembly Bill 45, which eliminated medical co-pays in California state prisons and jails, and The Dignity and Care Act (Assembly Bill 2533), which requires state prisons to provide free hygiene supplies, writing and mailing supplies, and notary access to those who otherwise cannot afford these essential items. This dossier documents a recent chapter in the protracted struggle against medical neglect and abuse at the California Institution for Women (CIW), where the suicide rate is presently more than eight times the national rate for people in women's prisons and more than five times the rate for all California prisons. Although CCWP has always been a statewide formation anchored by a San Francisco Bay Area office, an alarming spike in the number of preventable deaths at CIW in 2016 spurred the founding of a Los Angeles–based chapter of the organization. Through direct action and policy and media advocacy, activists inside and out have fought for, and in some cases won, changes to family notification policies, conditions of confinement on the "Suicide Watch" unit, and increased oversight (Senate Bill 960). Moreover, these efforts remind us how the conditions of incarceration undermine hope and mental health both for the imprisoned and for their loved ones on the outside. As this dossier also highlights, CCWP, together with Californians United for a Responsible Budget (CURB), Families United to End LWOP (FUEL), and other coalition partners, has helped lead a campaign to abolish the life without parole (LWOP) sentence in California, where more than five thousand people are presently serving this "living death sentence." These kinds of organizing efforts place the survival of the currently incarcerated at the heart of the project of prison abolition.

These fights to challenge conditions of confinement and push for decarceration also involve efforts to shift larger narratives about incarceration and gender-based violence. The coalitional campaign to DROP

LWOP, for instance, highlights the fact that the overwhelming majority of women serving LWOP sentences in California are survivors of violence; among them are women convicted of killing or "masterminding" the killing of their abusers as well as women convicted of "aiding and abetting" their abusers.* As this dossier shows, the visual storytelling project *A Living Chance* humanizes statistics and works to transform the conversation around extreme sentencing. In another register, trans, gender nonconforming, and queer currently and formerly incarcerated people in California's women's prisons are at the forefront of #MeTooBehindBars, a critical refusal of the carceral dimensions of the mainstream #MeToo discourse. This campaign shines a light on ubiquitous gender-based and sexual violence behind carceral walls, and, in turn, illuminates the foundational contradiction of promoting caging as a solution to rape and abuse. CCWP's narrative-shifting anti-violence work also takes place through the national coalition Survived and Punished (S&P), of which the organization is a founding member. S&P amplifies the stories of criminalized survivors of sexual and gender-based violence and insists that, as cofounder Mariame Kaba puts it, "prison is not feminist."

CCWP's abolitionist feminist politics are perhaps best summed up by its motto, *caring collectively*. Caring collectively for people in women's prisons over the last twenty-five years has meant refusing false and undermining dichotomies of "violent" and "nonviolent," victim and perpetrator, survival work and political resistance, and fighting to improve prison conditions and to abolish imprisonment. It has meant fierce, persistent organizing inside of prisons, advocating for "non-reformist reforms" that improve conditions of confinement and forge pathways for release, relationship building across walls and organizations, and "not mess[ing] over people in the name of politics," in the words of the Combahee

---

* Women are frequently cast as behind-the-scenes organizers and sentenced to long terms for harms they did not directly cause. Moreover, contexts of intimate violence are frequently disregarded. For analyses of how sexism exacerbates extreme sentencing, see especially Beth Richie, *Compelled to Crime: The Gender Entrapment of Battered Black Women* (New York: Routledge Press, 1995); and Alisa Bierria and Colby Lenz, "Battering Court Syndrome: A Structural Critique of 'Failure to Protect,'" in *The Politicization of Safety*, ed. Jane K. Stoever (New York: New York University Press, 2019).

River Collective.[2] And as CCWP touchstone and cofounder Shumate wrote in the first issue of the *Fire Inside*, "the battle must go on."
—Emily L. Thuma, Romarilyn Ralston, and Joseph Hankins

REFLECTIONS ON THE CALIFORNIA COALITION FOR WOMEN PRISONERS

To mark the twenty-fifth anniversary of the founding of CCWP, we asked members on both sides of the walls to share their reflections, either in writing or through conversation, on the organization's history, its contributions to the movement for abolition, and its practices of caring collectively.* Below are excerpts from conversations with and written reflections by more than two dozen CCWP members, the majority of whom are currently or formerly incarcerated in California's state prisons for women.

How did you first get involved with CCWP?

Mary Shields (MS): Happy [Charisse Shumate] stood up for us and did something. Something like twenty-four people had died in two weeks from medical neglect [at the California Correctional Women's Facility]. I worked in the infirmary, so I saw so many problems. Happy told me to remember everything, not to write anything down in case I got searched. So I remembered all the problems and told Happy later. She wrote it all down. She got everyone to do this, got us to remember the problems without writing them down, and then tell her. She organized all of us, got more and more of us to report the mistreatment. And she started getting really serious about reaching out to people outside. She kept going and going until she reached people who would help. She kept her notes in a legal folder so it couldn't be searched, but she still wrote

---

* For their example, we thank Liz Samuels and David Stein, Critical Resistance members who edited a similar compilation of reflections on the tenth anniversary of the founding of CCWP ally organization Critical Resistance. See Liz Samuels and David Stein, "Perspectives on Critical Resistance," in *Abolition Now! Ten Years of Strategy and Struggle Against the Prison Industrial Complex*, ed. CR10 Publications Collective (Oakland: AK Press, 2008), 1–14.

everything in code, just in case. Finally, she got in touch with a group of ladies who really wanted to know what was going on. That's how legal visiting got started. And Happy pulled me right into it. CCWP then became a group around '94 or '95. I still have the first *Fire Inside*.

Urszula Wislanka: To celebrate Mother's Day in the 1990s, I was given a leaflet asking to come to a meeting to support women prisoners' collective challenge to lack/abuse of health care in women's prisons. I had been a feminist my whole life, and advocated for US prisoners since the mid-1970s, but it had not even occurred to me that women can also be prisoners! I got involved in supporting the organizing effort of women prisoners, one expression of which was the *Shumate v. Wilson* lawsuit.

Aakifah Smith: Charisse Shumate was assigned to me when I first came to prison because I have sickle cell, so I was placed in her unit. She told me about the attorneys and the lawsuit she had in place. At the time I was young and too immature to understand the depths of the *Fire Inside*. However, I understood the impact Happy had on my life.

Fig. 1. Cover of the very first issue of the *Fire Inside*. Courtesy of CCWP.

Diana Block (DB): I first got involved when I attended an International Women's Day event in the San Francisco Women's Building in March 1996. This was CCWP's first public event since it had been founded in 1995 by women inside prison and advocates on the outside who were friends of mine. Angela Davis was the keynote speaker, and hundreds of people crammed the auditorium to hear her speak. The event greatly inspired me, and I decided to become part of building this new organization.

Mara Plascencia: When I aided a correctional officer by attempting to prevent a woman from attempting suicide, I was placed in AdSeg [administrative segregation] pending investigation. When CCWP discovered the injustice that I was dealing with, they immediately became proactive.

Hamdiyah Cooks-Abdullah (HCA): My first involvement with CCWP was in 2002 when I was released from prison after serving twenty years. Some

Fig. 2. Charisse "Happy" Shumate.

of the women I had befriended inside worked for LSPC [Legal Services for Prisoners with Children], and CCWP had office space inside LSPC's building. The work CCWP was doing always attracted me because the volunteers were going into jails and women's prisons, and I wanted to be a part of this work in any shape or form. I knew it would be difficult getting clearance so soon after my release, so I helped in every way I could—such as answering letters and phone calls, and giving presentations in schools and organizations throughout Alameda County on incarceration and the challenges I experienced post release. The volunteers and women I connected with inside helped fulfill my life after being away for so long. I considered myself very honored to keep working on behalf of the women and was blessed to be chosen as the executive director of CCWP in March 2005. I worked in this capacity until September 2008. We were a small but powerful force in the work around conditions of confinement for people living in women's prisons.

Debbie Lowe: Back in the year 2002 or earlier, I started getting visits [from CCWP members]. At that time in my life, I needed visits. Someone who loved and cared about me gave my name to CCWP . . . and today, I am still involved.

Laura Purviance (LP): My peers inside would share with me their copies of the *Fire Inside*, and I really appreciated a newsletter aimed at someone like me. That connection with the outside at the start of my fifty–life sentence has helped keep me motivated in making the most of my time while incarcerated.

Amy Moss: Over the years, I would come across the *Fire Inside*. I can't recall exactly how or when. I most likely was in AdSeg. Then I started reading more and more about advocating. Then I started a civil suit and started networking with others. . . . Now I'm in constant contact [with CCWP].

Jane Dorotik (JD): I have known and worked with CCWP since around 2003. What most impresses me is the willingness to solicit our voices in any and all initiatives toward reforming the system.

Susan Bustamante: I first got involved in CCWP through being interviewed by Adrienne [Skye Roberts] for the Living Chance project.* Being an LWOP, anybody who was willing to hear us caught my attention and my respect right off the bat. Knowing somebody's listening is really important because the lifers get heard by attorneys and the Board of Parole but not LWOPs. . . . And now, getting to be on the outside with everybody, that really shows me that I was on the right path back then. Being out, I'm even more on fire because I know who I left behind. And CCWP makes the way.

---

*   See section III of this dossier for more information on this project.

Fig. 3. CCWP members welcome Jane Dorotik as she was released from the California Institution for Women after twenty years of incarceration, April 23, 2020. Courtesy of CCWP.

Donna Jelenic: I first heard about CCWP several years after I got [to CIW], more than likely at one of our Long-Termers Organization meetings. Someone asked me if I wanted to read the *Fire Inside*. I remember writing an article and submitting it; they printed it. I can remember thinking, "They really care."

Anonymous: My first involvement was when I read a copy of *The Fire Inside* in 2010 at VSPW [Valley State Prison for Women]. That was my first year in prison, newly arrived from county jail. That newsletter gave me hope again when I was feeling hopeless, facing a twenty-six-year sentence that had been mishandled by public defenders. Conviction was, for me, something worse than what I actually was guilty of. I felt a great deal of shame, low self-esteem, and traumatic pain. I found myself engulfed in deep grief, and surrounded by many other women, fellow peers, especially [the] long-termers and lifers and LWOPs who were also grieving in the same way. Every issue of the newsletter has helped me feel less isolated and more hopeful and worthy to live on as I heal, change, grow, and transform.

Irma Noriega: I wrote [the letter-writing team] once about a child custody case and even though they couldn't personally help me, they sent me a whole packet full of resources. . . . I didn't expect that. It was awesome.

CCWP turns twenty-five this year. What do you want people to know about the organization's history?

Eva Nagao: CCWP is not just a coalition *for* women and trans prisoners, it is a coalition started and driven *by* women and trans prisoners.

Manuel La Fontaine (MLF): CCWP is a women and gender non-conforming–led movement, rooted in the human dignity and liberation struggle of people being held in captivity inside cages in California.

Tien Mo (TM): I think Charisse summed it up best: "When times get rough, hold your head up and know that you may be free or dead . . . before you see the change that we fight so hard for. But stay in peace with yourself that you are doing the right thing. It's not a 'me' thing, it's a 'we' thing." I believe that was written almost thirty years ago, yet still gives hope to all of us doing time in 2020. She fought and advocated for incarcerated people with AIDS, HIV-positive, and other medical issues, with strength and vigor, in the days when it was taboo to do so.

DB: We wanted to build an organization that took direction from the women/trans people inside and could also offer a place where former prisoners and women of color could develop their leadership. We wanted to fight the racism and gender violence that was central to the prison system and challenge the very existence of the prison industrial complex. We wanted CCWP to become a community as well as an organization. And we wanted to put visiting in the women's prisons at the core of our organization. Over the past twenty-five years, we have consistently upheld these values and organizing methods.

MS: [CCWP] has been my everything. Charisse's commitment to truth and to everyone getting a second chance is one of the things that really pulled us all together. And I think that commitment is still what pulls us all together. I try to live in a way that honors her and that commitment in every way I can. Even after all these years, our relationships with each other hold us all together. At the DROP LWOP rally last week, I saw Diana [Block], one of the first people Happy connected with outside, and we hugged. That connection, our love for each other, has been such a strong part of my life over these years. I want people to know to "reach back and touch one." If we reach back and touch enough people, we have a strong organization.

JD: This organization brings HOPE with a capital H to a segment of society (prisoners) that are mostly overlooked, vilified, misunderstood, and cast aside.

LP: The thing that most sticks out to me is the commuted—LWOPs who are now working with CCWP outside—these are outstanding human beings. They had been in contact with CCWP, and I can better appreciate *now* how that support helped them to show others in positions of authority that they deserved another chance. Those previously incarcerated people were group leaders, peer mentors, and community pillars who had far transcended the actions of their pasts which put them in prison. Seeing pictures and articles of them continuing the fight out there to help us who are still inside is so uplifting. That is the sort of legacy CCWP facilitates.

Amber Bray: One thing that I believe is incredibly remarkable about CCWP's history is the fact that they have hired a former LWOP to help coordinate various projects CCWP is pursuing, including the DROP LWOP campaign. I believe this speaks to their integrity and truly wanting to end a sentence that is a living death sentence.

Kelly Savage: CCWP actually comes inside the prison and listens and then isn't afraid to fight. Whether someone needs help with a commutation application or with parole or medical. And then the dedication—almost every single person in the organization is a volunteer.

Cyrus Dunham (CD): I want people to know that intergenerational, multiracial, cross-class, across-the-walls organizing is possible. I want people to know that it is possible to build a robust, revolutionary coalition that puts care above conflict, the collective above the individual.

Alicia Meza: CCWP has given me hope and inspiration to not give up, to keep fighting. And when I still felt weak, strength was given to me and showed me I am not alone. They opened up their hearts and found the positive out of my negative and helped me move forward. I wouldn't have made it this far without God or CCWP. Connecting with them was one of my greatest choices, with no regrets.

Ruby Padgett: I believe CCWP members are people who understand that one terrible decision does not define who a person is or becomes. Justice is for everyone. We should all be treated equally.

Tamara Hinkle: They sacrifice, push limits, and rearrange boundaries for a population that was once forgotten behind these walls.... Doors have opened, and life has been renewed!

One of CCWP's mottos is "Caring Collectively." What does this mean to you, and what does it look like in CCWP's work?

Romarilyn Ralston: I think Charisse Shumate, our founder, is the perfect example of "caring collectively." It was her caring, collectively, that got us where we are today. You know, she wasn't thinking about her own illness and her own suffering. She thought a lot about other people around her. And she rallied the troops and got people involved in being proactive about their own health care. You bring others in. And so it became an "inside-out" collective of people caring about each other. So I think we continue in that tradition. Even through some of the worst times of the prison regime here in California—the 1990s was one of the worst times, when prison expansion was off the charts; we built twenty prisons in twenty years—here we were, a few hundred, mostly life prisoners, caring about the health, the welfare, and safety of thousands of women in the state. And CCWP never folded.

Deirdre Wilson: The person who comes to mind is Chopper [Beverly Henry]. She touched so many people. She was a member from the very beginning and never lost that fierce, fighting, advocacy, rebel spirit. She's the epitome of the values of CCWP and the fierceness of challenging oppression and speaking your truth. The way she stood up for people and connected with people and was her totally authentic self.

She just drew so many people to her, and when she got sick it was a very powerful time. So many people came to see her. And it was painful, but it was a way for a lot of people to come together and celebrate what her life had been and the power, and the love, that she lived with.

Lanie Greenberger: This motto, "caring collectively," has special meaning to me as over the years I have observed/participated in campaigns wherein CCWP put forth the effort to represent *all* of us collectively. From those housed in AdSeg/SHU [Special Housing Unit] to transgender people to those suffering [from] mental illness and battered women. At no time did CCWP look the other way or think any challenge was too big or too small for their care. I must applaud CCWP's collective dedication to those of us serving LWOP sentences. When others simply dismissed us, CCWP took the bull by the horns and never let go until they succeeded. Conversation was opened and minds changed. Ultimately, LWOPs were commuted and released in numbers never imagined.

TM: "Caring collectively" is believing we are a part of something. We are bigger, stronger, more diversified, and simply better when we look at and care for one another. Alone, I am just a grain of sand, but all together, we can be the beach, withstanding whatever waves the ocean throws at us. CCWP embodies this. CCWP fights for the ones that are forgotten, the ones deemed unsavable by the system, trusting in the "we" vs. "I" concept. Being an LWOP, CCWP has advocated for me at various #dropLWOP rallies. I have been represented with letters, photos, banners, etc. The criminal justice system says "lock her up and throw away the key!" But CCWP, along with our voices, refutes that notion. We, as a collective, will not stand down.

Kelly Vaughn: From my own experience, CCWP has cared collectively for me in so many ways. When we meet, which has been consistently every six to eight weeks, I'm allowed to be open and honest about my life without judgment. They've been there when I needed help contacting my family, they've helped me with some legal situations, they help keep me focused by sending me educational books and keeping in contact with me through mail. The CCWP organization really is a huge part of my life. They give me hope for justice and faith for freedom.

Aminah Elster: "Caring collectively" expresses a movement wherein individuals understand that in order to dismantle the carceral system there must be a collective consciousness centered around empathy, humanity, love, and care for those inside women's prisons, jails, detention facilities, and those under community supervision.

MLF: CCWP is the epitome of a collective love struggle! CCWP has been and will continue to be my teachers, comrades, and partners in our struggle against the empire! CCWP shows us that another world is possible, if we struggle against patriarchy, capitalism, and exploitation collectively, and stay rooted in compassion, generosity, and wisdom.

CD: CCWP and the networks of care within it totally transformed my understanding of community. I experience a level of compassion, patience, and group-mindedness in CCWP that was something I'd been seeking for my whole life so far. It's much more how I imagined that a spiritual community would feel. We are a group of people united around a common cause—maybe a cause as simple as the belief that everyone has inherent value, that everyone deserves care, no matter what our messed-up world has told us. I see this common cause in the way we make decisions, in the way we navigate conflict, in the way we balance different beliefs and languages and orientations to the world.

HCA: It means that together, those of us who've experienced incarceration and those of us who haven't have the opportunity to support each other in ways that wouldn't be possible if we didn't care collectively. One of the memories that stands out for me that reflects the term "caring collectively" was one of the rallies we conducted outside of VSPW where an incredibly diverse group of us rallied around inadequate health care. We chartered a bus and rode together to support people inside. Once the rally began, we had a marching band leading us and the sisters inside all together, shouting through the walls in one voice, "We will be free!" This hope for freedom still lives in me almost fifteen years later.

Fig. 4. On January 26, 2013, more than four hundred people rallied outside of the Central California Women's Facility in Chowchilla to protest dire overcrowding. Longtime CCWP members Jayda Rasberry, Krys Shelley, and Colby Lenz can be spotted on the right-hand side. Photo credit: Daniel Arauz.

DROP LWOP! THE STRUGGLE TO END LIFE WITHOUT PAROLE SENTENCING

The following documents and photographs provide a window onto the ongoing campaign to end life without parole sentencing in California. These materials are but a limited sample of the struggle to expose the injustice of death by incarceration.

Fig. 5. CCWP members Tammy Garvin, Kelly Savage, Brandi Taliano, Laverne Dejohnette, and Susan Bustamante (left to right) speaking at an event in San Francisco in November 2019. All five women were serving LWOP until their sentences were commuted by former California governor Jerry Brown. Drop LWOP! Free them all! Photo courtesy of CCWP.

DROP LWOP FACT SHEET

The Life Without Parole (LWOP) sentence is inhumane, unjust, and costly.

LWOP affects thousands of Californians and their communities.

Approximately 5200 people are serving LWOP in California state prisons. About 200 of them are women and transgender people in Central California Women's Facility and California Institution for Women.

LWOP is unjust.

90% of people in California women's prisons serving LWOP were sentenced as "aiders and abettors" and/or under the Felony Murder Rule. This means they were NOT the main actor/perpetrator of the crime and may have been forced to be present when their abuser committed a murder.

The majority of people serving LWOP in California women's prisons are:
- Survivors of abuse (intimate partner violence, child abuse, sexual violence, and trafficking).
- People with no prior convictions.

> "The night of the crime, I was grocery shopping with my sister. I didn't know a crime was taking place…or that I would end up being a suspect and charged."
> -CeCe

People of color are disproportionately sentenced to LWOP.

LWOP is costly and inhumane.

The increase in LWOP sentences means that California prison populations are aging.

California spends approximately $138,000 per year on each prisoner over the age of 55 in the women's prisons. People serving LWOP are ineligible for elder parole and compassionate release even if they are elderly or terminally ill.

"LWOP is a living death sentence." - Kelly

While LWOP is promoted as a "humane" alternative, those sentenced to LWOP are sentenced to death by incarceration and not afforded the same legal protections as those sentenced to the death penalty.

As with death penalty sentences, the LWOP sentence deprives hope and discourages rehabilitation. People sentenced to LWOP are barred from the majority of self-help programs.

BUILD HOPE

SUPPORT JUSTICE

LWOP is exploitative.

People with LWOP sentences are only eligible for jobs that pay the lowest hourly amount, currently $0.08/hour, yet they are still required to pay restitution.

Those sentenced to LWOP have little recourse.

Prior to 1993, the Board of Parole Hearings (BPH) was required to review people serving LWOP after 30 years in prison. In 1993, the California Department of Corrections and Rehabilitation (CDCR) removed the BPH hearing requirement without required notification.

Beyond post-conviction appeals, the only opportunity for release is if the governor grants a commutation. Until 2016, only one person with an LWOP sentence had been granted commutation. This has started to change. Through the end of his term in 2018, Governor Jerry Brown commuted an unprecedented 283 people. People serving LWOP accounted for about half of that total. Of those serving LWOP whose sentences were commuted, 30 were women.

> "[My husband] nearly killed me too many times to count...The judge felt that anything dealing with [his] abuse had nothing to do with the trial. They just never hear about the domestic violence."
> -Laura

The recidivism rate for lifers is 0.5%, the lowest among people who are paroled. There is every reason to expect the same success from people whose LWOP sentence is commuted.

California has begun to recognize the injustice of the LWOP sentence.

It changed juvenile LWOP by passing legislation, including Senate Bill 394 in 2017, which entitles anyone who was sentenced to LWOP when under the age of 18 to a parole hearing by their 25th year of incarceration. While this is a start, the majority of the LWOP population is ineligible for this law.

Victims of crimes and their family members are remembered & respected.

People who are serving time for harming people are respectfully living their amends every day.

In 2019, we are calling on Governor Gavin Newsom to continue the unprecedented increase in commutations issued by Governor Brown.

California Coalition for Women Prisoners (CCWP), Californians United for a Responsible Budget (CURB), and over 100 allied organizations are calling on California legislators to DROP LWOP. Email: info@womenprisoners.org I Online at: womenprisoners.org

JOIN US IN THE FIGHT TO DROP LWOP

A LIVING CHANCE: STORYTELLING
TO END LIFE WITHOUT PAROLE

Started in 2014 by CCWP members, *A Living Chance: Storytelling to End Life Without Parole* is a multimedia project created in collaboration with people serving LWOP in California's women's prisons. Project cofounder Adrienne Skye Roberts describes *A Living Chance* as a project that uses audio recordings, interviews, letters, and porttraits that render "visible the struggles and resiliency of people who are, essentially, sentenced to die in prison." Check out the project's podcast: https://droplwop.com/a-living-chance-podcast/.

A Living Chance has created postcards, like the one pictured in Figure 6, featuring portraits of people serving LWOP on one side and their testimonials on the other. These postcards have been used in both individual commutation campaigns and broader efforts to educate people about the violence of extreme sentencing.

COMMUTATION for
TRACEE WARD
*Give survivors and youth of color
a chance at freedom.*

Fig. 6. Postcard from the Tracee Ward commutation campaign. Postcard by A Living Chance and CCWP, portrait by Billie Simões Belo. Accessed through Rebel Archives in the Golden Gulag, a public online archive.

BUILDING A STATEWIDE CAMPAIGN TO DROP LWOP

In September 2019 more than 125 people gathered in south Los Angeles to strategize about how to end LWOP sentencing in California. Directly engaging the voices of currently incarcerated people through videos and testimony, this group consisted predominantly of system-impacted and formerly incarcerated organizers, some of whom had themselves been sentenced to LWOP and recently commuted and released.

Over two days in informational panels and breakout sessions, attendees examined the history and effects of extreme sentencing in California and strategized how to dismantle the LWOP sentence as part of the larger fight to "make prisons obsolete."[3] They developed plans for broadening release strategies, changing the law through legislative proposals and ballot initiatives, and strengthening public education and outreach.

Fig. 7. Drop LWOP gathering, Los Angeles, September 2019. Photo courtesy of CCWP.

FIGHTING MENTAL HEALTH NEGLECT AND ABUSE AT THE CALIFORNIA INSTITUTION FOR WOMEN

The following documents and photographs provide a window onto organizing efforts to expose the crisis of mental health neglect and abuse at the California Institution for Women. These materials highlight a recent chapter in CCWP's twenty-five-year-long fight for the physical and mental well-being of people in California's women's prisons.

For Immediate Release – May 30, 2017

PSYCHOLOGICAL TORTURE CONTINUES AT WOMEN'S PRISON; FAMILIES, ADVOCATES DEMAND END TO NEGLECT & "SUICIDE WATCH" CONFINEMENT

On June 1, 2017, advocates and families will convene a vigil and rally at the prison, California Institution for Women (CIW), marking one year since the devastating death of twenty-seven-year-old African American, Shaylene "Light Blue" Graves. Graves was imprisoned at CIW at the time of her death and was only six weeks away from release. For days, Graves begged guards to move her to a different cell when she felt endangered, but CIW staff ignored her. Since 2013, at least fifteen women have died at CIW as a result of multiple forms of abusive practices which amount to psychological torture. These practices include ignoring desperate pleas for help by imprisoned people in mental health and medical crisis. Despite changes in CIW's top administration in 2016, reports of ongoing psychological torture at CIW continue.

Sheri Graves, mother of Shaylene, has been working with advocates at the California Coalition for Women Prisoners (CCWP) to bring more attention to the human rights crisis at CIW. "CIW staff failed to protect my daughter's life," she stated. "The fact that Shaylene's death is part of an ongoing pattern of disregard for human life at CIW makes this loss all the more devastating. Shaylene was an exceptional person with a big heart and so much promise. She was looking forward to her release and was working on her vision to begin a nonprofit organization called Out of the Blue to support people coming out of prison. In memory of Shaylene and all of the people who have lost their lives at CIW, we demand full transparency, full accountability, and an end to these torture practices."

CIW's suicide rate is more than eight times the national rate for people in women's prisons, and more than five times the rate for all California prisons. "Shaylene's death is part of a pattern of neglect and psychological torture at CIW," said Colby Lenz, an advocate at CCWP. "CIW uses "suicide watch" confinement as another form of solitary confinement, which has been identified as a form of psychological torture by incarcerated people, human rights experts, and legal advocates. As part of this torture, CIW punishes people in "suicide watch" confinement with intensive isolation that blocks them from visits and calls from families and friends. CIW also regularly fails to notify families about the status of their endangered loved ones, including blocking access to their legal and medical files even after death. Currently, "suicide watch" is overcrowded and CCWP continues to receive weekly reports of suicide attempts at CIW."

Shaylene Graves died shortly after thirty-five-year-old Erika Rocha hung herself at CIW in April 2016 after being forced in "suicide watch" solitary confinement. "I don't want any other family to go through what my family has gone through," stated Rocha's sister, Freida Rocha. Advocates and families demand the end of all forms of psychological torture within CIW, including the end of "suicide watch" confinement practices. As part of fulfilling the demand for transparency and accountability, the California Department of Corrections & Rehabilitation should make available public reports on compliance with the August 2016 Coleman settlement court order regarding mental health services and suicide prevention protocols. They also demand that those in confinement have full access to visits and calls from families and friends, and the immediate transfer of all medical and legal information to family members if their imprisoned loved ones are in life-threatening situations or have died while incarcerated at CIW.

HONORING THE DEAD, FIGHTING FOR THE LIVING

On June 1, 2017, the California Coalition for Women Prisoners sponsored a vigil and rally at the gates of CIW in Corona to acknowledge the one-year anniversary of the death of twenty-seven-year-old African American Shaylene "Light Blue" Graves and to protest the abusive conditions of confinement that have led to numerous preventable deaths at the state prison. Activists in the "free world" pressed their cardboard signs against a chain-link fence at the CIW so that incarcerated people out on the recreation yard could read them. Their coffin-shaped signs bore the names, dates of death, and causes of death of those who had recently lost their lives at the prison.

NO MORE PREVENTABLE DEATHS!
CARE NOT CAGES!

In the below image (figure 8), several dozen members and allies of CCWP are gathered just outside the gates of the CIW in Corona on November 9, 2019. The recent and preventable death of fifty-five-year-old African American prisoner Vicki Lee Hammonds brought them to the prison that afternoon. CCWP continues to partner with the loved ones of those lost to abuse and neglect at CIW to press the State of California to, among other things, end the use of isolation for those in mental health crisis, treat family members with respect and dignity in the case of death, establish ongoing independent oversight, and demand decarceration.

#METOO BEHIND BARS

In October 2017 #MeToo went viral, reigniting a national conversation about sexual harassment, abuse, and assault. In November 2017 four people currently or formerly incarcerated in California's women's prisons filed a lawsuit against the California Department of Corrections and Rehabilitation (CDCR), condemning sexual harassment and gender-based violence at the hands of prison guards. The lawsuit swiftly became the catalyst for a grassroots mobilization under the banner of #MeTooBehindBars. The following materials provide a window onto this ongoing campaign spearheaded by trans, gender nonconforming, and queer prisoners and former prisoners.

#MeTooBehindBars Fact Sheet

LAWSUIT DENOUNCES ASSAULTS AT CCWF

On November 9, 2017, a lawsuit was filed against the CDCR by four plaintiffs who are or were incarcerated at CCWF. The plaintiffs all identify as transgender, gender nonconforming, or queer. The lawsuit denounces two assaults where correctional officers used physical force, sexually harassed, and used homophobic and transphobic insults against the plaintiffs. Medical treatment was not provided for their injuries, and they were placed in abusive isolation cages where they were subject to further sexual humiliation and weren't able to access bathrooms.

Why was a lawsuit filed?

- The plaintiffs followed the prison's 602 grievance process to address the assaults. In some cases, their 602s were blocked from being processed, and in other cases the 602 process was exhausted but didn't result in any relief. The 602 process is controlled by the CDCR and rarely provides substantial relief for grievances.

- Many letters were written by advocates to CCWF's warden and the CDCR asking them to address the plaintiffs' grievances and to hold COs [Correctional Officers] accountable.

- A lawsuit was finally filed because CDCR did nothing to respond to these requests for relief and change.

- Plaintiffs recognize that the assaults are part of a larger pattern of excessive force by guards that impact many other women and trans prisoners. Their hope is that the lawsuit will help prevent such incidents in the future.

What specific changes are the plaintiffs hoping to accomplish with the lawsuit?

- Stop prisons from targeting gender nonconformity.

- Hold COs and staff accountable when they use excessive force. This could include reassignment, suspension, firing, and legal prosecution.

- End the use of force, intimidation, and other forms of retaliation against people who try to document and report CO misconduct. Protect whistleblowers inside prisons!

- End the use of punitive isolation cages with no access to toilets and no monitoring for health problems.

- Ensure that prisoners who are involved in any physical altercation with guards receive medical care as already mandated (but not implemented) by CDCR policies.

- Ensure the upholding of ADA [American with Disabilities Act] mandated policies and accommodations for incarcerated people with disabilities in all situations.

- Develop a whistle-blowing process that is managed by an agency external to the CDCR.

Why does the lawsuit specify that plaintiffs were all transgender, gender nonconforming or queer?

- Many women in prison are sexually violated and harassed. However, in the past few years there has been an increasing pattern of physical- and sexual-violence against transgender, GNC [gender nonconforming], and queer women prisoners at CCWF.

- These incidents represent a backlash against hard-won legal rights for trans people in prison, such as the right to access hormone therapy. They reflect CO resentment about changing cultural norms regarding gender identity.

- The incidents also retraumatize people who are survivors of sexual violence, homophobia, and transphobia before they were incarcerated.

- Winning changes in procedures for transgender, GNC, and queer people will support *everyone* who is subject to physical and sexual violence.

How can other people in women's prisons connect to the lawsuit?

- The legal team is continuing to collect stories from other prisoners about abusive attacks which could be used as amplifying material or to support a class action lawsuit in the future.

How does this lawsuit connect to the growing #MeToo movement?

- #MeToo represents a moment of exploding social awareness about the pervasiveness of sexual harassment and violence by those in power against vulnerable people. Women, trans, and GNC people inside prisons are vulnerable and often invisible targets of the guards, staff, and prison administration who control their lives.

- The inclusion of these stories from inside women's prisons provides a crucial dimension to the national conversation on gendered violence.

How can people support the lawsuit?

- CCWP and allied groups are committed to building a grassroots campaign to support the lawsuit. The campaign, anchored by loved ones and advocates, will educate and mobilize the public to demand an end to abusive and discriminatory behavior behind prison walls.

- To get regular updates about how to support the lawsuit and plug into the campaign, email CCWP at info@womenprisoners.org or write CCWP, 4400 Market St., Oakland, CA 94608.

Fig. 8. Rally outside of California Institution for Women, November 9, 2019. Photo credit: Sam Richardson.

Fig. 9. On October 30, 2019, more than sixty people affiliated with CCWP, the Young Women's Freedom Center, and Survived and Punished rallied outside the CDCR Office in Sacramento to decry prison as enabling sexual- and gender-based violence against trans, gender nonconforming, and queer people. Photo courtesy of CCWP.

AFTERWORD

If we think of abolition as not just eliminating incarceration, but meeting people's needs and supporting their ability to survive and thrive in the world, we have to understand that care, caring, and care work are crucial. In other words, we need to rethink care as crucial to abolition.

But care is often overlooked and unrecognized by those who chronicle instances of organizing and resistance within US prisons. Instead, prison resistance and organizing is frequently defined through a masculinist lens that privileges riots, hunger strikes, work stoppages, and lawsuits.

But care work in a carceral setting can be an act of resistance in and of itself. Jails, prisons, and other sites of confinement discourage relationship and community building. Instead, divisions—whether racial, geographical, or age—are highly encouraged and often function to allow prison injustices to continue unchallenged. Thus, the act of caring—and caring collectively—disrupts the orderly operations of an institution that relies on the divide and conquer strategy.

"Caring Collectively: Twenty-Five Years of Abolition Feminism in California" clearly illustrates that, in California women's prisons, care can—and does—lead to collective organizing, an aspect that has frequently been overlooked even by those studying prison organizing. Relationships formed the basis of the organizing that people in California women's prisons engaged in during the early 1990s to improve medical care. It was because of her relationships with other women that Charisse Shumate could ask them to remember and tell her about instances of medical mistreatment for her so that she could document and bring them to outside attention. Had Shumate not already had relationships with these women, they might not have been willing to risk retaliation for participating in these clandestine acts. But she had formed caring relationships with many women over her years in prison—and they trusted that she would use those stories to fight for them.

"It was her caring, collectively, that got us where we are today," reflected Romarilyn Ralston, a CCWP member who had been incarcerated with Shumate and continues to organize with the coalition after her release. "She thought a lot about other people around her. And she rallied the troops and got people involved in being proactive about their own health care. You bring others in. And so it became an 'inside-out' collective of people caring about each other."

This inside-outside collective became the California Coalition for Women Prisoners, enabling incarcerated members to identify their most pressing concerns and participate in building campaigns to address these concerns. They challenged sexual abuse behind bars, supported queer and trans people against attacks by prison staff, drew attention to the lack of mental health resources, and organized to eliminate life without parole sentences both for the 5,200 people serving these sentences and those who might be sentenced in the future.

People inside women's prisons also recall how CCWP provided not only assistance but also a lifeline to the outside world—through its visiting program, correspondence, and newsletter. These are aspects of inside-outside solidarity and organizing that are all too often overlooked; this dossier places them squarely within the context of abolition feminism.

—Victoria Law

NOTES

1. Romarilyn Ralston, quoted in "Reflections on the California Coalition for Women Prisoners" in this dossier.
2. Combahee River Collective, "A Black Feminist Statement," in *This Bridge Called My Back: Writings by Radical Women of Color*, ed. Cherríe Moraga and Gloria Anzaldúa, 4th ed. (Albany: The State University of New York Press, 2015), 210–18.
3. Angela Y. Davis, *Are Prisons Obsolete?* (New York: Seven Stories Press, 2003).

THE PRESENCE AND REACH
OF ABOLITION FEMINISMS

A REVIEW OF EMILY L. THUMA'S
ALL OUR TRIALS

Brooke Lober

In the summer of 2020, an abolitionist movement surged, took center stage, and gathered new participants in the United States and beyond. As the uprising against deadly anti-Black police violence exploded, newly energized social movement publics embarked on a strategic path: 2020 was a moment of clarity, with a target set on dismantling the most violent systems that secure a racist and sexist state. But if, to use Sara Ahmed's visceral term, the uprising was a "snap" for those exhausted by the constancy of police violence[1]—if we collectively snapped in the summer of 2020, attempting to break from an oppressive norm—we might note that what preceded this snap was a renewed ascendance of anti-violence feminisms in the US and across the globe.[2] From #NiUnaMenos to #MeToo, from the Women's March to #8M and the International Feminist Strike, between 2016 and 2020, feminist movements have instigated a massive cultural shift, highlighting the knowledge and practice of alliances anchored by BIPOC women, queer, trans, and nonbinary people who have always critically shaped racial justice and abolitionist movements as well as grassroots feminisms.

In taking to public space to end misogyny while exposing the entwinement of age, ability, race, and class in gender-based violence, intersectional anti-violence feminisms gained mass traction, contributing powerfully to the moment of renewed abolitionism that followed the police murders of Breonna Taylor, George Floyd, Toni McDade, and so many more. It wasn't the first time that feminism and abolition had converged. Feminist and gender-conscious formations have shaped recent anti-carceral organizing. Some abolitionist feminists, like Victoria Law, identify the reproductive, connective, and affective labor of women—both incarcerated and outside—as the fabric of abolitionist efforts.[3] But feminisms and gender/sex radical politics and analytics remain marginal in the official knowledge of prison and police abolitionism. Emily L. Thuma disrupts this elision in *All Our Trials: Prisons, Policing, and the Feminist Fight to End Violence* (2019), an invaluable contribution to the literature and practice of abolition feminisms. Thuma's investigation reveals the profound role that sex/gender plays in logics of incarceration and punishment; further, as Thuma shows, on these very grounds, feminist rebellion against raced and classed heteropatriarchal violence comes alive, both in the spontaneity of daily survival strategies and in the careful orchestration of organized resistance, behind and beyond carceral walls.

Drawing theory from practice, Thuma offers multiple routes for understanding power relations and their impact on social life. Mobilizing a feminist analysis of state power, Thuma's commitment to stage "a history of the carceral state from below"[4] resonates on every page. In *Remaking Radicalism*, a documentary reader of activism in the neoliberal era, social movement historians Dan Berger and Emily K. Hobson identify the construction of a "usable past" as "an interpretive strategy that approaches history as a renewable resource in the complex service of the present."[5] Thuma provides such a usable past, tracing grassroots feminist acts countering state violence that have grown their capacities in recent decades. The grassroots activism, cultural production, and moments of lived—often intimate—spheres in which life and death struggles occur all become sites of knowledge production in this perceptive account.

At the outset of each chapter, readers arrive at the scene of an action created by grassroots organizations that manifest resistance against gender-based violence and state forces that absorb and reproduce the conditions of a fundamentally sexist and racist society. One by one, accounts of these actions invite readers into scenarios of public life conjured by anti-carceral feminist movements of the past. Observe:

- In 1978 a group of Black feminist-led anti-violence activists march into the Washington, DC, streets, promoting women's empowerment and community-based responses to violence.

- In 1974 outside the fence of the North Carolina Correctional Center, a group called Action for Forgotten Women announces their solidarity with the incarcerated women inside, calling their support for the well-known, politicized prisoner and rape survivor Joan Little—while decrying the conditions of the prison itself—as the incarcerated women respond, cheering them on.

- In 1977 protesters gather at the Boston Statehouse, objecting to the construction of a special unit for women prisoners under the guise of mental health.

- In Seattle, in the spring of 1976, a newsletter addressing incarcerated women and children is simultaneously shipped to leftist and feminist bookstores as well as to jails and prisons, as it would be for the next decade.

- In 1980 the First National Conference on Third World Women and Violence, organized by the Black-led DC Rape Crisis Center, convenes in Washington, DC. The event sparks the creation of a new, national anti-racist, anti-violence network.

- At University of California, Santa Cruz, INCITE! Women of Color Against Violence hosts the first Color of Violence conference, turning away the overspill of attendants by the thousands and inaugurating the influential organization and network.

Each chapter connects these feminist mobilizations to wide-ranging accounts of meetings, marches, groups and coalitions, campaigns, trials, and the creation of counterpublics in print, song, film, and speech. Assembling an ambitious archive, Thuma invites readers into a history of resistance that indexes the expansion of the carceral state and the false promise of carceral feminism, placing these in dialogue with the rich and radical feminist pasts from which today's abolition feminisms emerge.

Thuma traces the key moment when overlapping race, class, and gender justice movements of the late twentieth century built on previous efforts, calling the crises of the repressive racial state and violence against women into public discourse. Against the normative historical narrative centered on white feminisms that dominates women's anti-violence movements, Thuma unearths specific historical moments and relations to show that, even as carceral feminism took shape in late-twentieth-century neoliberal policy, other, mostly unrecognized feminist movements worked to end violence against women while simultaneously challenging violent state practices wrought through race/gender power. These movements were broadly leftist, made up of projects and organizations led by Black, Indigenous, and migrant women of color as well as working-class and radical white women; many of these organizations were socialist, and many were lesbian led. It was not unusual for these groups to be more project based than ideologically attuned—many did not name themselves "feminist," but all of them, in speech and in action, produced a critique of sexist oppression. With an expansive, undogmatic conceptualization of the history of abolition feminisms—which were not yet named as such in the historical period the book tracks—Thuma frames this work as a history of "anti-carceral feminisms." As readers will likely consider and reconsider, Thuma writes, "the anti-carceral current of the 1970s and early 1980s and the feminist prison abolitionism of the twenty-first century share a genealogy, one that reminds us of the interdependence of struggles, the multiplicity of feminisms, and the power of coalition."[6]

Thuma's electrifying first chapter, "Lessons in Self-Defense: From 'Free Joan Little' to 'Free Them All,'" provides an alternate genealogy of feminist anti-violence activism that supplants the dominant white and carceral models, effectively producing a new "center" for feminist anti-violence history. Here, Thuma produces an account of interactions and combinations of racial justice movements for self-determination and feminist resistance to abuse with careful attention to the effect of these cases on the nascent feminist anti-violence movement.

The chapter brings together four famous defense campaigns of women of color who defended themselves by killing rapists and abusers, and whose release from incarceration became popular causes: Joan Little, Inez García, Dessie Woods, and Yvonne Wanrow. Across these inter-related cases and campaigns, Thuma considers the term "self-defense" as an analytic for feminist anti-colonialism, anti-racism, and embodied resistance to sexual violence. The phrase self-defense was a key term for twentieth-century social movements. It indicated varied logics and practices of individual and collective empowerment, from feminist tactics for resisting individual assaults to the collective resource dis-tribution and community protection invoked in the name of the era's most iconic movement: the Black Panther Party for Self-Defense. The multivalent notion of self-defense was deployed in these four popular campaigns to amass coalitions constructed across lines of politics and identity: "More than a legal strategy, 'self-defense' was a shared and galvanizing rhetoric that transected the radical social movements of the era."[7] Thuma explores self-defense with a deep analysis of four high-profile causes célèbres for anti-racist feminisms—movements that now, as then, often go unrecognized as feminisms at all. Unfolding the analysis, Thuma introduces the reader to the combined oppressive forces of sexism and racism and the theory of intersectionality that arose to name these conditions, centering campaigns focused on, filled with, and often led by women of color.

As Thuma shows, in each of the four cases, structures of race and coloniality conditioned the heteropatriarchal attacks from which the women successfully defended themselves and for which they were incarcerated. Beginning with Little, Thuma synthesizes each woman's story as the "product of historical processes,"[8] weaving sociopolitical critique with social movement theory to explain the circumstance of oppression and resistance signified by each defendant's life experience, her case, and the campaign that arose to defend and free her. Thuma provides a material analysis of the conditions of criminalization: we learn that Little's incarceration hinged on petty theft, economic crimes of a young Black woman's surviving in a racist and sexist environment, and a "war on crime" which would deliver her to prison. There, she would be subjected to sexual assault by a prison guard who she stabbed and, unknowingly, killed before fleeing. Tracing Little's campaign, Thuma uncovers a vast web of social movement activism: from the historical self-defense case of Rosa Lee Ingraham, which became a rallying cry for Black and leftist radicals of the 1940s, to Rosa Parks's long-standing anti-rape activism and contribution to the Little defense campaign. Further, by situating the Little campaign in the context of previous campaigns to free political prisoners—including the Panther 21 and Angela Davis—Thuma works against the grain of dominant understandings of what feminism was in the late twentieth century. In the historicization of this era, the solidarity against racist/sexist violence that was a feature of racial pride and power movements is often ignored or actively denied, but the Little campaign provides evidence that counters this dominant narrative. As Thuma notes, women and men from revolutionary struggles, including Attica Brothers Legal Defense, the Puerto Rican independence movement, and the Black Panther Party, energetically joined with feminist individuals and groups to produce a national mobilization on Little's behalf.

Thuma reveals shared opposition to converging gender, race, and class oppression among many well-known and some previously unrecognized figures and groups. In 1973 Davis had just won her exoneration. In characteristic manner, she used the coalition built around her own case to advocate for others, directing the newly formed National Alliance Against Racist and Political Repression to campaign for Little at a national scale. Through writing and activism based in Black feminist theory, Davis de-exceptionalized her own case, bridging the designations of "political prisoner" and "social prisoner." Meanwhile, the cultural organizing work on behalf of Little was exemplified by Bernice Johnson Reagon, whose song "Joan Little" hailed the politicized prisoner as "my sister" and "our mother." The anti-racist activist Anne Braden was known to critique white feminists for colluding with anti-Black racism, especially through their refusal to counter the mythology of Black male violence and interracial rape—a story Thuma engages in this chapter, highlighting Braden's organizing for Little's freedom with the Socialist Women's Caucus of Louisville. As in subsequent chapters, Thuma shines as a historian when she reveals an unknown detail that illuminates an obscured realm. For example, she recounts the unknown story of leftist white women who organized, against the prevailing norm of white-dominated feminist movements, to produce affinities with Little's case, acting strategically to turn liberal groups like North Carolina NOW toward this Black-led freedom campaign. Thuma's emphasis on this story asks us to reconsider the contradictions of white-dominated feminisms, complicating the "collectivity" of what historian Emily Hobson names "collective defense."[9] Here as throughout, Thuma opens the fabric of movements past to reveal, not simplistic unities, but the complex texture of collective labor necessary to create coalitional justice formations.

Thuma surveys both the anti-racist feminisms that aligned around these four defense campaigns, and their contrast, in a white-dominated feminist movement that continuously reproduced a "decidedly racist edge," as Davis commented of Susan Brownmiller's book *Against Our Will*, published immediately following the Little case. Following the case of García, Thuma shows how a more self-consciously identified feminist movement, incorporating many of the most well-known white women activists of the era, would nonetheless merge with the militancy of anti-racist, anti-colonial political prisoner campaigns. García, who set out to exact revenge on the two men who raped her and brutalized her friend, celebrated the fact of her killing as a victory in the service of her own honor. The movement that arose to free her was made up equally of radical feminist, anti-racist, and anti-imperialist activists, many from Latinx organizing initiatives. While the Inez García Defense Committee was linked with the white-dominated mainstream women's movement of the time, they allied with politically radical Bay Area–based organizations, including the Third World Women's Alliance, Concilio Mujeres, the National Conference of Puerto Rican Women, and the San Francisco gay men's group Combatting Sexism as well as the Black Panther Party. In doing so, they performed the painstaking "bridge" work that would soon become known as the hallmark of women of color feminism.

After detailing the coalitions that arose and produced specific readings of race and gender power in the organizing for Woods and Wanrow, whose defense campaigns more stridently decried the colonial nature of violence against women, Thuma offers a key analysis of the nascent feminist anti-violence movement—one that it is crucial to learn from now. In the final portion of the chapter, Thuma critically reassesses this movement in a pivotal moment. Just as the neoliberal state was increasing demands on nonprofit organizations, turning the women's anti-violence movement toward service provision and away from "advocacy," the prison system was poised to massify, with a new war on crime that would utilize feminist opposition to sexual violence to grow its reach. Thuma shows the ways that these four cases became "lessons" inspiring feminist debate and fissure, with anti-carceral feminists increasingly refusing to collude with state responses to intimate violence.

Chapter 2, "Diagnosing Institutional Violence," introduces an entirely new scene that is critical for understanding the production of women as carceral targets. Thuma meticulously traces evidence gleaned from newspapers, activist ephemera, interviews, and state policy to present a case study of a successful coalitional campaign that reveals the undertheorized antagonism between gender self-determination and the gendered violence of the "prison/psychiatric state." Thuma pulls this term from the Coalition to Stop Institutional Violence (CSIV), activists who "advanced a critique of the power of the carceral state and of psychiatry to define legitimate and illegitimate violence, and normal and deviant gender behavior."[10] Thuma charts the grassroots organizations that anchored a successful campaign, meanwhile empowering a multiracial group of several hundred women with varying proximities to criminalization and incarceration. They successfully prevented the construction of a center for so-called "violent women," specifically targeting dissident women prisoners, which would have functioned as a wing of the Massachusetts state prison system. By telling the story of the CSIV and their victory in preventing the construction of a carceral psychiatric hospital, Thuma offers an example of the ways that, by working to dismantle violent state institutions, anti-carceral feminisms intervene in sexist discourses that secure the gender norm.

This chapter reveals the anatomy of a social movement body that produced an abolitionist victory; at the same time, it shows us the figure of the madwoman, often a racialized sexual dissident, and reveals her relation with the institution of the prison/clinic. Studying the CSIV's activism as, what Cherríe Moraga famously named, "theory in the flesh,"* Thuma emphasizes the strategy to overturn the punishment state's use of the term "violent." Questioning the state's definition of violent women on grounds of both gender freedom and political freedom, activists launched a protest against what they cannily renamed the "violence unit"—the CSIV effectively reversed the directionality of so-called violence by claiming that disobedient incarcerated women were not violent but rather righteously rebelled against oppressive conditions. They resituated the will to violence in the state strategy of prisoner control.

To show how psychiatric violence operated and was resisted in this historical moment, Thuma details the history of behavior modification as a technique that merged the institution of medicine with the carceral state. As Thuma shows, this involved the deployment of pathologizing prisoner categorizations and diagnoses and the application of psychiatric drugs to control dissident prisoners. Referencing historian Alan Eliado Gómez's formulation of the "dialectic of prison rebellions and oppression," Thuma maps the appearance of eugenic rhetorics of the biological basis of resistance and the psychiatric control of prisoners onto the volatile historical moment of the 1960s and 1970s, during which the rise of insurgent racial pride and power movements flowed through the porous cracks of prison walls. Thuma introduces historical examples that contest popular memory of the formidable prison movement as an exclusively male province. For example, she details a 1974 rebellion in a Bedford Hills women's prison in New York, where techniques of the racialized pathologization of prisoners, punishment of prisoner activism, beatings by guards, and solitary confinement produced an oppressive atmosphere. When one incarcerated woman, Carol Crooks, was targeted for her legal advocacy to expose the abuses

---

* "Theory in the Flesh" is a section title from *This Bridge Called My Back*, 1981.

of the prison, a solidarity movement among women prisoners arose, after which Crooks and twenty-two more women were transferred to a psychiatric medical lockdown facility. Presenting multiple instances of women prisoners' and community-based feminist resistance against units labeled "special," "alternative," "medical," and "control units," Thuma considers numerous locations where psychiatric prison facilities were the subject of feminist insurgencies within and beyond the sites of the prisons themselves. Further, Thuma recognizes the gendered control of women as a strategy of counterinsurgency, exemplified by the prison/psychiatric state's targeting of women political prisoners like Assata Shakur, who was incarcerated in the maximum security unit (MSU) at Alderson, a "prison within a prison" that previewed the rise of many such "special facilities" aimed at dissident women. As members of the campaign to shutter the Alderson MSU asserted, "such units were designed to 'quell prisoner activism by removing political organizers from the general population and by threatening more severe conditions of confinement for those who might question or challenge institutional authority.'"[11]

Thuma enumerates the forces that discipline women through the production and punishment of subversives: perverse, unruly, and resistant women whose mistreatment was a mechanism for the control of women prisoners, providing an "other" that could tether all women to the operation of a norm. She further demonstrates the ways that "deviant" women and "dissident" prisoners were interpolated to justify institutionalization, medicalization, and psychiatric treatment. Carefully mapping a nexus of groups that came together to protest the "violent unit," Thuma names the multiple sectors that mobilized feminist rebellion against state control, citing Cathy Cohen's notion of a "politics of deviance," which identifies the political nature of women's activities otherwise deemed nonconformist, misbehaving, unruly, rebellious, deviant, queer, and insane—activities that make women targets for the prison/psychiatric state. Thuma contrasts state control against the ethics of gender self-determination as lived among incarcerated, activist, and politically dissident women as well as in the communities from which these groups emerged. Further, Thuma's research into the CSIV reveals their world-building practices of "self-help and mutual aid,"[12] which provided for the enactment of collective care and interconnection that would counter what Ruth Wilson Gilmore names the "organized abandonment" that conditions the rise of mass incarceration as governance.[13] Such practices of collective care, in this proto-abolitionist context, formed the basis of a nascent politics of transformative justice that would offer an experimental grounds for prefiguring alternatives to punishment as a response to interpersonal harm and abuse.

Another world-making project, that of producing women's prisoner newsletters, offers the raw material for chapter 3. This chapter reveals the contours of a convergence: the print culture of the radical left, the Women in Print Movement, and the anti-prison activism that spilled beyond the newsprint, taking form in the lives of women embroiled in carceral systems. As Thuma shows, prisoner newsletters formed as a component of activist counterpublics replete with concrete actions— but the newsletters themselves became the site of not only reporting but also action, forming a key tool for organizing on both sides of prison walls, across an archipelago of otherwise siloed spaces. The newsletters exposed the conditions that incarcerated women survived in while connecting them to each other and to activists who produced collective support structures to serve incarcerated women's needs.

This chapter emphasizes the importance of lesbian community organizers through a comparison of two newsletters. With the first, *Through the Looking Glass,* Thuma shines a spotlight on Rita "Bo" Brown before she became an underground revolutionary who eventually served time for her robberies on behalf of the Black Liberation Army, as part of the multiracial George Jackson Brigade. In the early 1970s, Brown was a young white working-class dyke who had developed an anti-racist politic. Recently released from federal prison—time she served for mail theft—Brown moved to Seattle and cofounded the Women Out Now (WON) prisoner project, which mobilized legal support and reentry services for women released from incarceration at the Pierce County prison about an hour south of Seattle. The coalition magnetized radical feminist activists, from students at the University of Washington to representatives of the Lesbian Resource Center, to the local chapter of Call Off Your Old Tired Ethics (COYOTE), the sex workers' rights organization. These groups allied to directly serve incarcerated women and published a newsletter that would run for more than a decade, circulating behind and beyond prison walls.

The second lesbian-run paper, *No More Cages*, was published by New York's Women Free Women in Prison Collective. Thickening the historical analysis that weaves together all these chapters, Thuma notes that the collective was one outcome of the uprising and legal struggle around the persecution of Carol Crooks at Bedford Hills. The collective continued exposing the classed, raced sexism of the prison regime for a decade after it formed, connecting incarcerated women with those outside and amplifying the voices of women prisoners. The group was sometimes made up of as few as four women, but the strength of their connections in lesbian communities sustained their radical efforts for years. Groups like Dykes Against Racism Everywhere (DARE), the Black and Latinx lesbian organization Salsa Soul Sisters, and Asian Lesbians of the East Coast all contributed to the sustainability of the Women Free Women in Prison Collective.

Such organizations could sometimes be the only link that incarcerated women had to each other and to those outside, and they took risks to write for and to receive the publications. The repressive tactics mobilized by authorities, including the federal Bureau of Prisons, which banned any writing that could be considered either political resistance or homosexual content, sometimes threatened the well-being of women who read the newsletters. As a rare forum through which incarcerated women could share their writing with each other and with social movement publics, the newsletters were key emergent spaces for gathering knowledge of state violence, like the racial/sexual abuse that happened within women's jail and prison facilities. Thuma writes that "prisoners testified to sexual harassment, abuse and coercion and identified practices that were part of the 'normal functioning of the prison' as forms of violence, including body cavity searches, inadequate or absent medical care, rules limiting verbal and physical interactions, and behavior modification regimes."[14] The newsletters were also spaces of richly textured communication about resistance against intimate partner violence, as criminalized survivors who had defended themselves against battery and rape found public support in the readership. Additionally, the newsletters exposed the homophobia and the psychiatric violence—and their overlap—that characterized a significant component of the abuse of women prisoners. In all, Thuma writes the papers are "evidentiary archives of the systematic character of state-sponsored sexual violence and coercion in US prisons."[15] As a body of literature, they represent a formidable starting point for anti-carceral feminist analysis, upending state-sponsored responses to the abuse of women and questioning the punishment system, recognizing it as a contributor to the conditions of violence that beset women and other sexual others.

The newsletters were politically leftist, internationalist, and radically queer. They connected many incarcerated women with the plight of women political prisoners, like Lolita Lebron and Assata Shakur, effectively linking the revolutionary left with people targeted by the state for "crimes" too often categorized as outside the sphere of the political. A powerful strand of anti-carceral feminism emerged from the organizations producing these newsletters and supporting incarcerated women via the mobilization of radical lesbian politics. Thuma shows that such individuals and groups transgressed normative gender modes that would mark out "the prisoner" and "the lesbian" as marginalized others. They also resisted contemporary lesbian feminist norms in multiple ways, including rejecting trans-exclusionary biological essentialism—evidenced by the fact that they sometimes counted transgender women within their networks for activism and for support while incarcerated. In both their queer feminist and leftist orientations, the women's prisoner newsletters formed a counterpublic and a counterculture with its own common sense, a desire to overturn the patriarchy of the state in a quest for justice for women prisoners and their loved ones, to transform the lived circumstances of oppressed, stigmatized, and caged people the world over.

Thuma's final chapter, "Intersecting Indictments," takes an unexpected turn, cementing the political stakes of anti-racist, anti-patriarchal, and revolutionary movements. It begins with two case studies, presented as a translocal approach to understanding Black women–led, multiracial, and mixed-gender feminist anti-violence organizing. With characteristic detail, and focus on the quotidian labor of grassroots organizing, Thuma illuminates the trajectories of two organizations that positioned Black feminists both at the center of a movement and as a bridge connecting women's and Black liberation struggles. The Coalition for Women's Safety, which emerged in Boston in response to a spate of horrific murders of young Black women, was powerfully guided by the visionary politics of the Combahee River Collective. The famous collective steered the Coalition's anti-patriarchal politics of Black liberation, bringing feminist and anti-racist organizations into a careful and complex practice of refusing state racism and sexism. Hundreds of miles away, the DC Rape Crisis Center, which began as a white-dominated women's liberation project, transformed to become a space for the expansion and radicalization of feminists of color, led by a formidable cohort of Black women activists.

Telling the story of the Coalition for Women's Safety, Thuma offers an account of the impressive complexity of public anti-violence organizing among Black communities and their allies in the late 1970s. In a moment of anger and uprising, in response to a spate of brutal murders of young Black women, the Coalition for Women's Safety successfully combined practices of community empowerment, self-defense, and opposition to state violence. Thuma shows how members of this coalition were able to humanize the victims of the brutal murders—who were blamed in public discourse for the murderous violence, as is the case in so many femicides—in tandem with their politics of uplifting the dignity of the women who were killed, activists mounted a freedom struggle, joining the defense campaign that mobilized against the indictment of obviously incorrect suspects, including the famous wrongful indictment of Willie Brown. Instead of seeking to punish individual bad actors through state action, the Coalition featured public mourning and anti-sexist empowerment as responses to the attacks. This portion of the chapter is especially valuable for students of Black studies and women's studies who have surely encountered the writing of the Combahee River Collective but know less of the practical work of its members and the guidance they provided to empower the nexus of Black, feminist, and lesbian movements to which they contributed.

Next the chapter turns to the DC Rape Crisis Center, a community-based institution through which Black feminists powerfully occupied multiple strands of a tangled web of radically engaged, practical movements for ending violence. As members of an "anti-establishment" movement for peer-led rape crisis response, they prefigured the next decades of activism in their recognition of the traumatic character of police responses to racial/sexual violence. Their multi-issue work magnetized women of color and working-class women committed to a broad and comprehensive, active feminist movement. Their Violence Against Women Taskforce, advertising their activities in anticipation of a march against violence (itself a precursor to Take Back the Night), wrote of their world-making approach: "Rather than rely on the criminal justice system as the only way to deal with violence against women, solutions involving empowerment of women, education of men, and community action are being promoted instead."

Taking us to the murder of the young Black nationalist and feminist anti-violence organizer Yulanda Ward, the book ends with a question and a provocation. Ward was a Howard University undergraduate and luminary of the housing justice, anti-poverty, Black liberation, and feminist anti-violence movements. She chaired the coalition on housing, participated in a Marxist-Leninist group with fellow DC Rape Crisis Center director Loretta Ross, and by all accounts, energized the coalitions that arose to oppose both patriarchal violence in intimate life and police violence, at once. She was murdered in a suspicious "robbery," in which nothing was stolen from her, but an execution-style gunshot ended her life. Soon, her apartment was thoroughly searched by the FBI, while those accused, and later acquitted, of the robbery were subject to no such scrutiny. At the close of the 1970s, movement participants recognized this as a new fold in COINTELPRO-style operations, now directed at the Black-led women's movement, poised as it was to oppose both state violence and the violence of poverty as well as ubiquitous violations of women. In this final moment, Thuma lifts up the story of Ward, highlighting the war on Black women as a real manifestation of the patriarchy of the state and recognizing the revolutionary nature—and state repression—of Black feminist organizing.

Thuma's text is not only a tour de force—which it surely is—but also a reflection of the author's attunement to her own role as a true teacher and a subtly powerful, generous contributor to abolition feminism. It is an invaluable contribution to the combined scholarship and activism that is our practice in social movements today. It is a resource and a guide for anti-carceral feminist action, the sustenance of abolition movements.

NOTES

1. Sara Ahmed, *Living a Feminist Life* (Durham, NC: Duke University Press, 2017).

2. For an account of the feminisms that soared across Latin America and beyond, beginning with the #NiUnaMenos movement in 2016, see Verónica Gago, *Feminist International: How to Fix Everything*, trans. Liz Mason-Deese (London and Brooklyn: Verso Books, 2020).

3. Victoria Law, *Resistance Behind Bars: The Struggles of Incarcerated Women* (Oakland, CA: PM Press, 2009).

4. Emily L. Thuma, *All Our Trials: Prisons, Policing, and the Feminist Fight to End Violence* (Urbana, Chicago, and Springfield, IL: University of Illinois Press, 2019), 3.

5. Dan Berger and Emily K. Hobson, eds., *Remaking Radicalism: A Grassroots Documentary Reader of the United States, 1973–2001* (Athens: University of Georgia, 2020), 2.

6. Thuma, *All Our Trials*, 163

7. Thuma, 17

8. Antonio Gramsci, *The Prison Notebooks*, trans. Joseph Buttigeg (New York: Columbia University Press, 2001).

9. Emily K. Hobson, *Lavender and Red: Liberation and Solidarity in the Gay and Lesbian Left* (Oakland: University of California Press, 2016).

10. Thuma, *All Our Trials*, 57.

11. Thuma, *All Our Trials*, 62

12. Thuma, *All Our Trials*, 56

13. Gilmore's key concept appears in many of her talks and texts, including *Golden Gulag: Prisons, Surplus, and Opposition in Globalizing California* (Berkeley and Los Angeles: University of California Press, 2007), 178.

14. Thuma, *All Our Trials*, 105

15. Thuma, *All Our Trials*, 110

FROM CAGES

FOR CAT BROOKS & CARROLL FIFE

Asantewaa Boykin

We are raising
Free babies from cages
Carving maps and scales
In concrete walls
And
Blue skies from stone
We named them after stars, constellations, and
Ancients
So when lost they can find their way back
We pave their roads with blood
Marking landmines along the way
Whispered affirmations as the slept
Some of us androgynous
Gender bending out of necessity
Without the privilege of either
Filing diligently at steel bars
Till our nails broke
And palms were sore
We hid freedom songs in lullabies
Wisdom in wives tales
Survival skills in parables
And vowed to tell them the truth
Even

When
It hurts
We lose sleep watching them breathe
And lose our own
Watching them leave
To expand the engraved maps
We left them

To the ones we bore
For the ones who bore us
Extended and blood
My loves
Be free

PART TWO:

THE VIEW FROM HERE

CORONAVIRUS CHRONICLES

April Harris

Edited and introduced by Colby Lenz and Alisa Bierria

INTRODUCTION

The California Department of Corrections (CDCR) didn't just fail to prevent a COVID crisis in prisons, they actively facilitated it. Prison guards and other staff increased COVID infections through a series of deliberate refusals: refusing to provide incarcerated people with masks, cleaning supplies, and hand sanitizer; refusing to wear masks themselves; and refusing to end the transfer of people between different prisons, including ICE detention centers. When all family and legal visits came to a halt, essential pathways for less-surveilled communication were eliminated, and information about what was unfolding behind bars became harder to access for family members, friends, the press, and organizers. The more prisons are able to block information about the conditions inside, the more deadly those conditions become.

In this carceral context of medical violence, terror, and suppression of information, April Harris, a Black woman incarcerated for decades at the California Institution for Women (CIW), became COVID positive and was sent to CIW's hellish COVID-quarantine unit, one of many that dotted California prisons and the rest of the United States. A key organizer inside, April made the decision to methodically chronicle what she witnessed and experienced. She entitled her daily journal entries *Coronavirus Chronicles* and sent them to Colby Lenz, a long-time volunteer community organizer and legal advocate at the California

Coalition for Women Prisoners (CCWP). When April initially reached out to Colby after testing positive, she was frantically trying to connect with her parents before being moved to an unknown site at the prison, especially after prison staff said that she wouldn't be allowed an opportunity to reach out to anyone. April and Colby's relationship had been cultivated for years and included their collaborative organizing a few years earlier to address an alarming suicide crisis at CIW enabled by the institution's active violence.[1] This volume's portfolio, "Caring Collectively," provides a window into CCWP's legacy of inside-outside relationship building and community organizing, which created a foundation of trust, skills, and shared political goals needed to quickly and deftly address this latest chapter of carceral deathmaking.

April could only send her chronicles out via JPay, a predatory prison company that provides email under prison surveillance, and as a result, some emails arrived many days after they were sent, and others were lost. Sending the information via a monitored medium also put April at risk of staff retaliation. Further, like everything needed in prison to support incarcerated people's survival and connection within an anti-survival/anti-connection structure, maintaining the ability to send email after being moved to quarantine required collective action. April kept her journal on a digital tablet, but once in quarantine, she lost access to the Wi-Fi and kiosks required to send messages. After people reported hazardous conditions in the initial COVID-quarantine unit to their families, the prison moved the entire unit of COVID-positive people to an unused, dirty building, where they blocked their access to communication with outside support. Only after sustained organizing exposed CIW's attempt to conceal the unfolding violence were people finally given a few minutes each to use the kiosks, make phone calls, and take showers.

Along with organizing mutual aid and pressing for emergency releases, CCWP members on the outside coordinated with incarcerated members at CIW and the Central California Women's Facility (CCWF) as well as with organizational partners, such as the Stop San Quentin Outbreak Coalition and Survived and Punished, to strategize how to share information from the inside as widely as possible. As a consequence, April and other incarcerated people were interviewed by multiple news media sources, providing the public with a very different account than CDCR's official reports.[2] Organizers also highlighted messages from incarcerated people through press releases, rallies, and social media campaigns that exposed the fact that prison staff were denying people the basic resources needed to survive, such as emergency medicine, clean water, and electricity. The information released from inside confirmed that prison "health precautions" only reproduced and exacerbated the racist carceral architecture that facilitates premature, gendered, and deliberately facilitated death.

This dimension of carceral deathmaking cannot be represented by COVID prison statistics alone. The rising numbers of COVID infections and COVID-related deaths that CDCR and other prison systems reported are likely an undercount[3] and do not capture how prisons contributed to the expansion and transformation of what counts as a "COVID-related death," such as suicide attempts as a consequence of COVID prison–related torture conditions and despair. April's journal entries detail a *prison within a prison*, showing us how the intensified violence of punitive quarantine was layered and interlocked with the ongoing violence of "regular" prison, a maze of carceral brutality.

Coronavirus Chronicles provides an archive of experiences written against the law, placing April Harris within a tradition of Black radical prison letters as well as a legacy of women and girls documenting their lives within conditions of captivity or confinement, including Harriet Jacobs, CeCe McDonald, and Anne Frank. April's inventories and time-specific logs also echo Ida B. Wells's method to "turn the light of truth" upon the maddening sexual/racial terror of lynching through research and accounting. The steady practice of documenting all she witnessed "with this eye and this eye," including the complex practices of care and resistance enacted by others incarcerated in quarantine, was also a survival tactic that helped keep April tethered to herself through the psychological torment of "doing time" that warps the speed and experience of time.

Throughout *Coronavirus Chronicles*, April's unique voice and storytelling skills ring clear with her wit, grief, despair, and shade. We are so honored to help distribute April's indispensable inside-out resource and powerful testimony. Her journal has been edited for length and anonymity with her permission.

—Colby Lenz & Alisa Bierria

May 16, 2020
Don't look like I'm getting a shower tonight, so I'll sync this tomorrow.

It's 10:00 p.m. and I have gone nine hours with no mattress. They wouldn't allow us to bring a mattress and they are ignoring all of my calls to get one. The officer told me to hold on numerous times. I am logging all of this. I even got his name. He is about to leave and go home, yet my bunkie and I have no mattresses. I am so sleepy but I have to wait up to catch someone.

It's midnight... still no mattress.

In 25 years I have filed ONE grievance. That shows you how much I complain. Since contracting this virus I have been treated with disgust and disdain. In 25 years I have never slept or went without a mattress. Now that I have this virus, I'm not allotted one. I have a documented chrono from medical that I am supposed to have two mattresses. I am being denied even just one. It is 12 midnight and the first watch staff continues to ignore me. I have told four officers since 1:30 p.m. that I do not have a mattress to sit on or sleep on. Now everyone is sound asleep but me. I have absolutely nothing to sleep on.

No water for four days.....enough is enough. I don't know how to file a lawsuit against this place but I'm going to start with a 602*. I already have back problems and now my back is hurting so bad. I am emotional and all over the place. I have asked for mental health twice and have been ignored. This is hands down the worst experience I've had in 25 years of being incarcerated.

---

*   A "602" refers to an administrative appeals form and process that incarcerated people can attempt to use to challenge any action, condition, decision, policy or regulation made by the California Department of Corrections (CDCR) that has a "material adverse effect upon [their] welfare and for which there is no other prescribed method of departmental review/remedy available." Exhausting the administrative appeals process is typically required before incarcerated people can file lawsuits in court based on prison law violations.

I have also been asking for toilet paper and sanitary supplies since 1:30 to no avail. I have not had one sheet of toilet paper in almost twelve hours. A few rooms are screaming for toilet paper.

2:00 a.m. Still no mattress. My bunkie fell asleep on the floor waiting. I just put a cover over her.

2:26 a.m. Just got a mattress and rooms got toilet paper. He told us to step back...we did..he threw the mattresses in the room then his partner started using his foot to kick them into the room further. They both laughed. The one who wasn't kicking the mattresses looked at my bunkie and said, "Don't ever say that I didn't do nothing for you." Just evil. We had no disinfectant to wipe his boot prints off the mattresses so we used our body wash and most of the toilet paper roll he gave us to clean them. They really hate us and they are not hiding it.

I'm going to sleep.

May 17, 2020
7:16 p.m. I see that the men in the Federal Prison Terminal filed a lawsuit against the prison for the mishandling of the [c]oronavirus. It was on the news.

Today the nurses are asking us different questions. Instead of just, are we feeling sick, chills, and fever, now they are asking us if we are feeling like hurting ourselves or others. That is new.

May 18, 2020
2:22 a.m. I cannot sleep. I am coughing uncontrollably. It's a very dry cough that feels like I'm gagging every time I cough. When I sit up, I feel so much better. My bunkie feels nauseous and is running a fever. I gave her four Tylenol and some crackers. She finally went to sleep. I'll try sleeping sitting up. I don't cough when I'm sitting up. In a few hours I will wash my face mask and pillowcase. This feeling is horrible.

6:54 a.m. These women banging and screaming nonstop is driving me crazy. It NEVER stops. I understand everyone's frustrations though. However, it's giving me anxiety. Sometimes I have to turn the volume up all the way on my [TV]. Sometimes I even have to turn the fan all the way up to drown out the noise.

May 19, 2020
11:46 a.m. The person across the hall just set their room on fire. I seen the flames and them sitting in the fire. They just evacuated us. We are outside right now. I cannot stop crying. I feel so bad for this person. I think they are ok. The staff was so scared she passed us up while it was burning. We had to bang on the door to get out.

It's **1:23 p.m.** and we are still outside. The smoke got in my lungs. It's burning. [The associate warden] walked by and inmates were trying to talk to him and he started yelling for us to back up and [that] he was busy.

2:29 p.m. Just got back in my room. Soot is all over my room. All over my property. We're going to try to clean this up and I'll be back.
   It's so hard to breathe. I keep coughing. I cannot believe what I saw. Now that I'm sitting down, I can give you details of what happened.

11:30 a.m. The person [who set the fire] waves at me. I wave back. We are directly across the hall. My bunkies bring up that this person has been refusing vitals, meds, and food. I've noticed it as well. About ten minutes later someone asked the staff to turn on the power. Apparently, their power went off. Then you could hear banging on the door. That's normal, but this time it was really close. I walked to the door, and they are staring at me but there are large flames behind them. I was in shock for about two seconds. I could not believe what I was seeing. It was like out of a movie. And they were so calm just looking at me. Finally, I snapped out of it and I started screaming, "Their room is on fire. Their room is on fire." Then fear came. I thought they were going to die, and I was going to watch the person burn. I kept screaming. The girls heard me and a friend down the hall started yelling "Fire!!" Two staff (a man and a woman) opened their door. When that door opened it was worse than I thought. At first it was black smoke pouring out of the room. [X] came out and I could see flames reaching the ceiling. I just kept staring. I put on my face mask because I couldn't breathe. The staff left and the room was just burning. (It was two mattresses with the cotton pulled out.) I watched it burn for about two seconds. Now everyone is screaming and scared and choking.

The man came back with the fire extinguisher while the lady was opening the doors one by one. Let's stop here... Yes, you heard me right. One by one. They have one button that will open all of these doors at one time in case of an emergency. I would call this an emergency. However, she opened each room one by one. I watched her with this eye and this eye. I watched so hard I watched her run right past me. We had to knock to get the man's attention to let us out. When I finally got out, I saw [X] handcuffed sitting in a chair by the door. I asked them what's wrong and they said, "Everything." It was just so sad.

5:20 p.m. Twenty more women are moving in right now. The staff just said that twenty new bodies are here.

8:04 p.m. Thirty more women are coming....

May 20, 2020
7:30 a.m. An inmate asked for her kiosk time and was told no, that they don't have the manpower. Some of these women haven't showered in four days. The Lt. said yesterday that we were going to be allowed to shower and contact our family. This staff is saying no. An inmate ran out of her room when they opened her door for breakfast and is refusing to go back in. She is crying saying that she wants to talk to her family. It's a lot of commotion. The guy officer (I cannot see his name because of his white suit) started kicking another inmate's door yelling (602 it. 602 the shit. Do your paperwork.) He lost it for a second.

I just asked the officer giving us ice right now what the officer's name was that was kicking the door. Her name is [P], she said and I quote, "Now you know I'm not giving up my officer's name to you." They are wearing these white jumpsuits that are hiding their name tag.

So they are denying showers again and kiosk times. I asked for a 602 a few times and they said there is none. They haven't given me a grievance form and I have been asking since May 12th.

8:00 a.m. They just placed a sign that reads "Red line" on the room across from me that had the fire.

These women are breaking. It's so sad. I'm trying to be strong. Trying to be the voice of reason. But sometimes I feel like ...I don't know.

8:00 p.m. They just announced that everyone will get showers and kiosk. Some lady is apologizing for the actions of the other staff.

Can you find out if all of my complaints go in one 602 or do I separate them[?] Thank you.

They are letting people out for kiosk time. I'm hoping it goes well so I can get my turn. If so I'm going to send these emails to you. However, I will continue to document everything for you. And I will send those emails when I can. You never know around here.

Thank you for everything.

I'm boiling water to drink right now. They give us one cup of ice very early in the morning. You cannot drink ice. So I have to boil water. I have a water jug that I brought with me. So I'm filling that up.

There is still so much soot all over my room. It's making my cough worse. I have a dark concrete floor and now it's light gray from the fire. I keep wiping it up but I only have a few sanitary supplies. I have nothing to get it up with. We removed it from the main things but it's still a lot of it in here. I hate this place. (sad face).

10:30 a.m. They are outside spraying for bugs. Some rooms were infested with bugs coming through the window cracks.

May 20, 2020
12:24 p.m. Women are protesting because they are refusing showers. It has been four days for some, five for others. This is crazy. Women are threatening to kill themselves. There was already a girl in Harrison who slit her throat open and her chest. This quarantine is real.

2:33 p.m. They have been banging on the door for a medical emergency for almost an hour. No one has come to check on us or to see what the emergency is. They do not do security checks on us. Someone could be dead in their cell and they wouldn't know. The banging is so loud. I swear about two hallways are banging at one time trying to help each other. No one is coming... This is crazy. This is sad on so many levels. I will never forget this. Never.

3:30 p.m. Someone is yelling for help over and over and over. No one is coming. This one is scaring me. She keeps screaming. It's piercing. I pray I never need help behind this door. Now people are trying to help her so they are beating on their doors. What if they left us? Makes you think... And it gets louder...It's so loud I'm getting a headache.

All four hallways are banging now. When they did my vitals my heart rate was 125 beats per minute. That shows my anxiety.

4:07 p.m. Staff just responded to the screams for medical help. Now medical is here putting her on a stretcher. I hope she is OK.

5:09 p.m. It is finally quiet. This is the first time since we've been here it's been so quiet. I think they banged themselves to sleep. The first moment of peace.

When chow comes they'll be at it again. So I'm going to get a nap in while I can.

7:08 p.m. Inmates are sitting down in the hallway. Officers are yelling, "Get the fuck up." The inmates are not moving. They are protesting in the hallway. Madness all over again. It never stops. It reminds me of those civil rights stories when they refused to move and the police were screaming insults at them. The officer threatened to pepper spray them. Let me block my door. I'm coughing enough.

It's **7:33 p.m.** They handcuffed the girls in the hallway. Now the inmates are turning on each other. I think I'm watching the unity we once had pack its bag and leave. Now the inmates are arguing with one another. It was us against them, now it's us against us.

7:47 p.m. Another medical emergency is being called and no one is coming again. I think someone is having a seizure. They will not come. You can really die in here. I will never be the same after this. They treat us like animals. I just pray that no one else sets their room on fire to get their attention.

Officer [C] just walked down here while they were yelling medical emergency and he ignored them and grabbed a cart. Today is May 20th.

The girl had a seizure. Everyone is yelling to the roommate to put her on her side. To hold her head. We are doing medical ourselves because the staff will not call them. Just when I thought I've seen it all. I just got sad.

8:43 p.m. Water is coming into all of the rooms. Not mine yet but you can see people pushing it out into the hallway. No one knows where it's coming from. There goes the banging. There goes my headache.

Someone just yelled that they have legal mail to send out and the officer said, "Oh well, we are busy." Whoever is trying to get their legal mail out has been trying for a few days now. I hear her ask almost every day. She's getting denied the opportunity to mail out her legal work. My bunkie has had her mail in the door for two days and they will not pick up regular mail either.

9:30 p.m. The girls are busting out their windows. The girl next to me has officially lost her mind. I can hear glass breaking while she is screaming. And she is one of the quiet ones. People are complaining that all of their stuff is wet from this mysterious water. Well, I won't be getting any sleep tonight. I can hear her ripping the screen off her window. She didn't think this all the way through because there are obvious bars on the windows as well.

They picked up our regular mail. I was just thinking...I don't think that all these staff are evil (trust me some are pure evil) but I honestly think that they are so overwhelmed. Administration puts a lot on them and some of them cannot work well under pressure. I'm watching the staff break down. When that man this morning started kicking that door he had really lost it. He took his home problems and work problems out on that door.

May 23, 2020

6:03 a.m. There is a rumor that the California Coalition for Women Prisoners are coming to protest outside of the prison today. The staff has done numerous security checks since my last entry (all of a sudden).

12:58 p.m. Everyone is screaming, "Help us!" out of their windows. They are protesting outside. I'm not on that side to be able to see. It does feel good to know that people care. Some of those people are my friends. Colby Lenz, Itzel Gutierrez, and Laura Hernandez to name a few. I'm feeling overwhelmed right now, but I'm smiling at the same time.

1:14 p.m. Women are still screaming out of their windows. Now they are yelling, "Let us out. Let us out." Someone yelled out "You guys should at least be on one accord." I thought that was funny.

2:44 p.m. Someone is screaming medical emergency. Now everyone is banging. No one is coming. [X] and [X] yelled to write down the time. It's room 200. Here we go. Here is my fear..........

2:53. p.m. Officers are coming. Wow it took them 9 minutes to respond. More inmates are writing this down.

The inmate is trying to kill herself but her roommate was the one calling medical emergency. They handcuffed her and just walked her by my room. I think she's going to suicide watch. Nine minutes was the fastest they have ever responded. Usually it takes them longer to come. They have an officer station right outside of our hallway. Not far at all.

I read that we are being taken care of and provided with everything we need. That goes to show that they are the real criminals. People wouldn't be trying to kill themselves if that was the case. Of course they are going to say that. Until inmates come up pregnant by staff or rape charges are brought against these officers THEN they admit that they have a problem. CIW has or had the highest suicide rate in the nation (mic drop). That speaks volumes by itself. Other than that they admit to no wrongdoing.

7:38 p.m. Just received one roll of toilet paper and they are passing out indigent bars of soap. Someone somewhere is doing something.

This situation is so sad. I can only imagine how those who are awaiting results feel and those who are awaiting testing. The anticipation has to be overwhelming and scary at the same time. There is a walk of shame where they dress you in yellow or blue gowns and parade you across the yard with about six astronaut-looking people escorting you with white suits and head gear. And the walk is far.

May 24th, 2020

12:03 p.m. They just started showers/kiosk down my hall. I'm surprised. Today is May 24th and I thought I wouldn't get a shower until the 26th. So again, somebody somewhere is doing something. I am so grateful to everyone who has been calling up here trying to make our voices heard.

12:32 p.m. The guard [H] just announced that two Associate Wardens are on their way. He said that he will be working tonight as well. He also said that he will be giving us sanitary supplies and another cup of ice. He said not to make him look bad in front of the A.W.'s.* He is going to give us what we have coming. Mind you he is one of the ones I appealed to for a mattress when I got here. So there you have it......
It all makes sense now. The reason we are getting a shower is because the A.W. (two of them) are on their way. This goes back to me saying that they are so comfortable in the way CIW is ran that they just say anything. Who tells you that because certain people are coming you will receive what you have coming? CIW is the gift that just keeps on giving. So when the A.W. arrives today they will see that we have been well taken care of. Then you will see in the newspaper that CIW inmates are receiving all that they need. It's over a hundred of us positive. Pick one, any one, and they will tell you a different story from what CIW's public relations is saying. I'm going to write down all the good that we will receive today. I must admit that we are being treated

---

* A.W. stands for associate warden.

a lot better now compared to when we first tested positive. That treatment was deplorable.

12:52 p.m. He just passed out supplies.

1:03 p.m. He just announced that if we ever need supplies to just ask him (this is good).

1:17 p.m. He just yelled, "Thank you for your cooperation ladies."

May 25, 2020
7:56 a.m. I am really thankful for everyone's prayers and warm thoughts. I feel like there has been a shift in how we are being treated. We are not being treated good but we are no longer being treated bad. If that makes any sense. Slowly (at a snail's pace) we are getting things without the inmates having to scream and fuss. I feel as if the voices of the Coalition, the media, and our families are being heard. So when I do leave and the next wave of positive cases move here it will not be as bad as it was for us.

May 26, 2020
9:59 a.m. Family and friends have emailed me saying that they have not received page two of my chronicles. The fire. Told you. It's a cover up. However, I will not be silenced. I keep copies.......

10:17 a.m. A girl was on the phone when I was getting out of the shower and I overheard some of her conversation with her family. She's in room 203. She was telling her mom that she doesn't have a TV, tablet, book, or bunkie. Can you imagine staring at a wall for 14 days with no one to talk to? She was crying so hard my heart went out to her. She has to be losing it in there. I wish I had a book to give her but I would've gotten into trouble for that. I don't know why I just assumed that everyone had something to keep themselves busy. Today I learned something different. It is officially our 14 day since testing positive anniversary.

2:53 p.m. We're getting ice yet again for the second time today. I'm thinking that maybe this is a thing now. Everyone is shocked but grateful. Things are definitely improving. We got supplies, showers, and ice twice.

I really don't know how I caught this virus. I was constantly washing my hands and for most of the day my job requires that I wear gloves. When I was working hard and got really hot I was guilty of sliding my mask down to get some air. Sometimes I left it down a little bit longer than I should've. I'm replaying all of this over in my head. Especially being a porter having to clean behind everyone. After this I'll probably brush my teeth with my mask on. This experience was horrible. Seriously though I will take better measures to protect myself moving forward.

I think that there will definitely be a second wave here. Worse than the first one. This is a controlled environment. The only way that we get anything is through staff. Checking their temperatures did not stop them from infecting us. Like I stated earlier taking my temperature allowed me to walk around clueless that I was infected and possibly infecting others. There has to be a better way. I have no suggestions but clearly their way did not work. I need one of those astronaut looking outfits.

7:38 p.m. OK so one of the girls that is moving back because she tested positive ran down here and said that she was moving to Miller B RM 31. The two girls that originally came from that room heard her. They still have all of their property in that room. That just set everyone completely off. They are moving people to our rooms with all of our property. I always try to convey to people outside of prison that our property is equivalent to a homeless person's cart. That cart is all that they own in this world. Take it from them and they will fight you as if their life depended on it.

This quiet unit is no more. My stomach is in knots. The Lt. promised us that we would be allowed to return to our rooms. That is why we left our property. Seven people who were not from our unit are moving into our rooms right now. It just took a turn for the worse. People are screaming that they are going to hang themselves. The banging is the loudest since I've been here.

Someone called chest pains. The officer is here. He is calling for the ambulance. I feel sick. I feel as if we are being so punished for having this virus.

7:51 p.m. The ambulance is here. She had a seizure. Stress.

8:00 p.m. They are bringing our property over here. That means we lost our rooms. That means some of our property is going to be missing. That means that we are displaced. This is so messed up. Everyone is crying so hard.

It's so many Sgts here right now. So much commotion.

8:09 p.m. They are bringing property. My heart is breaking. People are seeing that their property is not all coming back. Just like I said things are missing. This is by far the worst night. I cannot write anymore. .

May 27, 2020

9:52 a.m. Some girl just sat down in front of my door refusing to go in. It's room 203. The staff and medical are here trying to get her in. She wants ibuprofen but they are telling her that you cannot take that being positive with covid19 [*sic*]. She said it's the only thing that helps with her headaches. She went in.

10:24 a.m. The staff just slid some paperwork under all of our doors. Two pages (front and back) of puzzles and yoga exercises. I'm so over this place.

2:01 p.m. All is quiet here. Everyone is just so broken right now. I've been hearing carts come in but I'm not sure if it's new cases or not. I was hearing the girls talk and one of the women who left last night tested on Friday and got her results Tuesday.

As for my symptoms the rash is almost completely gone and I only cough about once or twice a day. It is not a hard cough at all. We'll see what the results are soon. I keep looking in the mirror like I'm going to grow a second nose or something. My bunkie has no cough and her rash is gone.

6:04 p.m. The staff just opened my door and gave me two trash bags. That's new. Everyone got two bags for trash. I always wondered where they expected us to put our trash.

8:50 p.m. The girls are discussing how to protest. Everyone is yelling out suggestions. Should they refuse to eat or refuse vital checks. This has been going on for a minute now with no solution. It's exhausting. I do not think anything will work. They do not care. It is blatantly obvious.

All of this is exhausting. I'm going to bed. I'll sync this tomorrow. Hopefully.

May 28th, 2020

6:49 a.m. I just seen on the news that eight inmates have passed away from covid at the federal prison Terminal Island. The officials stated that one inmate had recovered then passed away. It said that 70% of the inmate population is positive for covid. Seven deaths at CIM.* Now eight there.

8:55 a.m. Last night someone in our hall was informed that there was a death in her family. They allowed her to use the phone at 9:30 p.m. last night.

The counselor is here right now talking to her. I guess her son called up here. How sad. On top of dealing with the madness here. To lose someone then have to lock in a 10 by 8 cell to grieve alone with absolutely no comfort.

10:35 a.m. More women are asking to see mental health. One girl said being locked in the room like this is driving her crazy. The staff said that they will call mental health.

8:50 p.m. When I synced my tablet I received videograms of my parents. Two awesome people. Made me laugh out loud. How did I get so blessed? What a bright light in my dark place. They gave me the

---

* CIM is Correctional Institution for Men, a prison located just a few miles from CIW.

extra strength I needed to see this through. They are my constants. My rocks. I love them dearly.

May 29th, 2020

6:37 a.m. All night someone kept crying and screaming, "Let me out!" while pulling and hitting on the door. That went on all night. That was extremely heartbreaking. I don't know how much more people can take. Even being incarcerated we are not used to being locked down like this. On a normal day our door opens at 6:15 a.m. and stays open all day. At 3:30 p.m. our door locks for about 45 minutes for count then it opens back up. We are free to come and go until 8:45 p.m. So basically we are only locked down for 45 minutes a day. Here we are only out for 20 minutes a day. Huge difference.

I feel like I now have PTSD from this experience. It goes from complete silence to extremely loud and sharp banging and screaming. You never know when it's going to happen. Someone's cup dropped hitting the concrete floor and it scared me so bad. I could literally feel my heart beating hard in my chest. That has happened to me a few times.

10:51 a.m. Mental health just came (one guy) making an all call in the hallway. Everyone is asking to speak to him. He is passing out coloring papers and puzzles. One person asks why they never came to check on us. She is explaining the fire and no one checking on us after that incident. He said that he is not sure why. That mental health is supposed to be here Mon–Fri. They clearly do not come here.

12:15 p.m. They just passed out canteen slips for the month of June. They raised the price on so many items. The staff said it is because of the coronavirus. Some items went up 25¢.

5:28 p.m. The nurses just told us the test might come back Monday. I have made up my mind that I do not know where I am at. Sometimes it feels like a zoo, a mental ward, or a concentration camp. I quit trying to figure it out.

6:30 p.m. All is quiet in my hall. The other hallways are going crazy.

7:57 p.m. Someone is screaming "help!" The guards are coming. I'm surprised they came. He is calling for an ambulance. Rm 191. She's having difficulty breathing. I pray that she is OK. The window I have to look out of is so small and rectangular.

8:10 p.m. The ambulance just arrived.

May 30th, 2020
6:26 a.m. Today makes 19 days in isolation. I wish that I started documenting from the 12th when I first tested positive. I did not start documenting until the 16th.

6:43 a.m. They started showers in my hall.

9:09 a.m. Just finished my shower. I'm not doing too well mentally today. I woke up around midnight and watched church on TV for a little bit. I did the same thing this morning. It's helping me some. My bunkie and I pray a lot.

9:26 a.m. They passed out ice and picked up trash. The staff is being unusually pleasant. Honestly, second watch staff isn't that bad. It is third watch staff that is rude and lacks compassion.

When I was at the kiosk I saw the guard pushing a cart. On that cart was two trash cans full of trash and two igloos of ice with the lids off. That is so unsanitary. He was passing out ice and collecting trash at the same time operating off of the same cart. There was no lid on the trash cans or on the igloos.

I found it very interesting that when I logged into the kiosk it gave a statement that our emails are being read and monitored. It went on to say that our emails are not protected by attorney client privilege.

6:39 p.m. Watching the news. So sad. The world has gone mad.

9:42 p.m. More women moved in. What I did see in all of this is that friendships were formed amongst these women. All day you will hear everyone checking in with one another.

June 1st, 2020

12:58 p.m. Mental health is passing out sheets of paper to color.

4:14 p.m. The staff just announced that 18 people will be moving back to their units tonight. That is a good thing but the anticipation is overwhelming. I pray that I am one of them. You can hear everyone praying.

4:27 p.m. They passed up my door. Even if I don't go at least some people get to leave. I'm kind of sad. All of my friends are leaving. A few of us are still here. My bunkie is here with me.

4:55 p.m. A girl is trying to hang herself. Most of the women in my hall are leaving. Everyone is in an uproar. People are scared and upset because this can only mean that we are still positive. Another one is refusing to lock in. It's chaos. The staff is laughing.

Those that are leaving are happy. I'm so happy for them to get out of here.

6:22 p.m. My test came back positive. Again......I'm so broken right now.

7:39 p.m. Everyone from my hall is finally gone. With the exception of like five of us. I waved bye to everyone. It's quiet now. I was getting used to the noise. I got this. I will be OK. Maybe I'll test again soon. This is so sad. I'm really trying to be strong. I keep talking to myself. I keep encouraging myself. I started today off so hopeful......

June 4th, 2020

8:57 a.m. Last night was the first night that I did not cough. I haven't eaten in three days but I got a good night's sleep last night. That is a major milestone for me being that my cough would not go away. I did not cough at all. I think it's all the water I've been pumping into my body. I boil the water and leave it in bowls to drink throughout the day. Up to this moment I still have not coughed.

10:50 a.m. Just found out that I might not test again until the 9th. So heartbroken. I have been in the belly of the beast for almost a month now. This is pure torture on so many levels mentally, physically, and emotionally. I got this though.

12:19 p.m. They are in my hall retesting. It's not that many of us. Let's see. The guard keeps yelling names. He passed my door. The suspense. Not me. Not today.

12:34 p.m. I think they are finished with my hall. I don't know. I'm running out of food. I only bought enough food to last me two weeks. I'm getting close to a month now. I don't shop again until the 19th. I cannot dare eat the food they give. So I just don't eat to preserve the little I have left until I am really hungry.

It's quiet again (sad face). I don't understand what God is doing. Then again I can't even understand how He runs the physical world that I can see, so how am I to understand the vastly more complex world that I cannot see. There is this poem that I love. And it definitely applies to my situation.

I walked a mile with pleasure and she chatted all the way, but left me none the wiser with all she had to say.

I walked a mile with Sorrow and never a word said she, but Oh the things that I learned when Sorrow walked with me.

I'm going to lay [*sic*] down. The highs and lows of expectation are pretty exhausting.

June 5th, 2020

6:54 a.m. Another night without a cough. I made myself a humidifier. I boil a bowl of water and place a towel over my head. Now that feels good. So I don't know if it's the humidifier, vitamin C, or all of this water I am drinking. But I'm thankful that my cough is gone.

I purchased a few books from the kiosk the other day so I have been doing a lot of reading. I got The Wizard of Oz, A Tale of Two Cities, Oliver Twist, A Christmas Carol, Peter Pan, The Jungle Book, The complete works of William Shakespeare and a lot of studies on the apostle Paul. So now I can at least keep myself busy. I started with the Wizard of Oz. So many details I didn't know.

10:17 a.m. The other hallways have been going crazy since yesterday. I can only imagine what they are going through. You would think that things would have gotten better. That a system would now be formed. Clearly that is not the case.

June 6th, 2020
7:25 a.m. A woman (I recognize her voice) is going off out there. She is letting these guards have it. It's distant but I can hear her clearly. Something about the showers. I know that battle all too well.

11:50 a.m. Someone just announced that the warden is walking around.

12:08 p.m. The guard just did a security check. With the warden walking I feel like a director is off to the side saying, "And scene." This is when they pretend to care. They smile and ask how you're doing.

6:57 p.m. There are a lot of women who refuse their vitals now. I think they are pretty much over it. I don't know. But I can hear the women refusing and the nurses complaining about it. I still get mine checked. I made a promise to myself to just go through the process no matter how hard it is.

June 7th, 2020
7:21 a.m. There is a woman that is out for her shower and she just went absolutely crazy. She's screaming that she can't take this. She is slamming her door over and over. Guards are trying to calm her down right now. She is the same one that tried to hang herself last Monday. She is also the one I spoke of who doesn't have anything in her room to keep her entertained. I don't know her or her name but she has really had a very hard mental ride here. All I know is that she is in room 203.

In England long ago they proved that isolation caused mental issues. Their prison was called 'The Stir,' hence the phrase 'Stir crazy.'

June 9th, 2020
9:14 a.m. The nurse just said that I will probably get retested tomorrow. They have so many different answers to the same question. I am so

grateful to my family and friends that I even know what the [c]orona-virus is. This place has given us absolutely no information. The nurses always say that they have to ask the big boss. They say that everyday [*sic*] to every question anyone asks. The lady who just came from crisis is scared to be alone in a cell. I hear her beg any and everyone to bunk her with someone. Said she can't do this alone. Guards tell her that medical is in charge of bed moves now, and medical tells her that they have to talk to the 'Big Boss.' I'm so sick of the 'Big Boss.' I feel like going to Emerald City and talking to The Oz myself.

9:53 a.m. I asked for a grievance form and received one for the first time in 30 days.

6:24 p.m. I'm listening to the girls talk to one another. Everyone is talking about drinking bleach tomorrow for testing. Someone said she has been scrubbing the back of her throat with soap and a toothbrush. This is extremely dangerous. That shows the level of desperation in this place. I heard one girl say that she puts bleach on her toothbrush every morning. I can only try to discourage them from doing something that can be so lethal. However, I learned that desperate causes = desperate measures. Well, know that I will stay positive for the remainder of 2020 before I take that ride. I have had enough in these last two months of things inside of me that don't belong there.

June 10th, 2020
9:29 a.m. A good friend of mine who has done thirty years is paroling today. Ms. Beverly has weathered many storms with me. So sad that I could not say goodbye to my dear friend. As her journey continues, I wish her the best. Goodbyes like this are hard because you grieve the friendship as well because you know that you will never see that person again. All the memories, the laughs, and the tears are what is now cherished. Everyone sets out to his own path.

6:33 p.m. I just found out that a friend of mine died here. She had throat cancer. I am beyond devastated. She was so young. Our dream was to make it out of here alive. She didn't.

It is Wednesday night and I've yet to be retested.

June 11th, 2020
8:43 a.m. The nurse told me that I am to be retested today. We shall see.

10:15 a.m. I just retested. It's to a point now where it doesn't even hurt me anymore. Got past that hurdle now it's a waiting game.

There was a doctor out there answering questions. Well basically explaining what Covid19 [*sic*] is. Finally someone tells us after a month.

June 12th, 2020
6:49 a.m. I woke up in a bad place. Grieving the death of my dear friend Madonna Watson. May she rest in Paradise.

June 13, 2020
3:35 p.m. I'm hearing that the prison is saying that we were taken care of. Of course administration doesn't know what has gone on over here. I will challenge CDCR to a lie detector test any day.

6:39 p.m. So hopeful. A nurse just winked at me and said, "You should be getting out real soon." Maybe the results came back. Like Paul I am a prisoner of hope.

June 14, 2020
8:35 a.m. They just told me to pack my things. This only means that my test came back negative. Thank God... I'm nervous... why am I nervous. My hands are shaking.

I cannot believe it. I am free from THAT prison. The minute I hit that sunlight...... I felt it. I felt the difference. I mentally paroled.

I'm back in general population. I am so overwhelmed, but as I settle back in, I'm not quite the same. The more people talk to me I learn that I really don't care about the small stuff. I just don't want to be bothered with anyone anymore. I guess this too shall pass and I will feel different later. I feel like being a hostage really made an impact on who I am. From an isolated solitude emerges a different person. I was in a physical and mental cage.

Being back in general population I look around and the people I see haven't been through what I've been through. They are oblivious to the torture I endured just several yards away. We are all inmates but only a selected few know what I mean.

They threw me out of RC* to go on with serving my time like nothing happened. I walk away knowing secretly the torture they inflicted and the things I need not trouble myself to repeat.

I documented everything because I do have a voice regardless of whatever circumstances I find myself in. I wish that I would have found my voice twenty five years ago. I'm so thankful to my family and friends who continued to encourage me throughout this journey. I have since learned that the voices in our lives dictate our choices. I chose not to break. I may bend but I will never break.

I'm signing off on April's Coronavirus Chronicles. I do not plan on a sequel (smile).

NOTES

1. For a detailed account about the suicide crisis at the California Institution for Women and the inside-outside organizing and caregiving led by members of the California Coalition for Women Prisoners, please see Colby Lenz, "State-Sanctioned Suicides and Life-Making Resistance in Carceral Contexts," in *Abolition Feminisms, Volume 2: Feminist Ruptures against the Carceral State*, ed. Alisa Bierria, Jakeya Caruthers, and Brooke Lober (Chicago: Haymarket Books, 2022).

2. Jason Fagone, "Women's Prison Journal: State Inmate's Daily Diary during Pandemic," *San Francisco Chronicle*, June 12, 2020, https://www.sfchronicle.com/bayarea/article/Woman-s-prison-journal-State-inmate-s-daily-15334701.php; Eileen Guo, "Inmates Witnessed a Suicide Attempt. They Received Coloring Pages Instead of Counseling," *Washington Post*, July 26, 2020, https://www.washingtonpost.com/national/they-witnessed-a-suicide-attempt-they-received-coloring-books-instead-of-counseling/2020/07/25/e4490bfe-cdbd-11ea-bc6a-6841b28d9093_story.html; Madison Pauly and Stacey Dyer, "'The Officers Were Taking Our Toilet Paper': One Woman's Life in Prison Right Now," *Mother Jones*, April 3, 2020, https://www.motherjones.com/coronavirus-updates/2020/04/stacey-dyer-california-women-prison/.

---

* RC is short for Reception Center, which is where people are first imprisoned while waiting for a long-term location.

3. The Marshall Project, "A State-By-State Look at 15 Months of Coronavirus in Prisons," *Marshall Project*, July 1, 2021, https://www.themarshallproject.org/2020/05/01/a-state-by-state-look-at-coronavirus-in-prisons.

Photo by Esmat Elhalaby, Oakland, CA, 2020

A WORLD WITHOUT SWEATSHOPS

ABOLITION NOT REFORM

Minh-Ha T. Pham

"COVID-19 showed us how the entire planet is knit together ... [The] riveted gaze that we all have to put on it makes it possible and necessary for us to look at all of the other ways that the world is knit together—and what divides us."

—Ruth Wilson Gilmore, prison abolitionist and scholar

Ruth Wilson Gilmore's words—especially her choice to use a sartorial metaphor—makes me think two things. First, if COVID-19 showed us how the planet is knit together, it has also shown us that essential workers and, in the context of this discussion, garment workers—a labor force that's 85 percent women and largely women of color—are the ones doing the knitting. That is to say, the deep and extensive social, trade, capital, and labor systems that link the world together are fueled by the labor power of poor and working-class women of color workers, usually to their detriment. Second, Gilmore's comments, made during the online event "A World Without Prisons" with fellow abolitionist and organizer Mariame Kaba, suggests that a world without sweatshops must be understood as part of, and in relation to, a world without prisons.

Sweatshops and prisons are linked and co-constructed. Garment sweatshops in prisons have existed for centuries—as early as the 1700s—and continue to operate around the world in the United States, China, Thailand, Peru, England, Italy, and elsewhere. Prison workers have manufactured products for labels including Gap, Adidas, Tommy Hilfiger, Calvin Klein, Victoria's Secret, and JCPenney. While these brands would prefer we didn't know the carceral conditions in which some of their products are made, other brands like Prison Blues (the US), Stripes Clothing (Netherlands), and Carcel (Denmark) advertise them as part of their brand identity.[1]

These brands claim to offer on-the-job training, but people held captive in prisons aren't employees. They're not entitled to unemployment benefits, sick leave, paid time off, and they're not protected by labor or health and safety laws. Incarcerated and nonincarcerated garment workers are paid substandard wages and are subject to extreme forms of surveillance and discipline including physical and verbal abuse, cut wages, and job loss. Incarcerated workers also face the added threat of having their sentences extended if they get sick or don't make their quotas.

Today, prison garment factories also produce cloth face masks and other personal protective equipment (PPE). People incarcerated in state and federal prisons across the US sew masks for fellow prisoners, guards, and governmental agencies.[2] In California, prison workers sew masks for as little as eight cents an hour, twelve to fourteen hours per day, every day. The masks are sold to a wide range of state agencies from the California Highway Patrol to the Departments of Consumer Affairs, State Hospitals, and Parks and Recreation. The masks, which help finance the Prison Industry Authority, have become a lucrative revenue stream for the agency. In May 2020 the Franchise Tax Board placed a single order for seven thousand masks totaling $17,150.[3]

Although commercial garment workers and prison workers are a key point of production for life-saving masks, they rarely have access to them. Without adequate PPE, space for social distancing, or sick leave, garment sweatshops inside and outside prisons have become COVID hotspots. Going into the summer of the pandemic in May 2020, prison factories in states including Louisiana, Maryland, and California reported hundreds of COVID cases and a significant number of deaths among prison workers.[4] In December 2020 a study by the Marshall Project found that one in five incarcerated people across all US state and federal prisons had tested positive for COVID.[5]

ORGANIZED ABANDONMENT

Sweatshops, like prisons, are what Gilmore has theorized as "forgotten places."[6] Forgotten places are constituted by racialized patterns of organized abandonment in which state and corporate sectors work together to extract value from people and places largely of the global south, in the creation of profits that benefit people and places largely of the global north. Garment sweatshops are distinct from prisons in that the processes of abandonment derive from three extractive sources: state, capital, and culture—specifically neoliberal or "free-market" feminism.

Beginning in the late 1970s and accelerating in the 1980s and 1990s, trade liberalization or deregulation policies that gradually eliminated import quotas and reduced tariffs restructured the global economy. These policies enabled western companies to simultaneously minimize their production costs and maximize their profits by seeking out cheaper labor and cheaper source materials in other parts of the world. In this period, the centers of apparel production moved from the US and Europe to factories in the global south in designated export processing zones (EPZ), especially in Mexico, Central America, Asia, Micronesia, and Haiti. Factories in EPZs are exempt from most labor health, and safety regulations, taxes, and trade duties.

Race- and gender-based incentives also led western brands to move their production offshore. EPZs promised a ready, docile, and cut-rate labor force. Local and foreign governments represented poor women of color as naturally suited for the demanding and "unskilled" work of apparel production by emphasizing their "nimble fingers" and their compliant dispositions.[7] In the words of a Malaysian investment brochure written for western brands: "The manual dexterity of the oriental female is famous the world over. Her hands are small and she works fast with extreme care. Who, therefore, could be better qualified by nature and inheritance to contribute to the efficiency of a bench-assembly production line than the oriental girl[?]"[8]

The racial, gendered, and sexualized association of apparel production with Asian women and other non-Western women and women of color provided a cultural basis for slashing work safety conditions, worker protections, and wages in garment factories. Sweatshops are structurally built into the racialized, gendered, and colonial structure of international trade and labor arrangements that are designed precisely to extract from, neglect, and forget an array of human and environmental resources—skill, knowledge, time, health, wages, clean water, clean air—from the people and places of the global south.

In the 1990s, in the midst of the implementation of liberalization policies, garment sweatshops proliferated globally. Factories in Saipan, a US territory near the Philippines, produced 20 percent of the clothes sold by US brands.[9] Saipan was an attractive manufacturing site for brands like Tommy Hilfiger, Gap, Nordstrom, J.Crew, the Limited, Eddie Bauer, Liz Claiborne, and Levi's because it was both exempt from US trade and labor laws and *included in* from US supplier status.[10] In other words, factories in Saipan provided US fashion companies with below-cost labor, no tariff and import barriers, and unrestricted "Made in the USA" labels. Saipan garment workers, predominantly women, were recruited from the Philippines, China, Bangladesh, and Thailand with promises of good wages but instead were paid two to three dollars per hour, or 50 percent of the US federal minimum wage at the time. In 1999 a class-action lawsuit against eighteen US brands turned up more than one thousand safety violations and millions of dollars in stolen wages.[11]

Around the same time, it was reported that Kathie Lee Gifford's line of children's clothing for Walmart was being made by children in Honduras.[12] Workers as young as thirteen years old were paid thirty-one cents an hour to work twenty hours a day.[13] Closer to my home in California, seventy-two Thai garment workers were discovered to have been held for years against their will in a residential complex in El Monte (just east of Los Angeles). They were forced to work seventeen to twenty-two hours per day sewing clothes for then-popular US brands such as Anchor Blue and B.U.M. Equipment.[14] Workers were paid seventy cents per hour, but much of their income was garnished by the factory owners to pay off illegitimate recruitment fees as well as food and rent.[15] The media treated the El Monte case as an outlier in the US garment industry. In fact, the El Monte case wasn't too far from the norm. It not only demonstrates the carceral qualities that prisons and sweatshops share but also serves as a stark example of how sweatshops are racially gendered sites of carceral violence. A survey of Los Angeles garment factories in the same period found that 96 percent were in violation of health and safety regulations (72 percent were judged serious enough to result in injury or death).[16] Two decades later, the reality of the US garment industry is much the same. In 2017 the California Department of Labor found violations at 85 percent of the garment factories it visited in Los Angeles and that workers were owed "$1.3 million in back wages, lost overtime, and damages."[17]

SWEATSHOPS AND FREE-MARKET FEMINISM

Along with sweatshops, the early years of apparel trade liberalization produced a wave of pro-sweatshop feminist thinking and writings. Articles in prominent media such as the *New York Times*, AP News, and *Slate* endorsed sweatshops using the language and logics of feminist empowerment and included headlines such as "In Praise of Cheap Labor"; "In Principle, A Case for More 'Sweatshops'"; and "In Honduras, 'Sweatshop' Wages Better Than Nothing for Many Workers."[18] Briefly, the pro-sweatshop feminist position holds three core beliefs: the right to paid employment is an essential feminist principle; garment work "modernizes" global south women and global south countries (e.g., bringing "fashion" and a technical education to poor and often rural women of color and bringing technological infrastructure to their countries); and garment work is liberatory (e.g., paychecks, however small, free garment workers from patriarchal cultural and family expectations). In this upside-down worldview, sweatshops lift women of color out of socially, culturally, and economically impoverished circumstances. The reality is that sweatshops pull workers deeper into poverty, precarity, and abandonment at the hands of a powerful global network of international monetary organizations, corporate actors, and local factory owners and governments.

Like carceral and imperialist feminisms, pro-sweatshop feminism operates from a white supremacist, paternalistic logic, which claims that sweatshops and global free-trade capitalism are civilizing feminist projects that save Black, Asian, Latin American, and Indigenous women from Asia and the Americas from their respective patriarchal and "undeveloped" cultures to western liberalism and global capitalism. This colonial ideology is now widely promoted on the world stage. As Hester Eisenstein has documented in her research, "international financial institutions—including the World Bank, the International Monetary Fund, the United Nations, and a raft of NGOs like CARE— along with corporate entities like Nike" have now co-opted neoliberal feminist discourses to declare that sweatshops offer a "solution to the world's problems" by providing jobs to women in and of the global south.[19] Like all civilizing missions, the oppressive reality of racism and colonialism is whitewashed by a moral-capitalist discourse about women's "freedom."

Western neoliberal feminism isn't always as crude or explicit in its support of sweatshops. For example, in the 2010s western feminists were surprised to learn that their "girl power"–themed fashion collections and statement T-shirts had been made in sweatshops in Bangladesh, Sri Lanka, and Mauritius, where workers were paid poverty wages when they were paid at all.[20] Some of these garments were created to help fund US and European activist organizations and charities. The public and media generally treated these incidents as ironic revelations about a complex global supply chain. Meanwhile, the feminist entrepreneurs involved in these stories promised to do better. Danielle Newnham, cofounder of F=, a British nonprofit that claims to be "all about inspiring and empowering girls," and the designer of "Girl Power" statement T-shirts made by Bangladeshi garment workers for pennies per hour, promised to find another supplier *if presented with sufficient evidence*: "[W]e are always concerned if anyone is treated badly—our entire mission is based on empowerment and if we receive evidence of poor treatment, we would look for another supplier immediately."[21]

Newnham expresses a common neoliberal feminist position. For her and other feminist entrepreneur-activists, sweatshops are isolated problems specific to individual bad factories that can be resolved by adjusting individual corporate and consumer behaviors ("we would look for another supplier immediately"). By treating sweatshops as flaws rather than structural features of the global fashion industry, neoliberal feminist positions tacitly legitimize the trade liberalization policies, corporate business strategies, and racially gendered geopolitical ideologies that gave rise to (and continue to sustain) the conditions that make sweatshops not only possible but inevitable.

Similar individualizing feminist strategies have been implemented in the COVID-19 era. In the early weeks of the pandemic, a wide range of western brands from H&M and Gap to Oscar de la Renta and Balmain scrambled to protect their bottom lines from the inevitable drop in consumer spending by abandoning their suppliers. By March 2020 a long list of brands had "cancelled" their orders and exercised their contractual right to refuse to pay for an estimated $40 billion worth of almost-complete and completed apparel orders.[22] (Some of these orders had already shipped.) The media and many activist groups viewed these cancellations as examples of brands behaving badly, of brands acting outside the range of normative corporate conduct. But the right to withhold payment—indeed, brands' unilateral right to amend any part of the contract—is enshrined in standard contracts between global north buyers and global south suppliers and protected by international trade and labor governing bodies that have restructured the global economy to privilege corporations.

Other standard conditions that protect buyers and exploit suppliers' structural vulnerability include canceling purchase orders "in whole or in part without [supplier] authorization and at [the buyer's] sole and absolute discretion."[23] This clause is taken verbatim from a Kohl's contract dated on March 2020. Canceling the order doesn't preclude the buyer from taking possession of the order mid-production or, in the event that the order's already been shipped, taking possession of the order postproduction. Many contracts also stipulate that "the cost of the Goods, the cost of any fabric, or any other cost at all"—including the cost of labor—becomes the supplier's responsibility once orders are canceled.[24] For example, an Arcadia (e.g., Topshop) contract states, "If we suspend or cancel an order we will not be legally responsible for any direct or indirect damage or loss this may cause you."[25]

In the COVID era, brands specifically invoked a contractual provision called "force majeure." A common feature in many kinds of contracts, force majeure is a legal doctrine that excuses the parties from their contractual obligations due to impediments beyond their control. Contracts between fashion brands, their various subcontractors, and garment factories are distinct in that the force majeure event is defined in vague terms and that the contracts provide buyers *the exclusive right* to invoke force majeure. Arguably the one-sided terms of the contract would give suppliers grounds for legal action, but these contracts also provide buyers protections against such actions by requiring "legal action to be filed in the courts of the country where the brand is headquartered, not the supplier's country" and requiring that the supplier "pay the brand's attorneys' fees if it loses."[26] Racialized exploitation is not the unlucky outcome of a few brands behaving badly but a contractual condition of participating in the global fashion economy for poor countries and millions of racialized and gendered workers in and from the global south.

The contractually binding organized abandonment of garment workers directly led to an unprecedented loss of jobs and wages in garment industries around the world beginning in February and March 2020. Numerous media outlets characterized the situation as a humanitarian crisis.[27] Bangladesh, the world's second-largest apparel exporting country, saw the biggest losses in jobs, wages, and export revenue. In March 2020, "orders for over 900 million garments worth $2.9 billion [were] cancelled."[28] By the end of June, Bangladeshi factories reported that 1,931 brands had suspended or "cancelled" $3.7 billion worth of orders.[29] In Myanmar, 150 of the country's 600 factories shut down.[30] In Cambodia, 200 of 600 factories shuttered.[31] In Viet Nam, an estimated 30 to 50 percent of garment workers, or about one million workers, lost their jobs.[32] And in the Philippines, approximately 60,000 workers, or 30 percent of the garment industry, were let go.[33] Most garment workers were dismissed without their owed wages. In Bangladesh, "72.4 percent of furloughed and 80.4 percent of dismissed workers were sent home unpaid."[34] While brands were quick to abandon garment workers (as they always are), they didn't abandon their investors. Several weeks after Kohl's reneged on its orders with Korean and Bangladeshi suppliers (apparel orders worth $100 million and $50 million respectively), the US's largest department store paid $109 million in dividends to its stockholders.[35]

By October 2020, about 40 percent of the garment workers who were laid off at the beginning of the pandemic due to contractually binding organized abandonment were still out of work,[36] and many more were still waiting to be paid an estimated $3.19 to $5.78 billion in back wages.[37] As staggering as these numbers are, they don't include homeworkers or other workers left off of official factory payrolls, nor do they account for outstanding overtime and severance pay.

In response, activists—a predominantly multiracial network of young women in the global north—launched social media campaigns[38] to pressure brands to commit to paying for their abandoned orders in full.[39] Hashtags like #PayUp and #PayYourWorkers began trending on social media platforms in posts naming and shaming specific brands for their COVID-19–induced cancellations. The public and media have credited the hashtags and the online campaigns with recovering a significant portion of garment workers' wages. A *Vogue* article praised social media activists for "unlock[ing] around $1 billion in Bangladesh and $15 billion globally, which accounts for over one-third of the $40 billion worth of wages owed to garment workers at the beginning of the Covid-19 crisis." According to *Vogue*, the #PayUp campaign is "a true sign of the power of social media activism" and "really does show the deep impact that a single hashtag can have on an entire industry and population."[40]

The reality, though, is less rosy. There's no direct or primary data on how much of the money recovered by social media campaigns actually made its way back to garment workers.[41] In Bangladesh as late as December 2020, garment workers who have been on the street protesting their lost wages and jobs since April 2020 still had not been paid. In the words of one garment worker named Salma: "[W]e have been protesting for our wages multiple times. We were beaten by the factory-backed goons, water cannoned by the police, been promised 19 different dates to settle what we are owed. But nothing materialised."[42] In India, recovered wages were being garnished to repay employers for relief money workers received while they were unemployed. "Workers say they are being offered the choice of less money or working extra shifts for free to pay back their bosses, who dangle the threat of unemployment if employees refuse."[43]

There's no doubt that these campaigns helped raise the public's awareness about the abandoned orders and that they succeeded in pressuring some brands to pay up—or at least pressured them to issue press releases promising to pay up. But by calling out specific brands, these campaigns individualize a systemic problem. The mass abandonment was a consequence of brands acting within their *legal right*—at least as they interpreted them. Their contractual agreements include clauses that allow for the possibility of canceling orders anytime, including postproduction, and even dropping suppliers altogether. These are long-standing entitlements, outcomes of decades of western corporate political lobbying and other corporate-driven and corporate-funded policy-making activities. The abandonment of garment workers is built into the unequal trade and labor arrangements between consumer countries in the global north and supplier countries in the global south.

In failing to identify the institutional sources of organized abandonment—economic liberalization policies and free-market ideologies—these campaigns are unable to intervene in, much less challenge, the global fashion supply chain's power structure. In some ways, they ultimately legitimize it. The myth of corporate social responsibility rests on two wobbly pillars: that global capitalism can be ethical and that corporations can and should regulate themselves. Such approaches reinforce the supply chain's top-down power relations under the guise of a feminist and humanitarian concern for protecting and caring for a predominantly women of color labor force.

Misdiagnosing the sweatshop problem also lets other agents of this extractive industry off the hook. Along with international trade, financial, and corporate entities, supplier countries and sweatshop factory owners play a significant, if more localized, role in global fashion's extractive operations. In the middle of the pandemic, local governments and factory owners not only failed to protect garment workers in their factories, they also intensified the conditions of organized abandonment. Promises to help workers in the form of government-provided disaster relief funds or factory-provided severance pay have mostly rung hollow. When workers speak up to demand their legally entitled compensation, they're typically met with retaliatory harassment, violence, and job loss.

Factory owners particularly targeted unionized workers and labor organizers. A report by the Business & Human Rights Resource Centre found over 4,870 cases where unionized workers and labor activists in nine factories in India, Bangladesh, Myanmar, and Cambodia were dismissed during the pandemic.[44] These factories produce clothes for major US and European brands like H&M, Primark, Inditex (Zara), Levi Strauss & Co., MANGO, BESTSELLER, Michael Kors, Tory Burch, and Kate Spade (Tapestry). Some of those targeted were fired just days after joining a union.

A notable example involved Cambodian garment worker Soy Sros, who was arrested and jailed for fifty-five days after posting a Facebook message critical of her factory's plan to lay off eighty-eight unionized workers.[45] Sros is an employee at Superl Holdings, a factory in Phnom Penh that makes luxury handbags for Michael Kors, Jimmy Choo, Kate Spade, Coach, and Versace. For months, labor activists in Cambodia and elsewhere pleaded with these brands to intervene on Sros's behalf and to protect workers' rights to demand better working conditions. Brands ignored their calls, hiding behind the long and convoluted subcontracting system that was designed precisely to allow brands to evade responsibility for their factories' labor conditions.

Prison abolitionists critique reforms that seek out "gentler" and/or "fairer" formations of imprisonment and punishment. They distinguish reforms that ultimately legitimize and reinforce the prison system, or "reformist reforms," from other reforms that shrink the scope of carceral systems and enable bigger shifts toward abolition. I argue that free-market feminist sweatshop reforms should be understood as reformist reforms. They pursue gentler, fairer, and more inclusive forms of upstream labor and resource extraction (from the global south to the global north) rather than the abolition of this extractive industry altogether.

Reformist reforms that only ask brands to pay workers their owed poverty wages don't interrogate, much less challenge, the sociopolitical economic order under which workers in a $2.5 trillion industry are paid poverty wages in the first place. Calling for "inclusion" and "diversity" at the top of the supply chain in the modeling, fashion design, and media industries ignores the underlying racial, gendered, and geopolitical inequalities that garment workers bear no matter who is on the runway or at the top of a masthead. Likewise, knee-jerk calls to boycott fast fashion isolate sweatshops to a specific sector while giving a pass to designer and luxury markets, whose products are often made in the same factories, under the same conditions, and by the same hands as budget and mass-market fashions. The "boycott fast fashion" logic at best misunderstands and at worst distorts the structural reality of fashion production under global capitalism. And in doing so, it elevates elite fashion brands and consumers as fashion's moral leaders and as garment workers' western and tacitly white saviors. Sweatshop reformist reforms share a common theme: they facilitate the racial, regional, and class hierarchies that make women and girls of the global south disproportionately—and almost entirely—vulnerable to the organized abandonment and violence of global fashion.

SWEATSHOP ABOLITION IN PRACTICE

Sweatshop abolition cannot be achieved through an individualist analysis or an individualist response. Abolishing sweatshops requires building solidarity across the various units of the supply chain; across geopolitical and hemispheric divisions; across multiple forms of carceral/capitalist institutions; and across race, gender, and class differences. Essentially, it means shifting away from individualist free-market feminism towards radical anti-capitalist women of color feminisms that have always insisted on structural critiques of capitalism, colonialism, racism, and patriarchy, and on prioritizing the collective, the collaborative, and the relational. Sweatshop abolition dismantles and remakes rather than improves the conditions that underwrite the organized abandonment of garment workers—the social, material, political, economic, and environmental relations that currently hold together global fashion supply chains. Sweatshop abolition works to end exploitation, not to lessen the degree of exploitation (e.g., fighting for a minimum wage, or even a living wage, that just covers workers' basic needs). Indeed, abolition isn't about doing, getting, or wanting the bare minimum for workers. Abolition opposes and antagonizes "the bare minimum" to demand, in Gilmore's words, "a future that has some sense of all the voluptuous beauty that life should hold."[46]

We can look to examples of sweatshop abolition currently in practice within garment worker cooperatives for guideposts toward sweatshop abolition. Two visionary examples include the Los Angeles–based group Homework for Health (H4H) and the Chicago-based Blue Tin Productions.[47] H4H and Blue Tin share fundamental organizational features. Both co-ops challenge the vertical structure of the garment factory model. Workers, not brands or factory owners, determine their employment conditions. Pricing, production schedules, payment structure, and whether to take a job or not are decisions that get made collectively rather than handed down from above.

H4H began in late March 2020 as a health and economic justice initiative between the Garment Worker Center and Al Otro Lado, a social justice legal organization serving indigent deportees, migrants, and refugees. It began as a means of organizing in and against the crisis of COVID-accelerated abandonment. As the name suggests, H4H workers make and sell cloth face masks at home. They share decision-making power, materials (e.g., fabric and elastic bands), workloads, and profits. While H4H workers produce fewer masks, they earn far more per mask than factory workers. In 2020 and 2021, garment factory workers in Los Angeles made $5.50 per hour making masks. H4H workers made approximately $5.50 per mask.*

H4H garment workers also have access to and can participate in various workshops focusing on online payment systems, photographing

---

* On September 27, 2021, California passed Senate Bill 62, known as the Garment Worker Protection Act (GWPA). The new law, effective in 2022, abolishes the piece-rate pay system and requires that garment workers are paid the state's minimum hourly wage. The GWPA also makes factories and brands jointly and severally liable for violations of the act.

and posting photos of masks online, web design, Spanish- and Eng-lish-language acquisition, and personal and business income taxes. The emphasis on workers' personal growth and well-being means that members choose how they work (one member, Yeni, often sews by hand) and when they work. H4H's organizational structure not only allows but encourages workers to prioritize familial and community responsibilities above work responsibilities. In Yeni's words: "I don't rush myself to do a very quick job [...] to get more work. What I want is only to maintain the work, to get an income, pay my taxes, and take care of my kids at home. That's enough for me." Paulina, another H4H worker, states: "I don't know how many masks I make an hour or a day. That's the awesome thing [about Homework 4 Health]."[48]

Blue Tin opened its doors in January 2019. Its current four mem-bers—all immigrant women from Nigeria, Turkey, Philippines, and Iran—work together in a studio in Chicago sewing collections for smaller labels with smaller runs. Blue Tin prioritizes designers who use sustainable fabrics, know the supply chain for their fabrics, design for nonnormative bodies, and/or have limited resources. Blue Tin offers a sliding scale production rate.

Like H4H, Blue Tin places their members' personal well-being over profits. Hoda Katebi, founding member of Blue Tin, explains: "Usu-ally a company will grow and then think about labor and sustainability, but that goes against the core of what we're trying to do at Blue Tin . . . We're developing Blue Tin's culture and organization *around* ethics and sustainability. We're trying to imagine what that world can look like where clothes can be made not only without violence but with care."[49] This ethic of mutual care and responsibility means that members might stop working to comfort another member suffering personal distress. Katebi related a couple of instances where Blue Tin lost a cli-ent because members decided to "stop production to walk together, to get ice cream," and in another case, assist a member to leave an abusive relationship by helping her look for an apartment. Blue Tin envisions itself as "a place where we can learn and grow and not just [a place] to earn a paycheck." Like H4H, Blue Tin organizes a variety of work-shops based on members' interests, such as postmenopausal self-care, domestic violence, and somatic coaching (a holistic mind-body-spirit approach to self-improvement and self-healing).

Homework 4 Health and Blue Tin Productions oppose fashion's extractive structure not by reforming it but by building entirely new relations and conditions of living and labor. Their practices recall Leanne Betasamosake Simpson's observation about the opposite of dispossession: "[W]hat's the opposite of dispossession in Indigenous thought again? Not possession, because we're not supposed to be capitalists, but connection, a coded layering of intimate interconnection and interdependence that creates a complicated algorithmic network of presence, reciprocity, consent, and freedom."[50] For H4H and Blue Tin Productions, "presence, reciprocity, consent, and freedom" are potential abolitionist principles for future social and labor practices.

NOTES

1. For more on prison garment factories, see Chiara Spagnoli Gabardi, "The Ethics of Fashion Brands Made in Prisons," *Eluxe Magazine*, August 25, 2017, https://eluxemagazine.com/culture/articles/fashion-brands-made-in-prisons/; Annie Kelly, "'Virtually entire' fashion industry complicit in Uighur forced labour, say rights groups," *The Guardian*, July 23, 2020, https://www.theguardian.com/global-development/2020/jul/23/virtually-entire-fashion-industry-complicit-in-uighur-forced-labour-say-rights-groups-china; Elizabeth Paton and Andrea Zarate, "Made on the Inside, Worn on the Outside," *New York Times*, February 21, 2019, https://www.nytimes.com/2019/02/21/fashion/prison-labor-fashion-brands.html.

2. Hannah Dreier, "'A recipe for disaster': American prison factories becoming incubators for coronavirus," *Washington Post*, April 21, 2020, https://www.washingtonpost.com/national/a-recipe-for-disaster-american-prison-factories-becoming-incubators-for-coronavirus/2020/04/21/071062d2-83f3-11ea-ae26-989cfce1c7c7_story.html.

3. Wes Venteicher, "California prisons sell coronavirus masks to the state. Are the prices too high?" *Sacramento Bee*, May 10, 2020, https://www.sacbee.com/news/politics-government/the-state-worker/article242614381.html.

4. See Venteicher, "California prisons sell coronavirus masks to the state"; Cary Aspinwall, Keri Blakinder, and Joseph Neff, "Federal Prison Factories Kept Running as Coronavirus Spread," *Marshall Project*, April 10, 2020, https://www.themarshallproject.org/2020/04/10/federal-prison-factories-kept-running-as-coronavirus-spread; and Luke Broadwater, "As coronavirus spreads in Maryland prisons, a small team of inmates makes 24,000 masks, other protective gear," *Baltimore Sun*, April 27, 2020, https://www.baltimoresun.com/coronavirus/bs-md-pol-prison-masks-20200427-fewq4quw6bd63n7fbdcx66rkj4-story.html.

5. Beth Schwartzapfel, Katie Park, and Andrew Demillo, "1 in 5 Prisoners in the U.S. Has Had COVID-19," *Marshall Project*. December 18, 2020, https://www.themarshallproject. org/2020/12/18/1-in-5-prisoners-in-the-u-s-has-had-covid-19.

6. Ruth Wilson Gilmore, "Forgotten Places and the Seeds of Grassroots Planning," in *Engaging Contradictions: Theory, Politics, and Methods of Activist Scholarship*, ed. Charles R. Hale (Berkeley and Los Angeles: University of California Press, 2008), 32.

7. See Edna Bonacich, Sabrina Alimahomed, and Jake B. Wilson, "The Racialization of Global Labor," *American Behavioral Scientist* 52, no.3 (2008): 342–55.

8. Quoted in Diane Elson and Ruth Eleanor Pearson, "'Nimble Fingers Make Cheap Workers': An Analysis of Women's Employment in Third World Export Manufacturing," *Feminist Review* 7, no. 1 (1981): 93.

9. Philip Shenon, "Made in the USA? Hard Labor on a Pacific Island," *New York Times*, July 18, 1993, https://www.nytimes.com/1993/07/18/world/made-usa-hard-labor-pacific-island-special-report-saipan-sweatshops-are-no.html.

10. See Shenon, "Made in the USA?" and Steven Greenhouse, "Suit Says 18 Companies Conspired to Violate Sweatshop Workers' Civil Rights," *New York Times*, January 14, 1999, https://www.nytimes.com/1999/01/14/us/suit-says-18-companies-conspired-to-violate-sweatshop-workers-civil-rights.html.

11. Greenhouse, "Suit Says 18 Companies Conspired to Violate Sweatshop Workers' Civil Rights." The garment worker pay gap has worsened since the 1990s. In 2020 garment workers making cloth face masks in Los Angeles were paid five dollars per hour or about 40 percent of the state's twelve to thirteen dollar per hour minimum wage.

12. Stephanie Strom, "A Sweetheart Becomes Suspect," *New York Times*, June 27, 1996, https://www.nytimes.com/1996/06/27/business/a-sweetheart-becomes-suspect-looking-behind-those-kathie-lee-labels.html.

13. Associated Press, "Kathie Lee Fights Back On Sweatshops," *Seattle Times*, May 2, 1996, https://archive.seattletimes.com/archive/?date=19960502&slug=2327066.

14. Julie A. Su and Chanchanit Martorell, "Exploitation and Abuse in the Garment Industry," in *Asian and Latino Immigrants in a Restructuring Economy*, ed. Marta Lopez-Garza and David R. Diaz, (Stanford, CA: Stanford University Press, 2002), 22.

15. John F. Harris and Peter McKay, "Companies Agree to Meet on Sweatshops," *Washington Post*, August 3, 1996, https://www.washingtonpost.com/archive/politics/1996/08/03/companies-agree-to-meet-on-sweatshops/b52ea250-f428-4f13-9e7a-389622d9a92f/.

16. Edna Bonacich, "Organizing Immigrant Workers in the Los Angeles Apparel Industry," *Journal of World-Systems Research* 4, no. 1 (1998): 10–19.

17. Natalie Kitroeff and Victoria Kim, "Behind a $13 Shirt, a $6-an-hour Worker," *Los Angeles Times*, August 31, 2017, https://www.latimes.com/projects/la-fi-forever-21-factory-workers/.

18. See Freddy Cuevas, "In Honduras, 'Sweatshop' Wages Better Than Nothing for Many Workers," *AP News*, July 16, 1996, https://apnews.com/article/fb4d8d420e730a16623275241409a11b; Paul Krugman, "In Praise of Cheap Labor," *Slate*, March 21, 1997, https://slate.com/business/1997/03/in-praise-of-cheap-labor.html; and Allen Myerson, "In Principle, A Case for More 'Sweatshops,'" *New York Times*, June 22, 1997, https://www.nytimes.com/1997/06/22/weekinreview/in-principle-a-case-for-more-sweatshops.html.

19. Hester Eisenstein, "The Sweatshop Feminists," *Jacobin*, June 17, 2015, https://www.jacobinmag.com/2015/06/kristof-globalization-development-third-world/.

20. As examples, see Tansy Hoskins, "The Feminist T-shirt Scandal Exposes an Entire System of Exploitation," *The Guardian*, November 3, 2014, https://www.theguardian.com/sustainable-business/sustainable-fashion-blog/2014/nov/03/feminist-t-shirt-scandal-exposes-entire-system-exploitation-elle-whistles-fawcett-society; Sirin Kale, "How Much It Sucks To Be a Sri Lankan Worker Making Beyonce's New Clothing Line," *Vice*, May 17, 2016, https://www.vice.com/en/article/d7anay/beyonce-topshop-ivy-park-sweatshop-factory-labor; and Simon Murphy and Redwan Ahmed, "'Girl Power' Charity T-shirts Made at Exploitative Bangladeshi Factory," *The Guardian*, March 1, 2019, https://www.theguardian.com/business/2019/mar/01/charity-t-shirts-made-at-exploitative-bangladeshi-factory.

21. Murphy and Ahmed, "'Girl Power' Charity T-shirts Made at Exploitative Bangladeshi Factory."

22. Elizabeth L. Cline, "Fashion's $16 Billion Debt to Garment Workers Should Spark Reform, Not Sympathy," *Forbes*, October 13, 2020, https://www.forbes.com/sites/elizabethlcline/2020/10/13/fashions-16-billion-dollar-debt-to-garment-workers-should-spark-reform-not-sympathy.

23. Jeffrey Vogt et al., "Farce Majeure: How Global Apparel Brands Are Using the COVID-19 Pandemic to Stiff Suppliers and Abandon Workers," (Berlin: Worker Rights Consortium/European Center for Constitutional and Human Rights, September 2020), 5.

24. Vogt et al., 6.

25. Vogt et al., 6.

26. Vogt et al., 4.

27. For example, see Soutik Biswas, "Coronavirus: India's Pandemic Lockdown Turns Into a Human Tragedy," *BBC*, March 30, 2020, https://www.bbc.com/news/world-asia-india-52086274; Brooke Roberts Islam, "The True Cost of Brands Not Paying for Orders During the COVID-19 Crisis," *Forbes*, March 30, 2020, https://www.forbes.com/sites/brookerobertsislam/2020/03/30/the-true-cost-of-brands-not-paying-for-orders-during-the-covid-19-crisis/; and Sarah Kent and M. C. Nanda, "Fashion's Humanitarian Crisis," *Business of Fashion*, April 1, 2020, https://www.businessoffashion.com/articles/global-markets/fashions-humanitarian-crisis.

28. Ruma Paul, "Garment Exporter Bangladesh Faces $6 Billion Hit as Top Retailers Cancel," *Reuters*, March 31, 2020, https://uk.reuters.com/article/health-coronavirus-bangladesh-exports/garment-exporter-bangladesh-faces-6-billion-hit-as-top-retailers-cancel-idUKKBN21I2R9.

29. Sushimita S. Preetha and Zyma Islam, "Bangladesh: 1931 Brands Have Delayed & Cancelled $3.7 Billion Worth of Orders from Garment Factories During COVID-19," *Daily Star*, June 29, 2020, https://www.thedailystar.net/business/news/you-suffer-we-survive-1920733.

30. Reuters, "Coronavirus cuts a swathe through Asia's garment industry, leaving thousands out of work," *South China Morning Post*, May 19, 2020, https://www.scmp.com/news/asia/southeast-asia/article/3084963/coronavirus-cuts-swathe-through-asias-garment-industry.

31. Reuters, "Coronavirus cuts a swathe through Asia's garment industry."

32. Tomoya Onishi and Yuichi Nitta, "Vietnam Garment Makers Hung Out to Dry as Global Orders Vanish," *Nikkei Asia*, April 19, 2020, https://asia.nikkei.com/Business/Companies/Vietnam-garment-makers-hung-out-to-dry-as-global-orders-vanish.

33. Bernie Cahiles-Magkilat, "30% of Garment Workers to Remain Jobless Till Dec." *Manila Bulletin*, August 20, 2020, https://mb.com.ph/2020/08/20/30-of-garment-workers-to-remain-jobless-till-dec/.

34. Clean Clothes Campaign, "Un(der) Paid in the Pandemic." (Amsterdam: Clean Clothes Campaign, August 7, 2020), 5.

35. Mei-Ling McNamara, "Anger at Huge Shareholder Payout as U.S. Chain Kohl's Cancels $150M in Orders," *The Guardian*, June 10, 2020, https://www.theguardian.com/global-development/2020/jun/10/anger-at-huge-shareholder-payout-as-us-chain-kohls-cancels-150m-in-orders.

36. Matt Blomberg, "Pandemic Seen Rolling Back Conditions in Asia Garment Factories," *Thomas Reuters Foundation News*, October 21, 2020, https://news.trust.org/item/20201021120504-od7au.

37. Clean Clothes Campaign, "Un(der) Paid in the Pandemic."

38. See Simon Glover, "Brands Named and Shamed Over Cancelled Orders," *Ecotextile*, March 31, 2020, https://www.ecotextile.com/2020033125899/materials-production-news/brands-named-and-shamed-over-cancelled-orders.html. Also see the Worker Rights Consortium COVID-19 tracker at https://www.workersrights.org/issues/covid-19/tracker/.

39. A number of brands such as American Eagle Outfitters, Bestseller, URBN (Urban Outfitters, Anthropologie, and Free People), Gap, and Debenhams demanded retroactive discounts as a condition of payment. See the Worker Rights Consortium, "Updates and Analysis," May 1, 2020, https://www.workersrights.org/updates-and-analysis/#May01Asda; and Simon Glover, "Debenhams 'demands 90% discount on order,'" *Ecotextile*, May 11, 2020, https://www.ecotextile.com/2020051126067/fashion-retail-news/debenhams-demands-90-discount-on-orders.html.

40. Brooke Bobb, "This Hashtag Unlocked $15 Billion of Lost Wages Due to Cancelled Orders from Gap, Levi's, and Other Brands," *Vogue*, July 10, 2020, https://www.vogue.com/article/remake-payup-campaign-social-media-garment-workers-wages-gap.

41. My thanks to Mark Anner for speaking to me by phone about this on January 5, 2022. Anner is a labor scholar and board member of Re/make (the nonprofit organization that launched the #PayUp campaign).

42. Quoted in Redwan Ahmed, "'I thought about killing my children': the desperate Bangladesh garment workers fighting for pay," *The Guardian*, December 10, 2020, https://www.theguardian.com/global-development/2020/dec/10/i-thought-about-killing-my-children-the-desperate-bangladesh-garment-workers-fighting-for-pay.

43. Anuradha Nagaraj, "Indian garment workers cover bosses' lockdown losses," *Reuters*, October 22, 2020, https://www.reuters.com/article/us-india-workers-trfn/indian-garment-workers-cover-bosses-lockdown-losses-idUSKBN2771PK.

44. Alysha Khambay and Thulsi Narayansamy, "Union Busting & Unfair Dismissals: Garment Workers During COVID-19" (London: Business & Human Rights Resource Centre, August 2020), https://media.business-humanrights.org/media/documents/files/200805_Union_busting_unfair_dismissals_garment_workers_during_COVID19.pdf.

45. Annie Kelly and Harriet Grant, "Jailed for a Facebook Post: Garment Workers' Rights at Risk During COVID-19," *The Guardian*, June 16, 2020, https://www.theguardian.com/global-development/2020/jun/16/jailed-for-a-facebook-post-garment-workers-rights-at-risk-during-covid-19.

46. Ruth Wilson Gilmore and Naomi Murakawa, "Ruth Wilson Gilmore on COVID-19, Decarceration, and Abolition," (Chicago: Haymarket Books, April 17, 2020) video, https://www.haymarketbooks.org/blogs/128-ruth-wilson-gilmore-on-covid-19-decarceration-and-abolition.

47. See Homework 4 Health, https://www.homework4healthla.org; Blue Tin Productions, https://bluetinproduction.com.

48. Yeni and Paulina, Zoom conversation with author, November 18, 2020.

49. Hoda Katebi, phone conversation with author, December 21, 2020.

50. Leanne Betasamosake Simpson, *As We Have Always Done: Indigenous Freedom Through Radical Resistance* (Minneapolis: University of Minnesota Press, 2017), 185.

"THE SOAP, THE SHOWER CURTAIN, AND THE MOPPING UP"

Tabitha Lean

(CW: sexual violence)

The air was thick and damp and heavy. The moisture from the shower was carried along warm wafts and drifts of steam that circled upward, sailing along the planes of the ceiling, resting uncomfortably amongst the cracked and peeling paint, where water damage had swollen the plaster and bubbles of moisture had burst it open like war wounds revealing the bloodied flesh beneath. The fluoro lights overhead buzzed persistently, flickering intermittently casting random shadows that stretched and shrank against the grey walls—walls that reeked of institutional bleakness and misery.

The whole place was devoid of any real character, and yet somehow the architecture contained within it centuries of violence, pain, and oppression. It was difficult to breathe in this space—the air was too thick and the damp, black, overgrown mould infiltrated your lungs like fingers creeping across the surface of your breathing organ and filling it with spores, turning your insides black, while the musty smell tapped annoyingly at the edges of your nostrils begging to be let in. In here, you learnt to breathe in shallow breaths through your mouth, because the blocked drains let off a stench that could rot all of your senses from the inside, leaving you with the taste of filth and death for days.

I stood steady with my eyes closed tight, head tilted upwards (I always loved the feeling of rainfall on my face especially when it was coupled

with the moon's crepuscular rays bathing me in its twilight beams—
oh, for those days). This was a rare moment of solitary. Everything
was communal in here no reflective space, certainly no privacy. Hot
water streamed from the shower nozzle: the kind of stream that comes
out in fits and bursts, splutters even—the kind of inadequate pressure
that gives out just enough to get you wet, but leaves you holding a
grudge against the hard and rough lime scale on the chrome plugging
all the little holes closed. But in this place, you have to be grateful for
anything that can wash away the grime that burrows its way into your
open pores like a fungus, clogging your skin with its omnipresence. I
could hear the girls in the yard, someone had a basketball, bouncing
it repeatedly up and down the court, the sort of repetitive sound that
grates on your nerves, but in this place consistency is hard to come
by, so you take what you can get. I could hear someone else swear-
ing loudly: cursing the other girls or the staff or the world—likely all
three. This place is built upon mountains of discontent. The women
in here are caught in endless cycles of punishment and pain, buried
in entrenched ruts of melancholy, and trapped in trauma so deep that
freedom from the familiar is near on impossible—scary, even.

The mirrors in this place had fogged over, and beads of conden-
sation dripped down in wandering trickly lines, intersecting and
growing thicker until those trails pooled along the chipped, cheap
melamine benches, stained and etched with women's markings. The
bathroom door was slightly ajar (Of course! Nothing worked how it
should in this shit hole) and wisps of steam filtered through the crack
into the corridor. The place was otherwise quiet, as quiet as it was
going to get. I hummed a familiar tune to give company to the sound
of water splashing down creating a symphony with the crinkle of the
worn, ripped shower curtain with its broken hooks, that left it hanging
slightly askew, barely holding back the sploshes of water. It seemed
that the state of that shower curtain epitomised the hopelessness and
dysfunction of this place.

Within an instant, the bliss bubble I had constructed had burst. It
was as swift as a needle piercing a balloon but without the bang or the
tears of the toddler left holding a flaccid crumple of latex. In a single,

well-trained move, my back was pressed against the wall pinning my body into submission. I

1

felt my shoulder slip along the slimy surface and winced. Fuck, I'd never get clean now. I felt the ooze of blood running down my back like little rivers following their natural water course. Drips of red hit the floor and were quickly overwhelmed and absorbed by the water—fuck those broken tiles. I gasped in shock as pain seared down my side like a hot knife running through butter. The water rained down on me—us—it ran across my face, drips perching along the ridges of my brows, welling along my eyelashes while mini streams poured along the lines of my neck, travelling down to my chest turning my breasts into rocky water falls.

My breathing was hard as their lips took possession of mine. The hot water was intoxicating and my body betrayed me and I felt warmth spread to the extremities. We were both interminably wet, hair saturated and their soaked clothes pressed against my naked body. I reached up, but with one swift

move my hands were pinned against the tiles. Their mouth and lips and hands roamed roughly across my naked form, along the curves and across all the soft edges. I thought if I just stood still, if I didn't react, didn't submit or respond or breathe even, they'd move on...but I very quickly realised that this wasn't the entree, I was the whole fucking buffet. So there I stood, eyes closed, holding my breath, counting slowly in my head...counting to the highest number I could go...and at 328 it was over...relief washed across me like the perfect wave, but instead of riding that crescent to the shore, I sank to my knees and sobbed; big, fat salty tears—you know, the kind of crying that twists your face and distorts all your features? Pain is so fucking ugly.

I huddled in the corner of the shower, rubbing the bar of grey soap pathetically against my knee, salty tears and shower water combined to rain down on me. The force of it was ripping my breath away. And then I could hear someone screaming. It was terrifying, blood curdling, and it just kept going on and on and on. With furrowed brow, I crawled along the floor, pathetically naked, rising to my knees, until I was staggering wet footprints across the room. I used the bench to haul my heavy body upright, and I saw myself in the mirror—it was me. It was me screaming. Instantly I clapped my hands to my mouth to stop the terror from escaping my throat, as if my hand could contain all of the pain and all of the panic, as if anything could. I watched the blood slowly ooze from the slit in my brow, and my eye was starting to bloat with a purplish-green hue. As if seeing through another lens, I saw the weight of depression clinging to my body, like an oversized coat I had borrowed in the winter. My mind wondered at how I had got to this place in this space in this time…it hurt to remember, it physically hurt, it hurt to the pit of my stomach and echoed through the valleys of regret down to my soul—it was as if each memory was so tightly stored away that I had to squeeze it out like the last bit of toothpaste in the tube. I wrestled with each memory, and tore the gaffer tape from the archives in my mind. My hands gripped the basin, knuckles white with the strain, while thick globs of blood slowly fell onto the porcelain.

I forced myself to think. I thought about how I had been lured into suppression. I thought about everyone who had fed off me and discarded me like week-old food. I thought about how my body had been stripped bare, a rotting carcass of my former self, an empty shell with no hope, no future, no fight left in me, not even a roar. I was battle weary. I was tired, so fucking tired. I was consumed by an ineffable sadness, a grief so palpable, and a weariness that sagged and oozed from every pore.

I had been assaulted, night after night in this place and to my surprise it was a wolf that brought me finally to my knees. But if I'm being fair, it had started before I came to this place. The violence—the brutality—it followed me as if I was pied piper leading every fucking rat to my door. I would always walk a little more warily. I would always sleep a little less deeply. I was changed on a molecular level. It was the ubiquitous slaps in the face I couldn't stand. And I longed for peace, because even though I've always chosen delirium over death, anything right now would be better than the reality.

2

And then someone flushed the toilet in the next stall, they cleared their throat. The siren rang for the girls to come back inside, it was time to line up, time to be counted. I bowed my head in submission as I glanced around the crime scene, letting the tidal wave of sadness wash over me, praying today wasn't the day that it drowned me, knowing I'd have to be prepared for it all to begin again tomorrow…because I am just a number—a sequence of six tiny, little numbers—numbers don't feel pain, numbers have no rights, numbers need no dignity.

Numbers…we are all just numbers inside.

Beware the calls for unity

QTGNC STORIES FROM US IMMIGRATION DETENTION AND ABOLITIONIST IMAGINARIES, 1980–PRESENT

Tina Shull

The shocking death of Roxsana Hernández in the summer of 2018 follows from a decades-long history of abuse and neglect of queer, trans, and gender nonconforming (QTGNC) migrants in US immigration detention. Hernández traveled with a Central American migrant caravan through Mexico in the spring of 2018, arriving at the US port of entry in Tijuana on May 9, seeking asylum in the United States. Customs and Border Patrol (CBP) immediately detained her, placed her in a freezing hielera (icebox), and transferred her one week later to Immigration and Customs Enforcement (ICE) custody at the private-contract Cibola County Correctional Center in New Mexico. HIV-positive, denied access to medical care, and bearing marks of physical abuse, Hernández died two weeks after entering the United States. An independent autopsy confirmed deep bruising and injuries consistent with the abuse she alleged and complications related to HIV.[1]

That August, queer and migrant rights groups led an action in Albuquerque, New Mexico, blocking traffic and demanding #Justicefor-Roxsana. Kris Hayashi of the Transgender Law Center stated: "This is a moment of moral clarity. Black and brown transgender migrants, fleeing persecution and seeking safety in the US, are being locked up, killed through abuse and neglect, and deported back to death

sentences by the United States government. It is past time for leaders of the LGBTQ+ movement to do what it takes to hold our government accountable and put our bodies on the line until all of our
people are free to survive and thrive."[2] The Transgender Law Center
filed a wrongful death tort claim in New Mexico. In October of 2019
Hernández's attorneys reported that despite the lawsuit, ICE deleted
footage of her in detention in violation of federal rules—yet another act
of impunity. Roxsana's story, and ICE's suppression of it, points to the
violence facing trans women across society more broadly and illustrates
the anatomy of migrant detention: isolation and routine denials of due
process, medical care, adequate nutrition, and communications with
the outside; vast discrepancies between written standards and practices
on the ground; physical and psychic assaults; and retaliation. In sum, a
system of state violence characterized by erasure and removal.*

As a historian, I explore how imperial and carceral logics have been
raced and gendered across time and place, and, as praxis, I work with
communities affected by detention to archive stories that resist and
upend these logics.[3] Echoing other abolitionists, I argue that QTGNC
stories from detention must be centered in efforts to end immigration
detention, informed by abolition feminism, a "liberatory vision" led
by women, trans, and gender nonconforming people of color to build
a world "free from all forms of violence, including those produced by
carceral logics and systems of surveillance, policing, punishment, and
exile."[4] Through an analysis of government documents, media sources,
migrant and activist testimonies, made objects, and acts of resistance,
this essay explores stories of QTGNC migrants in detention and their
collaborators since the eighties. I ask how stories in various forms serve
either to fuel or to counter state violence, and how QTGNC migrants
and collaborators wield them to forge what I call *abolitionist imaginaries*—alternate archives that illustrate both vision and praxis for a world
without violence. Beginning with an analysis of the contestation of

---

* QTGNC migrants are disproportionately subjected to the routine abuses of
medical neglect and sexual assault in detention. See reporting by Freedom
for Immigrants and Human Rights Watch at freedomforimmigrants.org and
hrw.org.

narratives surrounding Mariel Cubans detained on US military bases and in prisons in the eighties, and feminist, queer, and migrant rights organizing against Haitian detention through the HIV/AIDS crisis of the eighties and nineties, it explores the ways in which queer and trans people resisted from the inside and led "inside-outside" and coalition organizing on the outside to challenge detention in its entirety. Finally, I consider the role of storytelling in personal and activist responses to detention and calls for abolition in the late 2010s—and its relationship to trauma.

RACE, GENDER, AND CRIMINALIZED MIGRATION

Roxsana's forced migration, detention, and death—and the efforts of advocates to keep the crisis of trans detention in public view—provide a small window into the mechanisms of US empire and its maintenance of a vast complex of nearly three hundred local, federal, and private facilities that has grown tenfold since the mid-1980s and by early 2020 has imprisoned a high of over fifty thousand migrants a day and four hundred thousand a year across the United States.* Hers and a resurgent number of deaths in detention under the Trump administration raise urgent questions of how this system came to be and how it continues, obscured from public view. Systems of incarceration have always disproportionately targeted specific groups of people based on race, most clearly, but also on gender, class, dis/ability, and ideology. Together, these markers of difference have shaped immigration policy and detention practices. Historian Kelly Lytle Hernández argues that today's prison landscape must be understood as an extension of the United States's history as a white-settler colony. In this way, migrant detention operates within legacies of immigrant exclusion, slavery and Jim Crow–era segregation, Native American removal, and their

---

*   Due to the COVID-19 pandemic, detention numbers reached their lowest since the mid-2000s at 13,500/day in February 2021 but have been rising again under the Biden administration to 22,000/day as of January 2022. In 2019 the United States detained a record number of 69,550 migrant children in addition to the adult detention population. See ICE.gov.

attendants—white supremacy, patriarchy, and ableism—that are tied together in a process of "mass elimination" that is continuous and dynamic.[5]

Here I join a growing body of scholarship that theorizes the displacement and confinement of queer and trans migrants, not only to show how their liminality renders them more vulnerable in carceral systems but also how "a queer approach" can help us reimagine borders and belonging entirely. Labeled by the state as problem populations, QTGNC migrants are pathologized, criminalized, and subjected to higher rates of abuse, sexual assault, and death in the immigration detention system.[6] Detention itself is gender violence. As experiences of migration and confinement are starkly gendered, so are imperial logics shaping them. The US immigration system follows a paternalism that, according to A. Naomi Paik, "normalizes relations of domination in highly gendered terms of kinship, whereby the United States acts as the needed (if unwanted) guardian to infantilized refugees."[7] Such humanitarian terms obscure the violence of detention, but QTGNC migrants in detention tell otherwise.

In theory, immigration detention is a civil procedure distinct from the criminal legal system. Not subjected to punishment in a legal sense, migrants in detention are not "doing time." Instead, they are suspended in it, awaiting either deportation or release which can take months or years. They may be undocumented, or asylum seekers newly arrived in the US, or legal permanent residents targeted for removal for commission of certain crimes. In practice, detention looks and feels like prison, functioning within a larger context of mass incarceration in the US. Moreover, the criminalization of migration itself since the 1980s, a phenomenon called "crimmigration," has melded these systems together in ways that have made them increasingly indistinguishable— from local law enforcement's cooperation with ICE to the building of "mixed-use" facilities. Immigration violations now comprise over half of all federal charges, while many migrants now serve lengthy prison sentences for reentry before entering the administrative detention and removal process.[8] Whether administrative or punitive in name, "a jail is a jail is a jail."

The early 1980s marked an important turning point in the history of migrant detention—a time of real and perceived economic, social, domestic, and international crisis. Cold War–foreign policy and migration trajectories were inextricably linked, and the Reagan administration moved to enact stricter immigration enforcement policies of detention and deterrence in response to three asylum-seeking migrant groups in particular—Cubans, Haitians, and Central Americans.[9] Black and Indigenous migrants of color, and QTGNC migrants especially, pose a threat to the US imperial project and the white-settler nation as their literal presence embodies its failures. Mass migrations of these migrant groups during this time of perceived public crisis—themselves created and fueled by US Cold War–foreign policy, migration controls, and media and public panic—served to justify the Reagan administration's expansion of the detention system, obscure the impact of its foreign policies, and retaliate against and silence migrant voices and allied opposition. Caribbean and Central American asylum seekers stood at the center of the formulation of policies that have since fueled detention's growth.

However, alternative narratives abounded, from within spaces of detention and from inside-outside and coalition activism, illustrating the intersections of oppression facing migrant, racialized, and QTGNC groups. These acts of resistance sought to expose state abuses while envisioning alternatives to trajectories of US imperialism and prison doctrines embraced by subsequent administrations. Overlapping episodes of violence that mark the history of immigration detention inflict intergenerational trauma, but they also open possibilities for forming new solidarities and abolitionist imaginaries.

QTGNC MARIEL CUBANS AND THE RISE OF A DETENTION REGIME

The 1980 Mariel Cuban boatlift, a mass migration of nearly 130,000 Cubans to southern Florida during the summer of 1980, was a catalytic event for the rise of the contemporary US immigration detention system and for bringing queer migrant politics to the forefront of public debate. Coinciding with the Carter-Reagan election, the Mariel Cuban migration, as well as increasing arrivals of Haitians and Central Americans fleeing repressive dictatorships and US–backed civil wars, stoked public xenophobia and became an enduring symbol of crisis evoked by the Reagan administration to develop new policies of detention and deterrence in the early 1980s.[10] Overwhelmed by the Mariel migration and widespread rumors and media reporting of Cuban sexual deviance and criminality, the Carter administration did not grant Mariel Cubans immediate refugee status. Instead, they were given a temporary legal status and sent to four military bases across the country for processing. Here, I trace contesting narratives surrounding queer and trans Mariel Cuban migrants detained at Fort Indiantown Gap, Pennsylvania, and Fort Chaffee, Arkansas, in order to illustrate the liminality of camp life and possibilities for resistance. Government documents reveal how QTGNC migrants shaped detention policymaking and modes of retaliation that became embedded in detention's design. However, acts of resistance and oral histories also show how queer and trans migrants claimed lives within detention, challenging their indefinite detention and the US Cold War asylum regime more broadly.

The passage of the 1980 Refugee Act shortly before the Mariel boatlift began promised to align US asylum policy with the United Nations Refugee Protocol of 1967, opening possibilities for a broadening of the definition of "refugee." Previously, the US had predominantly granted refugee status only to those fleeing communism. However, despite the 1980 act, the retrenchment of the Reagan era saw a return to Cold War–priorities, and the act's promises of providing asylum seekers more due process went largely unfulfilled. Furthermore, in 1980 homosexuality was still grounds for inadmissibility in US immigration law. Mariel Cubans posed a dilemma: because they were undeportable due to strained US-Cuba relations, Immigration and Naturalization Service (INS) stopped screening migrants for homosexuality in the fall of 1980.[11] Susana Peña argues this ambiguous policy inflicted a "fractured gaze" on Cubans as "authorities had to see homosexuals in order to move them out of the media spotlight even as they claimed not to see the homosexuals in order to deny their existence to the media."[12] This uneven process of seeing and not seeing resulted in misreporting, distorted media narratives, and imposed segregation on detained QTGNC migrants, but it also opened spaces for them to maneuver within.

Oral histories reveal how Cubans navigated liminal spaces to affirm and demand respect for their identities. Some played up or performed queerness in order to receive exit papers to leave Cuba, hoping to be accepted "with open arms" by the US, while others who were imprisoned in Cuba for being gay were forcibly removed. Armando, for example, says he wore "the gayest outfit he could find" during his interview with Cuban police officers, while Antonio wore an "eye-catching outfit" and "spoke in a fake voice, exaggerating my mannerisms so that they would be convinced that I was a homosexual."[13] Armando does not remember being asked about his sexuality while screened by INS and sent to Fort Chaffee. However, the Cuban-Haitian Task Force, formed by Carter to manage the camps, weighed options for handling four "problem" groups slowing the resettlement process and receiving outsized media attention: the "criminal element," "unaccompanied minors," "mental illness," and "homosexuals." Under heightened public and official scrutiny, members of these groups experienced a range of segregation and punitive practices in detention that, in effect, confirmed their "deviance," heightened suffering, and prolonged detention times.[14]

At first, Cubans seemed fairly free to recreate social life in refugee camps. Single men, single women, QTGNC migrants, and families were housed separately, mostly by choice, and a black market of commodities, including sex, was not regulated.[15] QTGNC migrants were unofficially sent to Fort Indiantown Gap in Pennsylvania. Cuban-edited camp newspapers, *La Libertad* at Fort Indiantown Gap and *La Vida Nueva* at Fort Chaffee, acknowledge gender nonconforming groups, mostly in relation to sexually transmitted infection education. Reflecting the camp's homophobic gaze, an interview with a Cuban named Tamayo in *La Libertad* relates: "[P]roblems which occur with the homosexuals are being controlled, since generally they keep to their own side of the area or around their barracks, or get sent to other areas. Here in America, homosexuality is not a crime, so it seems gays are enjoying their newfound freedom, perhaps in an exaggerated way, and causing problems by agitating straight men and families, who do not like their children to see or hear certain things."[16] This assumption of freedom, however, became increasingly problematic.

Mark Segal, activist and founder of the National Gay Newspaper Guild and the *Philadelphia Gay News*, recounts how he was one of the first to learn of QTGNC Cubans detained at Fort Indiantown Gap through a friend at the Metropolitan Community Church (MCC). Wanting to get the "scoop," Segal and a friend drove out to the heavily guarded camp. Segal wore a black Nehru shirt with cardboard in the collar, posing as a priest and telling US Army guards that he was a representative of MCC there to help "resettle the homosexuals." Looking disgusted, a guard directed them to two barracks. Segal recalls: "It was like a party was going on in that place. There were drag queens throwing material around each other, they were trying on makeup . . . even in captivity, in an Army base, they felt that freedom. It was amazing." When Segal said they were from a gay newspaper, "the whole place lit up. A gay newspaper! Gay people are here! And they all came running over . . . it was very festive and very loud. And about half an hour later we found ourselves surrounded by the Army with rifles drawn." They left with their camera and tape recorder. A few days later, Segal received a call from a general demanding the tape and film, but it was too late. "We were the first newspaper in America to report on the gay Cubans in Pennsylvania."[17]

Despite stories of solidarity and freedom, detention became increasingly punitive. When Reagan entered office in January of 1981, five thousand Cubans who had been consolidated at Fort Chaffee remained—many were single men, Black, queer, and/or trans, and difficult to find sponsors for. Efforts to obtain sponsorship and resettlement for Cubans involved cultural training and expressions of heteronormative "American" values; by contrast, those who remained excludable were rendered invisible by continued detention.

The largely xenophobic reception of Mariel Cubans in the adjacent town of Fort Smith, Arkansas, highlights familiar anti-immigrant themes seen at various times throughout US history: foreign threats of criminality, financial burden, disease, and sexuality.[18] Preoccupations with disease and sexual deviance were intimately tied to race. Media reporting highlighted the spread of tuberculosis, gonorrhea, and syphilis in the camps. A local newspaper reported a rumor that twenty Cubans had raped a female police officer at Fort Chaffee, allegedly beginning with a local Ku Klux Klan (KKK) organizer reporting the incident to Governor Bill Clinton's office.[19] Similar stories abounded. After an uprising at the camp in April 1981 in which one Cuban was shot, the *Arkansas Democrat* ran an article that began: "Fort Chaffee—The insane who huddle under blankets are sedated lest they cut their wrists to get attention. Homosexuals swish along dusty streets in drag. Single young women bear children conceived in the American resettlement camp. These are the unwanted Cubans at Fort Chaffee." Republican governor Frank White, who unseated Clinton in 1981, sent this article to the White House relaying the "desperate need to resolve this situation" and demanding the camp's closure.[20]

Sylvia Gonzalez of the Cuban-Haitian Task Force noted that queer life at Fort Chaffee was "freer" than in Cuba or the United States. However, "we have to impress upon them that homosexuality is not an accepted thing by Americans at large . . . once they've been assigned a sponsor, you'll see that the eyebrows tend to grow out and the make-up fades as they prepare for reality." That gender nonconformity proved a liability outside the camp says more about the severity of discrimination across US and Cuban society, however, than it does about so-called freedom in detention. Working against pervasive anti-Blackness and homophobia, sponsor organizations pressed Cubans to demonstrate a willingness to "fit in" with US society. Paula Dominique of the Church World Service told the *New York Times*: "There are people who call up and request a white, college-educated Cuban who speaks English . . . We remind them that we're not a Sears catalogue."[21] Most sponsors preferred women, children, or families, but the majority of those held at Fort Chaffee were young, single males. Almost three-quarters were Afro- or dark-skinned Cubans; only 16 percent were reported to have spent time in jail in Cuba or the US.[22]

Top Reagan administration officials affirmed Governor White's request to remove Cubans from Fort Chaffee and the state. Chief of Staff James Baker reassured him, "Nobody wants these people," and Vice President George Bush wrote that handling the "undesirables" was a "high priority in the administration."[23] Such was official language as the administration scrambled to mitigate fallout from the visibility of the Mariel "crisis" but struggled to find a state or site willing to accept Cuban refugees. Considering a pitch for a private contract facility in Montana, they instead transferred the remaining Cubans at Fort Chaffee to prisons throughout the country in 1982. The administration labeled it an "interim" solution that would be "faster and millions of dollars less expensive" than building a new detention center.[24] However, as the Reagan administration committed to using carceral punishment to deter migration, thousands of Mariel Cubans remained imprisoned for years, and some for well over a decade.

In 1980 some Mariel Cubans had already began filing individual habeas corpus claims from within detention, and some won their release. In November of 1982 one thousand jailed Cubans filed a class-action lawsuit challenging their indefinite detention and claiming that undocumented migrants should have due process rights, but it failed. US government counsel Douglas Roberto said, "If the attorney general determines they are a danger to society, he doesn't have to let them out." In 1986 the Eleventh Circuit upheld the indefinite detention of Mariel Cubans in *Garcia-Mir v. Meese*.[25]

Nations such as the United States wield categories of refugee status as a tool of empire, but asylum claims can also be a powerful site of resistance. One such claim was that of Fidel Armando Toboso-Alfonso, who arrived with the Mariel boatlift and was paroled into the US in 1980. But INS redetained him and terminated his parole for possession of cocaine, deeming him deportable for this crime of "moral turpitude." In response, Toboso-Alfonso filed a political asylum claim in 1985 based on the 1980 Refugee Act's protection of members of "a particular social group," in this case, homosexuals. INS argued such a persecuted group did not exist, but Toboso-Alfonso demonstrated that Cuban police kept a file on homosexuals, thus documenting a decade of discrimination he faced in Cuba before arriving in the United States. In 1990 the court found he had experienced persecution in Cuba for being gay, and he won his freedom.

Matter of Toboso-Alfonso was the first successful asylum case defining homosexuals as a persecuted group and proved an effective challenge to the United States's Cold War refugee paradigm. Also in 1990, the United States repealed homosexuality as grounds for inadmissibility in immigration law. In 1994 Attorney General Janet Reno established this ruling as a new precedent for asylum cases, ultimately shaping a new QTGNC migrant politics in the United States.[26] Today, such asylum cases are a powerful challenge to the prolonged detention of QTGNC migrants and have secured the release of many, effectively saving lives.

Fig. 1. Two gender nonconforming Cuban individuals grooming in their barracks at Fort Chaffee, c. 1981. Courtesy of Charles Lee Hughes Fort Chaffee Photograph Collection, University of Arkansas Special Collections.

HUNGER STRIKES, UPRISINGS, AND INSIDE-OUTSIDE ACTIVISM

Some of the most effective challenges to immigration detention have come from inside-outside activism, in which outside collaborators follow the experience and leadership of those on the inside. This section considers a range of tactics employed in Haitian- and Mariel Cuban–resistance to detention and inside-outside and coalition organizing in the 1980s and early 1990s, as advocacy groups launched litigation, storytelling, and direct actions in support of migrant-led hunger strikes and uprisings inside prison walls. This discussion is far from complete, but it underlines various ways in which migrants inside and feminist, queer, and migrant rights organizations on the outside worked together to make detention's abuses visible and demand accountability from the state.

Detention experiences and modes of resistance illustrate state policing of queer bodies, including those with HIV/AIDS. The rise of the HIV/AIDS crisis was inextricably (and tragically) intertwined with Cuban and Haitian migration in the 1980s, especially at the intersections of public panic over Afro-Caribbean migration, contagion, and the development of detention policy. In 1978 US patients began exhibiting symptoms of AIDS, the same year the Carter administration established the Haitian Program, designed to detain Haitian asylum seekers and fast-track deportations. In 1982 the Center for Disease Control (CDC) reported a link between Haitians and HIV, less than a year after the United States announced new mandatory detention and Haitian interdiction policies. HIV/AIDS also disproportionately devastated resettled queer Mariel Cuban communities in Miami, Philadelphia, and San Francisco. In 1987 the same year that the United States legislated a ban on HIV-positive migrants from entering the US, the longest-lasting uprising of detained migrants—a two-week prison takeover—occurred in Oakdale, Louisiana, and the Atlanta Federal Penitentiary in Georgia, with negotiations led by queer Mariel Cuban migrants. This section concludes with a rare victory: the closure of the US government's Haitian HIV-quarantine camp at Guantánamo Bay effected by inside-outside organizing in 1993.

The US government's exceptional discrimination against Haitian asylum seekers since the late 1970s—as seen in mass rejections of Haitian asylum cases, long-term detentions in prisons and detention sites, medicalized quarantines, and being the only migrant group subjected to interdiction on the high seas—reveals the anti-Blackness underwriting immigration detention's growth since the 1980s. After Reagan took office, INS resumed a ramped-up version of Carter's Haitian Program—in direct refutation of a judge's ruling that the program was racist and discriminatory.[27] These moves were met with a new wave of inside-outside activism, critical public opinion, and ongoing legal actions seeking due process for detained Haitians. Haitian resistance during the Reagan era mirrored Mariel Cuban resistance, yet inside-outside and solidarity organizing was even more broad-based as groups connected Haitian detention to civil rights struggles, anti-imperialism, feminism, and HIV/AIDS, health, and dis/ability justice.

As Haitians wielded their bodies and voices to wage hunger and labor strikes in detention, the radical women's collective and feminist publication *Off Our Backs* worked to support Haitians across multiple detention sites and to share their stories with the public using an inside-outside approach. The collective formed a Creole-speaking Women's Task Force for Haitian Political Prisoners, who visited asylum-seeking Haitian women detained at the Krome facility in Miami and a federal prison in Alderson, West Virginia. In a series of articles in 1982, *Off Our Backs* stated solidarity with political prisoners and detained migrants in Haiti and the US resisting dictatorship and US imperialism, connecting struggles for freedom from slavery, colonialism, worker exploitation, and gender discrimination across time and place.

Off Our Backs details conditions of Haitian confinement in women's own words as they recounted horrific instances of reproductive violence and retaliation in detention. This includes pregnant women being systematically given injections to induce abortions upon arrival in Miami; Haitian and Cuban women held in "extreme isolation" at Alderson; deprived of physical contact and information; and wages of ten dollars a month for laboring in the prison's mattress factory compared to two hundred dollars a month paid to incarcerated citizens.[28] Haitian women at Alderson also experienced retaliation in the form of restricted phone and visitation access for trying to communicate with the outside world and routine harassment by INS officers.

The publication critiqued the prison's infantilizing of Haitian women, creating space for stories of suffering and resilience. Visitor and medical anthropologist Lani Davidson wrote in April of 1982: "They call them girls. They call the building in which they are imprisoned—a dank brick structure encircled by a 15-foot chain link fence—a cottage. Cottage 26. They say they are proud when 'their girls' walk unescorted over to the cafeteria, when they say 'I love you' in the hallway after English class, when they call their unit supervisor 'Mommy.'" Countering this were testimonies of "common anguish." One woman speaking anonymously for her protection shared: "Life is getting worse and worse in here. The only time we get out of here is to eat, to go to chapel once a week, and to the doctor's—if they say our complaint is valid. We can't call anyone except relatives, and no one can call us." Grave physical- and mental-health crises abounded, including suicide attempts, nervous seizures, bleeding lips and bruises, depression, weakness, fatigue, and hospitalizations. "Many refuse to eat," Davidson writes. "Boredom is one of the worst facets of women's lives here." However, these testimonies also reveal resilience. Women organized prayer services with "music played through paper-covered hair combs and songs written during the many long hours of anxiety and pain," while a visitor named Renee ran a "home-fashioned beauty salon," washing women's hair in a laundry sink. Davidson relays a message from the women: "We are not idle people, or stupid like they told us in Miami. We have our hands and our bodies and our minds. We are strong. In the death that they want us to have so much, we know life. You tell them they can never take that away from us."[29]

Organized and politicized, Haitians utilized group tactics of hunger strikes and sit-ins to resist their detention. The *Off Our Backs* task force coordinated across detention sites to amplify the women's demands. In response to rumors they would be transferred to Central America, women organized hunger strikes at Krome and Alderson in April 1982.

In a letter detailing the reasons for the strike, women at Alderson write: "Are we not human beings like all other human beings? . . . Or is it because we're black? They don't treat refugees from other countries like this." And, "We know that if we go back we will disappear within the blink of an eye . . . we prefer to die here." At Krome in Miami, forty-one women staged a hunger strike and "sit out," joined by men through a fence separating them. After sleeping outside for five days, several were hospitalized, and one force-fed intravenously. Protestors on the outside staged a May Day demonstration, and supporters in California joined the hunger strike as well. The article concludes, "A negative consequence is that surveillance and other security measures have been stepped up at Krome and Alderson."[30] Such a ramping up of abusive detention conditions, resistance, and state retaliation escalated throughout the Reagan era.

As mentioned above, several thousand Mariel Cubans remained imprisoned for much of the 1980s. Some were imprisoned since arrival, while others reincarcerated largely as a result of intense surveillance and policing targeting this migrant group. In the summer of 1987, INS District Director Louis Richard described those still imprisoned: "We've got everything from skyjackers, arsonists, rapists, murderers, aggravated assaults, crimes of virtually every type you can think of. A couple hundred are hard-core deviates that do strange things. They are psycho cases. I would be for keeping these people in jail for the rest of their lives before I would take a chance on letting one harm your child."[31] Reflecting homophobia and ableism underlying immigration restriction more broadly, these comments also reveal how Mariel Cuban migrants, in particular, were simultaneously criminalized and pathologized. However, testimonies of imprisoned Cubans shared with advocacy groups, lawyers, and the media detailing abusive prison conditions contrast sharply with official narratives.[32]

The 1987 Mariel Cuban Oakdale and Atlanta prison uprisings occurred against the backdrop of long-simmering resistance to Reagan's detention policies. According to Loyd and Mountz, between 1985 and 1989, there were at least twenty-five other "disturbances" across the detention system. In 1984 Cubans were put on lockdown in

Atlanta after setting fire to their belongings. In 1985 fifty-five Cubans staged a disturbance while on a bus transferring them to a federal penitentiary in Atlanta. And at the Krome facility in Florida in 1986, Cubans set fire to their belongings once again and were subsequently transferred to other sites including a "mixed use" Federal Bureau of Prisons (BOP)/INS facility in Oakdale, Louisiana.[33]

Not mere anarchy, the Oakdale and Atlanta uprisings of 1987 were a highly organized public plea, sparked in response to news that the United States and Cuba had negotiated to repatriate all remaining imprisoned Mariel Cubans. Newly available documents from the Department of Justice (DOJ) regarding the uprisings reveal DOJ and Attorney General Edwin Meese's retaliation against Cuban unrest as they closely monitored and refuted sympathetic media coverage of the standoff. As Cubans carefully staged negotiations, leveraging hostages, the media, and religious and pro-US messaging to demand compassion, they raised public awareness of the injustice of their prolonged detention. In a matter of hours, fifteen hundred Cubans took hostages and set fire to buildings of the detention center in Oakdale, with one thousand Cubans enacting the same two days later in Atlanta's federal penitentiary.

During negotiations, led by BOP Director Michael Quinlan and Meese, Cubans ran both prisons in a coordinated, theatrical manner, staging threats of violence to leverage media access, with support from the Coalition to Support Cuban Detainees in Atlanta and Cuban-American bishop Agustin Román from Miami. In the end, only one civilian was injured and negotiations ended peacefully with a promise to halt deportations and provide individual case reviews—which INS would largely renege on. The DOJ's continued racial profiling, antipathy, and dismissal of Cuban credibility exacerbated the crisis. As the longest prison takeover in US history finally drew to a close, mixed public reactions continued.

Media depictions of the uprisings, while increasingly sympathetic, augmented the "family man" identity of Cubans leading the prison siege, centering the voices of wives and children on the outside.[34] Bishop Román echoed this sentiment, arguing that deportation was inhumane due to Cubans' establishing families in the US. A Freedom of Information Act (FOIA) request I filed to obtain the DOJ's documentation of negotiations during the hostage and prison takeover, however, reveals that the lead Cuban negotiators were "homosexuals." The DOJ's notes describe "no real leadership," dismissing their horizontal organizing tactics. Meese's refusal to include Cuban advocates in negotiations and the Cubans' mistrust of INS stalled negotiations. An FBI psychological profile of Mariel Cubans, also in the DOJ's files, reveals the melding of the US government's raced, gendered, and ableist characterizations of the migrant group. Under "typical psychological characteristics" of the "Cuban majority," it lists:

1. Low tolerance for frustration

2. Impulsive; seek immediate gratification wishes

3. Concrete thinking; low-average intelligence

4. Willing to take risks without considering consequences

5. Psychologically naive; able to be influenced by more sophisticated manipulators

6. Criminal mindset due to time served in US and Cuban prisons

7. Exaggerated pride in masculinity and bravado

8. Emotionally labile; quickly shift emotions (sometimes in a matter of minutes) from one extreme to another

9. Minimal social skills; unable to function in a complex society

10. Unrealistic hopes and aspirations about life/freedom in US

11. Positive feelings for US but negative feelings toward US government

The memo continues by summarizing the "model Cuban prisoner" as someone who is "both culturally disadvantaged and developmentally retarded." While able to distinguish right from wrong, he is "primitive," but with "street sense," and "willing to lie and take advantage of situations." He "is only capable of holding the lowest paying jobs," and finally, he has "neither the self-discipline nor the patience required to better himself through more acceptable social ways."[35]

Seven years after Mariel, it was clear that top levels of US government had written off the humanity of "undesirable" Mariel Cubans still in custody. While the Reagan administration moved to retaliate and rebuild, inscribing a new carceral chapter in the detention of "criminal aliens," Mariel Cubans were once again dispersed across the US prison landscape and forgotten. Like other prison uprisings in US history such as Attica in 1971, the Oakdale and Atlanta uprisings were an organized attempt to gain control over prisons in the pursuit of a goal, yet remarkable in their transnational, anti-deportation politics. Lawyer Mark Hamm concludes, "The outstanding feature was respect for life and human dignity."[36]

The entanglements of "xenophobia, racism, nationalism, and fears of HIV/AIDS" in the late eighties and early nineties led to coalition organizing that brought QTGNC- and migrant-rights groups together in common cause.[37] In its lesser-known history, the AIDS Coalition to Unleash Power (ACT UP), a direct-action organization responding to the HIV/AIDS crisis, began building coalitions with immigrant rights groups and organized actions on behalf of detained migrants in Los Angeles and New York City. ACT UP members would also play a central role in the fight to close the Haitian refugee HIV-quarantine camp established at Camp Bulkeley at Guantánamo Bay, Cuba, in the early 1990s.

While ACT UP's legacy is largely remembered as single-issue advocacy for domestic medical and health-care reforms for white gay males, the ACT UP Oral History Project uncovers more intersectional moments. ACT UP Latino Caucus member Moises Agosto remembers he was initially drawn to the organization as it fit within a "grassroots movement" including the Latinx and African American community in New York. "That was where I wanted to go— communities that were already disenfranchised."[38] However, he also noted tensions within the organization, skepticism from communities of color toward ACT UP's more privileged members, and personal frustrations with a "lack of will" to include more women and racialized communities.

Two sites of ACT UP actions, outside of a hotel INS used to detain migrants in Los Angeles in 1988 and at the Varick Street detention center in New York in 1991, featured a range of storytelling tactics and mobilized a "coalition of voices."[39] In Los Angeles, ACT UP Education Cochair Larry Day addressed the crowd:

> Those of us gathered here today are here to speak with one voice: to say 'enough'—to say 'basta'—to the Immigration and Naturalization Service . . . We are here to demand justice for our immigrant brothers and sisters. Over the past few years, the AIDS-affected and the immigration-affected communities have witnessed similar political phenomena . . . This recent history has taught us that we are again in need of building and strengthening our coalitions so that our key issues are never again swept under the political rug.[40]

In New York, a series of ACT UP actions protesting the detention of HIV-positive Haitians at Varick Street and in the Haitian HIV-quarantine camp at Guantánamo Bay were recorded and produced as a series of episodes of Damned Interfering Video Activists (DIVA) TV. In these productions, formerly detained migrants shared their stories while advocates read letters and testimonies from those inside. Two ACT UP members, Betty Williams and Bro Broberg, located housing for Haitians released from Guantánamo Bay and paroled into the US. Williams recounts an emergency meeting of grassroots activists and members of the Haitian community to organize a trip to Guantánamo where, because of their shelter work with ACT UP, she and Broberg were authorized to provide mental health support to Haitians on hunger strike and threatening suicide. Williams recalls meeting with Haitians in an unused camp area: "We were never allowed in the camp, never, never, never, which actually helped us with the folks, because that's the way they treated Jesse Jackson."[41] While never an official program of ACT UP, Williams and Broberg resettled one hundred Haitians in the New York City area. By the mid-nineties, divisions within ACT UP and the Haitian advocacy community and difficulties faced in locating sponsors led to the disintegration of ACT UP's detention advocacy. Nonetheless, Karma Chávez asserts the importance of remembering and uncovering these histories. As "imperialism, poverty, homophobia, sexism, and racism promulgate what continues to be, for many, a deadly disease," "queer archive activism" such as DIVA

TV and conducting oral histories provides a "model for queer coalition building and AIDS activism that accounts for the complexities of oppression, repression, and illness."[42]

Ultimately, litigation and inside-outside activism led to the closure of Camp Bulkeley. As lawyer Michael Ratner recounts, a hunger strike organized and led by HIV-positive Haitians and joined by university students across the US galvanized a campaign to close the camp in 1993. In her history of Haitian detentions at Guantánamo in the early nineties, A. Naomi Paik argues that the US's "benevolent" premise of establishing the HIV-quarantine camp veiled its extraordinary forms of violence. However, paralleling the organization of imprisoned Mariel Cubans described above, Haitians resisted their detention at Bulkeley by organizing themselves into the Association des Refugies Politiques Haitians and modeled representative democracy to uplift testimonies from detention and organize a hunger strike as a collective way to, in Paik's words, "expose their living death."[43]

Litigating on behalf of Haitians, Ratner and his team at Yale Law School concluded that although their Haitian clients seemed to have "everything against them: they were immigrants at a time of intense anti-immigration hysteria, they were also Black, Creole-speaking foreigners; they had strong political ideas; and they were HIV-positive," their positionality brought together a wide array of constituencies. AIDS activists, Haitians, African Americans and civil rights leaders such as Jesse Jackson, refugee and human rights organizations, religious leaders, students, Hollywood and public figures concerned about AIDS, and anti-imperialists all contributed to the campaign. Ratner argues that this intersectional coalition building and their following the leadership of those in detention led to the campaign's success.[44]

STORIES TO END DETENTION

As QTGNC migrants have been subjected to increasing violence and have wielded their voices and bodies to resist detention in recent years, this concluding section contemplates the role of storytelling as resistance, its abolitionist potentials, and its harms. Whether personal expression or performative tactic to win an individual or a group's freedom, stories can challenge the system in its entirety, but the work of storytelling is fraught. In a landscape rife with trauma and retaliation, piecing together archival records is a fragmented and often dangerous process. My concerns here are shaped by my experience as a Soros Justice Fellow at the organization Freedom for Immigrants in 2016–18, where I collaborated with people in detention to document, archive, and mobilize their stories. Finally, I recount and reflect upon contestations surrounding community efforts to close the trans detention "pod" at the Santa Ana City Jail in California as a move toward abolition.

Stories are often critiqued for their singularity and as "trauma porn" contributing to tropes of migrant victimization. As Sujatha Fernandes cautions, stories can fuel neoliberal agendas, especially if "reconfigured on the model of the market to produce entrepreneurial, upwardly mobile subjects." Individual stories lacking context can also "shift the focus away from structurally defined axes of oppression and help to defuse the confrontational politics of social movements."[45] Speaking out can also risk retaliation, persecution, and even death—impacts that fall disproportionately on marginalized communities. Even if done anonymously or in relative safety, telling one's story often exacts a toll by reanimating trauma. However, humanities-based approaches to understanding immigration enforcement through storytelling— whether in narrative, art, poetic, multimedia, or another form—also offer great possibilities. Stories form an alternate archive to challenge the logics of imperialism and xenophobia, bring data to life, and help articulate the unspeakable traumas of immigration enforcement. Storytelling can also heal and empower affected communities.

Gretta Soto Moreno, a trans woman, artist, and asylum seeker from Mexico, was detained with men at the Eloy detention center in Arizona for over two years where she was routinely harassed and abused. In a moment of desperation, Gretta severely cut her genitalia with a razor and wrote "no more violence on trans women" in her blood on the wall of her cell. She was then transferred to the Santa Ana Jail in California in 2015, where the city had contracted with ICE to establish the only detention pod specifically for trans migrants in the country. Santa Ana's trans pod was a result of mounting advocacy for queer and trans people in detention in the late 2000s and early 2010s. As Karma Chávez argues, identity-based petitions to the Department of Homeland Security, such as that made by the National Immigrant Justice Center (NIJC) on behalf of thirteen queer and trans individuals detained by ICE in 2011, may lead to material improvements in detained migrants' lives, but they also reveal a potential pitfall of inside-outside organizing. By demanding review and accountability within the system's existing structures, petitions like NIJC's may divert more resources to reform efforts such as the creation of trans pods rather than abolition—inadvertently fueling the system's growth.[46]

A 2016 Human Rights Watch report based on interviews with twenty-eight trans women held in immigration detention between 2011 and 2015 describes conditions Gretta experienced as the norm. While detention may often echo abuse trans women have previously endured, incarceration further subjects trans women to gendered violence through traumas of solitary confinement, sexual assault, lack of access to medical care including HIV-related care and hormone therapy, and routine strip searches.[47] Despite its establishment as an alleged "safe" space for trans women, the Santa Ana trans pod routinely subjected migrants to these violences, including strip searches conducted by male guards.

Volunteers from the detention watchdog organization Freedom for Immigrants (FFI) began visiting Gretta at Santa Ana and worked for her release in 2016. Now Gretta sits on the organization's leadership council. She says having visitors and doing art helped her survive her time in detention. While at Santa Ana, she drew her account of an assault she witnessed (figure 2), supporting a complaint filed by FFI. Her artwork most often depicts women's shoes, birds, and flowers signifying freedom (figure 3) and is featured in a zine we published of poetry by people formerly detained and visitor volunteers.[48] In a poem titled "Unknown Identity," Gretta writes of her time in detention: "One thousand days of my freedom, I am sad with God / Oh not again blaming others for my mistakes / I go back to where I came from / I do not know, Lord, help me / At the end of the road I am free / I am a woman / But who binds me? / I do not know / I'll hide myself and pretend to be happy."

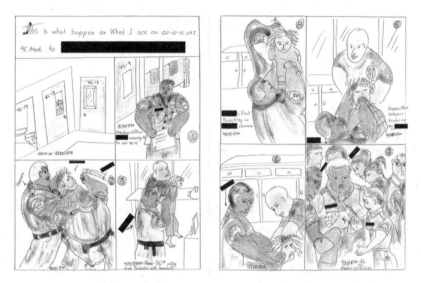

Fig. 2. "This is what happen or what I see on 2-10-16": Gretta's telling of abuse in the Santa Ana jail's detention pod for trans women. Courtesy of Gretta Soto Moreno.

Fig. 3. Artwork by Gretta Soto Moreno while detained at the Santa Ana Jail in California c. 2016. Courtesy of Gretta Soto Moreno.

As an outspoken activist, Gretta has recounted her story many times in her own asylum case and for journalists, legislators, legal briefs, and community members, undoubtedly leading efforts to end detention in myriad ways. I remember a time Gretta and I spoke to a congregation in San Diego, each of us sharing our experiences with detention. I remember the shock of the audience upon hearing Gretta's story, and the same sharp pain that shoots up my spine every time I speak publicly about my ex-husband's deportation and why I do this work. I wonder, what toll does telling take?

In 2016 the city of Santa Ana voted to end its contract with ICE and close the jail's trans pod, a result of years of mounting local activism and hunger strikes led by trans activists both inside and outside. This work has paved the way for Santa Ana's passing a sanctuary ordinance after Trump's election in 2017, its subsequent phasing out of its ICE contract, and now, efforts to close and repurpose the jail entirely. This illustrates the abolitionist potentials of QTGNC stories and queer- and trans-led activism.

However, tensions among those detained and community organizers arose as they debated the merits of closing the trans pod. Many were concerned that the pod's closure would result in the transfer of trans women to more repressive jails in Texas and New Mexico—such as Cibola, which opened after Santa Ana's closure and where Roxsana died in 2018—while others maintained that the closure was a crucial step toward abolition. Las Crisantemas, an organization of students at University of California Irvine and Cal State Long Beach founded to support QTGNC migrants in detention, took an abolition feminist stance to social media using the hashtags #EndTransDetention and #AbolishAllJailsPrisonsAndDetentionCenters.

Upon the pod's closure, Freedom for Immigrants, Las Crisantemas, and community organizations worked quickly to find sponsors for trans women detained at Santa Ana and to fight for their release rather than transfer. However, a small number of trans women were not released and instead were transferred to New Mexico. Debates over piecemeal reforms, e.g., working to end trans or child detention first versus working towards abolishing the entire system, are recurring and important. But working on campaigns to improve conditions or free individuals from incarceration does not necessarily run counter to or distract from longer-term goals of abolition. Instead, this work can be a radical act of collective political education.

This essay has explored how the resistance of QTGNC migrants in detention over the past four decades has sought to dismantle the logics and apparatus of US imperial power while showing the potentials of QTGNC stories for mapping abolitionist imaginaries. What role can historians, ethnic studies, and humanities scholars play in this work?

Organizations like the Queer Detainee Empowerment Project (QDEP) in New York, Las Crisantemas in southern California, and the Transgender Law Center in San Francisco argue that centering and advocating for QTGNC migrants in detention is the first step towards abolition. Others point to the global context of QTGNC detention, drawing lessons from the "victory" of the United Kingdom's near-elimination of trans detention in 2016.[49] Las Crisantemas supports QTGNC migrants in detention and works on individual campaigns to free people by selling artwork and hand-woven objects to raise money for their bonds as well as engaging in storytelling and media work that is inside-outside driven. Peace-building organization Activate Labs does similar work in its accompaniment of Central American youth and refugee caravan members, engaging both migrants in and those affected by detention in storytelling that is informed by participatory action research methods as well as conducting art-centered "trauma healing spaces" workshops.

What are the costs of extracting stories and made objects, and what is just compensation? On one hand, performative storytelling can reanimate trauma. On the other, community-driven storytelling can build solidarity, awareness, and healing. Feminist scholar and abolitionist Angela Davis asserts: "The trans movement is so important not because we need to acknowledge the pain and suffering, and how trans women of color bear the brunt of all violences," but, "It is also important that we realize what we are doing when we challenge the binary structure of gender . . . we recognize the possibility of challenging all other categories we take for granted." Art, she concludes, helps us go beyond these categories, even "if only for a short period of time," and "helps to create community among us."[50]

Fig. 4. A shoe woven out of food wrappers by a QTGNC asylum seeker from Ghana at the Adelanto Detention Facility c. 2018. Courtesy of the author.

Reflecting on scholar-activist attempts to make resistance to state violence visible, Julian Gill-Peterson credits ACT UP's intersectional and "sweeping critique of state power, the police, homophobia, racism, sexism, and poverty." Gill-Peterson asks how we learn to live with the "ghosts produced by the inheritances" of the HIV/AIDS crisis as the urgency of the epidemic has faded into what is now an endemic and "continuous biopolitical management of death in life." Are we "too late to intervene in the ways those who came before us did?"[51] Since 2020 the COVID-19 pandemic has thrown the violence of incarceration, and these questions, into sharper relief, but the pandemic also opened up new abolitionist imaginaries when detention numbers reached their lowest in 2021.

We may ask a similar question of histories of resistance to immigration detention, as bordering and carceral practices have become endemic to US society and detention numbers are again rising. Telling stories by creating and reassembling community-based material and digital archives are ways to explore these haunting questions as well as recognizing the outsized burden of storytelling on QTGNC, people of color, and other marginalized groups. In *Invisible No More*, Andrea Ritchie recounts stories of police brutality and state violence facing women and queer people of color, urging us to "mobilize what we learn to deepen our analyses of racial profiling, police brutality, and mass incarceration, and expand them along the axes of gender, gender identity, and sexuality alongside race, ethnicity, religion, class, nation, immigration status, and disability." What can these stories tell us about racism, colonialism, and gender-based violence? Ritche asks, "What gaps do they expose in our thinking and actions?"[52]

Gretta says, "People have power and I want them to begin using it to hold their government accountable for the abuse it does to people like me."[53] *

NOTES

1. Sandra E. Garcia, "Independent Autopsy of Transgender Asylum Seeker Who Died in ICE Custody Shows Signs of Abuse," *New York Times*, November 27, 2018, https://www.nytimes.com/2018/11/27/us/trans-woman-roxsana-hernandez-ice-autopsy.html.

* I would like to thank the Open Society Foundations, the Charles Warren Center at Harvard University, and the Goizueta Foundation and Cuban Heritage Collection at the University of Miami for their generous support of my research. I would also like to thank Gretta Soto Moreno, Freedom for Immigrants, the Transgender Law Center, the Queer Detainee Empowerment Project, Las Crisantemas, Activate Labs, and Emily S. Rosenberg, Christina Davidson, Courtney Sato, Hannah Waits, David Hernández, Jessica Ordaz, Martha Balaguera, Jenna Loyd, Karma R. Chávez, and Sandibel Borges for their constructive feedback.

2. Transgender Law Center, "Roxsana Hernandez," https://transgenderlawcenter. org/legal/immigration/roxsana.

3. See Immprint at imm-print.com and Climate Refugee Stories at climaterefugeestories.com.

4. INCITE! Women of Color Against Violence, "Abolition Feminism: Celebrating 20 Years of INCITE!" *INCITE!*, accessed March 30, 2020, https://incite-national.org/2020/02/05/abolition-feminism-celebrating-20-years-of-incite/; Mariame Kaba and John Duda, "Towards the horizon of abolition: A conversation with Mariame Kaba," *Next System Project*, November 9, 2017, https://thenextsystem.org/learn/stories/towards-horizon-abolition-conversation-mariame-kaba.

5. Kelly Lytle Hernández, *City of Inmates: Conquest, Rebellion, and the Rise of Human Caging in Los Angeles, 1771–1965* (Chapel Hill: University of North Carolina Press, 2017), 9; Kristin Garrity Sekerci and Azza Altiraifi, "A US immigration history of white supremacy and ableism," *Al Jazeera*, op-ed, January 31, 2018, https://www.aljazeera.com/opinions/2018/1/31/a-us-immigration-history-of-white-supremacy-and-ableism.

6. Eithne Luibhéid and Karma R. Chávez, *Queer and Trans Migrations: Dynamics of Illegalization, Detention, and Deportation* (Urbana: University of Illinois Press, 2020), 5; Lauren Zitsch, "Where the American Dream Becomes a Nightmare: LGBT Detainees in Immigration Detention Facilities," *William and Mary Journal of Women and the Law 22* (2015): 105–28.

7. A. Naomi Paik, "Carceral Quarantine at Guantánamo: Legacies of US Imprisonment of Haitian Refugees, 1991–1994," *Radical History Review* 115 (Winter 2013): 156.

8. Judith A. Greene, Bethany Carson, and Andrea Black, *Indefensible: A Decade of Mass Incarceration of Migrants Prosecuted for Crossing the Border* (Austin, TX: Grassroots Leadership and Justice Strategies, 2016), https://grassrootsleadership. org/sites/default/files/reports/indefensible_book_web.pdf.

9. Kristina Shull, "Reagan's Cold War on Immigrants: Resistance and the Rise of a Detention Regime, 1981–1985," *Journal of American Ethnic History* 40, no. 2 (Winter 2021): 5–51; Jenna Loyd and Alison Mountz, *Boats, Borders, and Bases: Race, the Cold War, and the Rise of Migrant Detention* (Oakland: University of California Press, 2018).

10. Shull, "Reagan's Cold War on Immigrants"; Loyd and Mountz, *Boats, Borders, and Bases.* See also Carl Lindskoog, *Detain and Punish: Haitian Refugees and the Rise of the World's Largest Immigration Detention System* (Gainesville: University of Florida Press, 2018).

11. Donnel Nunes, "Rules on Immigration by Homosexuals Eased," *Washington Post*, September 10, 1980.

12. Susana Peña, "'Obvious Gays' and the State Gaze: Cuban Gay Visibility and U.S. Immigration Policy during the Mariel Boatlift," *Journal of the History of Sexuality* 16, no. 3 (September 2007): 498–99.

13. Peña, "Obvious Gays," 482; 488.

14. Kristina Shull, "'Nobody Wants These People': Reagan's Immigration Crisis and the Containment of Foreign Bodies," in *Body and Nation: The Global*

Realm of U.S. Body Politics in the Twentieth Century, ed. Emily S. Rosenberg and Shanon Fitzpatrick (Durham, NC: Duke University Press, 2014).

15. Gastón A. Fernández, *The Mariel Exodus: Twenty Years Later: A Study on the Politics of Stigma and a Research Bibliography* (Miami: Ediciones Universal, 2002), 42–43.

16. La Libertad, August 1, 1980, box 36, Cuban Haitian Task Force Files (CHTF), Carter Presidential Library (CPL).

17. Mark Segal et al., "Mark Segal," LGBTQ Marielitos Oral History Project, William Way LGBT Community Center; *Philadelphia Gay News* 4, no. 21, August 21, 1980.

18. Erika Lee, *America for Americans: A History of Xenophobia in the United States* (New York: Basic Books, 2019).

19. "KKK allegation still unconfirmed," *Southwest Times Record*, August 16, 1980, A7, folder "Other Newspapers," box 42, CHTF, CPL.

20. Frank White to Rich Williamson, April 20, 1981, letter; Peter Arnett, "Cubans Caught in 'Beauty, Tragedy' of System," *Arkansas Democrat*, April 19, 1981, folder "General Correspondence," box 9, Francis S. M. (Frank) Hodsoll Files, Reagan Presidential Library (RPL).

21. Paul Heath Hoeffel, "Fort Chaffee's Unwanted Cubans," *New York Times*, December 21, 1980.

22. María Cristina García, *Havana USA: Cuban Exiles and Cuban Americans in South Florida, 1959–1994* (Berkeley and Los Angeles: University of California Press, 1996), 71; "Meeting with Governor White on Fort Chaffee," February 20, 1981, folder "CHTF Office of Public Affairs," box 12, CHTF, CPL.

23. George Bush to Frank White, June 3, 1981, letter, folder "Detention Center and Chaffee Working Files (2)," box 8, Francis S. M. (Frank) Hodsoll Files, RPL.

24. "Termination of Ft. Chaffee Operations," n.d., folder "Immigration Policy: Cubans and Haitians," box 10, James Cicconi Files, RPL.

25. Philip Erickson, "The Saga of Indefinitely Detained Mariel Cubans: Garcia Mir v. Meese," *Loyola Los Angeles International and Comparative Law Review* 10 (1988): 271.

26. Julio Capó Jr., "Queering Mariel: Mediating Cold War Foreign Policy and US Citizenship Among Cuba's Homosexual Exile Community, 1978–1994," *Journal of American Ethnic History* 29, no. 4 (Summer 2010): 99–100.

27. *Haitian Refugee Center v. Civiletti*, 503 F. Supp. 442 (S.D. Fla. 1980); Lindskoog, *Detain and Punish*, 56–62.

28. Lani Davidson, "Haitian Women Prisoners Stand Strong," *Off Our Backs* 12, no. 4 (April 1982): 15; 27.

29. Davidson, "Haitian Women Prisoners Stand Strong."

30. Maya Spencer, "Haitian Prisoners Stage Hunger Strike," *Off Our Backs* 12, no. 6 (June 1982): 12.

31. Mark S. Hamm, *The Abandoned Ones: The Imprisonment and Uprising of the Mariel Boat People* (Boston: Northeastern University Press, 1995), 80.

32. Elliott Young, *Forever Prisoners: How the United States Made the World's Largest Immigrant Detention System* (Oxford: Oxford University Press, 2021), 122–24.

33. Loyd and Mountz, *Boats, Borders, and Bases*, 112; Ari L. Goldman, "From Tiny Cuban Port to Louisiana Rampage," *New York Times*, November 23, 1987.

34. Young, *Forever Prisoners*, 147.

35. O.B. Revell and F.I. Clarke to FBI Director, November 29, 1987, memo, folder "30-03," box 1, Records Relating to the Oakdale and Atlanta Prison Riots, 11/23/1987-12/4/19 (OAPR), FOIA Request #60856, Record Group 60, NARA II.

36. Hamm, *The Abandoned Ones*, 18.

37. Paik, "Carceral Quarantine at Guantánamo," 155.

38. Moises Agosto Interview, ACT UP Oral History Project, December 14, 2002. Available at actuporalhistory.org.

39. Karma R. Chávez, "ACT UP, Haitian Migrants, and Alternative Memories of HIV/AIDS," *Quarterly Journal of Speech* 98, no. 1 (2012): 63–68. See also Guantánamo Public Memory Project, available at gitmomemory.org.

40. Actions and Events 1987–1997. Action: Los Angeles Resistencia Protest-Mardi Gras Hotel Immigration and Naturalization Service (INS) Detention Center AA88.0319.1 1988. MS ACT UP Los Angeles Records: Actions and Events 1987–1997, folder 15, box 4. ONE National Gay & Lesbian Archives.

41. Betty Williams Interview, ACT UP Oral History Project, August 23, 2008. Available at actuporalhistory.org.

42. Chávez, "ACT UP," 66.

43. Paik, "Carceral Quarantine at Guantánamo," 156–59.

44. Michael Ratner, "How We Closed the Guantanamo HIV Camp: The Intersection of Politics and Litigation," *Harvard Human Rights Journal* 11, no. 187 (1998): 211.

45. Sujatha Fernandes, *Curated Stories: The Uses and Misuses of Storytelling* (Oxford: Oxford University Press, 2017), 3–4.

46. Karma R. Chávez, "Protecting LGBT Immigrant Detainees: The Rhetoric of Identity and the Expansion of the Prison-Industrial Complex," in *The Rhetorics of US Immigration: Identity, Community, Otherness*, ed. E. Johanna Hartelius (University Park, PA: Penn State University Press, 2015), 70–90.

47. Adam Frankel, "Do You See How Much I'm Suffering Here? Abuse against Transgender Women in US Immigration Detention," Human Rights Watch, March 23, 2016, https://www.hrw.org/report/2016/03/24/do-you-see-how-much-im-suffering-here/abuse-against-transgender-women-us.

48. Alicia Partnoy, Christina Fialho, and Kristina Shull, eds., *Call Me Libertad: Poems Between Borders*, (San Francisco: Community Initiatives for Visiting Immigrants in Confinement, 2016), https://www.freedomforimmigrants.org/poetry.

49. Shana Tabak and Rachel Levitan, "LGBTI Migrants in Immigration Detention: A Global Perspective," *Harvard Journal of Law and Gender* 37 (2014); Rachel Savage, "UK should not detain 'at risk' LGBT+ asylum seekers: lawmakers," *Reuters*, March 21, 2019.

50. Angela Davis, "Radical Commitments: The Life and Legacy of Angela Davis" (Boston, Harvard Radcliff Institute, October 29, 2019).

51. Julian Gill-Peterson, "Haunting the Queer Spaces of Aids: Remembering ACT UP/New York and an Ethics for an Endemic," *GLQ: A Journal of Lesbian and Gay Studies* 19, no. 3 (2013): 280.

52. Andrea J. Ritchie, *Invisible No More: Police Violence Against Black Women and Women of Color* (Boston: Beacon Press, 2017), 233.

53. Tina Vasquez, "#ICEOnTrial: Advocates Rally to Hold Federal Agency Accountable for Systemic Abuses," *Rewire News*, April 11, 2018.

Maria Gaspar, "Disappearance Suit," Captiva, FL, 2018

THE POLITICS OF EVERYDAY LIFE

PALESTINIAN WOMEN INSIDE ISRAELI COLONIAL PRISONS

Samah Saleh

INTRODUCTION

Mariam was held captive in an Israeli colonial prison cell in the late 1960s for her involvement in the Palestinian resistance. She recalls a memory during that time that still sits with her today: when Israeli prison guards were celebrating Israeli Independence Day, their Palestinian captives were commemorating the Palestinian *nakba*, or the "catastrophe" of 1948. The prison staff put Israeli flags up around the prison, which made the Palestinian women angry. They felt that this was a provocation directed at them, and the women decided to collectively challenge it, strategically arranging to take down all the Israeli flags. They succeeded and celebrated their achievement and their assertion of agency, even as captives of colonial regimes. For them, taking down the flags was a means of performing their *sumud*, or steadfastness, inside prison. According to Palestinian critical theorist Lena Meari, sumud "is not definable" as a specific practice, but it can be approximated as "a Palestinian mode of becoming and orienting oneself in colonial reality." Sumud is a "constant revolution in becoming and its significance lies in its non-conceptualized features."[1] In response to their collective removal of the flags, the women were put in isolation for punishment and then moved to another prison with harsher conditions. However, as Mariam said, "*We never cared about their punishments.*" Important here is a reflection on the ways in which fear of punishment did not diminish the agency Palestinian women prisoners felt over their own actions and their role in the struggle. Continuing to resist, even while in prison, their collective commitment to sumud demonstrates the broader political and psychological gains prisoners have contributed to Palestinian liberation.

Palestinian women have been involved in resisting British imperialism and Zionist colonial settlement and land theft since before the 1948 nakba. Since then, women's participation in the struggle has grown and shifted along different axes of the national struggle. More recently, women have been a central acting force in the Palestinian intifadas and the continued struggle to end the Israeli occupation. Women from different classes were involved in both major uprisings, joining street demonstrations, hurling stones and shouting at the Israeli soldiers, or using their bodies as barricades to block the beating or arrest of their children and homes. Especially during the First Intifada, women played essential roles in popular and neighborhood support committees to effectively replace the institution of the Israeli Civil Administration in towns, villages, and camps.[2] These activities were a type of grassroots organizing that centered everyday actors in the broader political struggle. Committees formed during this period to mobilize women around issues of family and work, creating day care centers, after-school activities, clinics, health and education programs, literacy classes, and vocational training. They pioneered the unionizing of women workers and established women's industrial collectives. As a result, these committees reached women from all backgrounds and established a critical convergence of social movement as part of the political struggle.[3]

This extended to the Second Intifada but in a changed political landscape in which women enacted "maternal" roles,* took part in marches,

---

* As Penny Johnson and Eileen Kuttab wrote during the moment it unfolded, the Second Intifada differed sharply from the first in its gender-order: "The extension of women's roles in the First intifada was possible because the division between combatants and non-combatants was very fluid. In the second intifada . . . 'combatants' are highly defined by gender and age. As a result, women's reproductive role as bearers of the fighters, a politicized role already present in Palestinian political culture, is heightened, and the mothers

and supported families of the injured and the martyred.[4] The broader landscape of crisis, despair, and resistance during this epoch provided the grounds for women to move inward and outward: both to learn more about themselves and to come into contact with other women activists in various women's committees and other collectivities. These connections allowed them to gain confidence and legitimacy as actors of history making and encouraged them to speak up, network, interact, and become part of the public and political scene. In this era, women in the Palestinian movement challenged existing social discriminatory hierarchies and renegotiated gender norms in social and political fields of struggle.[5] Yet these generative elements also required women to put their bodies and livelihoods in the physical line of fire. Indeed, many were killed, targeted for arrest, detained, and harassed for being related to men who were suspected of being linked to armed groups or for participating in militant actions themselves.[6]

More than sixteen thousand Palestinian women have been held in Israeli prisons since 1967. At the beginning of 2011 the number of imprisoned women was 110, which fell to thirty-six in the wake of a prisoner exchange negotiated by Hamas. Today, there are approximately thirty-nine women in prison, but the number fluctuates according to the intensity of the political moment and the success of prisoner exchanges.[7] For example, when clashes with Israel intensify, the number of women in prison increases. Despite the longevity of the Palestinian struggle, the undeniable role women's movements have played as part of the broader national liberation movement, and the history of imprisonment Palestinian women have endured, few studies discuss women's experiences and stories of imprisonment. As Ismail Nashif has argued, women are oftentimes relegated to representations through the eyes of and in relation to imprisoned men.[8] In my own review of the literature, I have similarly found scarce mention of women's roles. The overwhelming trends in scholarship on the Palestinian political struggle seem to ignore underlying gender relations. When political prisoners are discussed, it is generally presumed that the discussion

---

of the martyr become symbols of resistance (Peteet, 2001), while actual mothers . . . face acute and agonizing dilemmas."

applies to both women and men, without consideration of the gendered dimension of imprisonment or the important ways that Israeli colonial-gendered violence or Palestinian cultural and social gender practices shape women's experience.

I undertook my research in a place that I belong to and where I have lived my entire life. I have experienced many incidents of Israeli attacks, violence, and turmoil while living in Palestine, and so I am part of the story. Alison Jaggar has argued that we are, in part, drawn to research topics and practices by our emotions, so the assumption that emotion will not be present in the research is unrealistic.[9] From a feminist perspective, as researchers, we must use research strategies that help us find a "voice for ourselves," or learn from women who have had common research experiences to help clarify the meaning that drives our work.

When I decided to research Palestinian women political prisoners in Israeli colonial prisons, it was hard for me to find previous research that focused specifically on women political prisoners. When I approached organizations related to political prisoners or representatives of political movements about my research plan, some insisted that I didn't need to research women former prisoners and that there had already been a lot of work around them. But when I asked to see the work, they faced the question with hesitation. Whenever they guided me to look at a specific work, it was always about political prisoners who are men. This experience gave me insight into how women's narratives and contributions are disregarded as a site of critical knowledge production relevant for the persistent sumud of the prisoner movement and the Palestinian people more broadly.*

In her novel *The Wild Thorns*, Sahar Khalifeh illustrates how the community perceives time in Israeli prison when one of the characters comments: "Inside they told me that prison was for me, and that those who don't go to prison, even for a day, will never become real men, even if they grow two moustaches rather than one."[10] This statement

---

* As I was carrying out my research, Nahla Abdo (2014) became the first scholar to publish work about Palestinian women political prisoners in colonial Israeli prisons.

reflects the strong association between prison and masculinity and how patriarchy has been deployed within the Palestinian political and social domain through the struggle. How then do we account for women prisoners who challenge normative gender expectations when they breach the social contract by entering what is considered the masculine domain? In other words, while gendered expectations restrict women to the realm of the "social" within the movement, what happens when they themselves become actors of political or armed resistance and/or become prisoners?

This article focuses on the politicization of everyday life for Palestinian women inside Israeli colonial prisons, which are sites of direct confrontation with the Israeli colonial regime and military apparatus. For many Palestinian women, their incarceration is the first time they will have prolonged interaction with individual Israeli soldiers. In this situation, Palestinian women feel they must present their political beliefs all the time, in all their daily activities. Therefore, daily routines and mundane tasks, in addition to reading, writing, embroidery, and social relations, become politically charged acts of contest and perseverance. Palestinian women insist that they are using the time of their imprisonment as a means of resistance and that the experience of prison is not breaking them but instead it can be utilized to learn and grow in preparation for the outside world and in service to the ongoing struggle for freedom.

This research examines how imprisonment shapes the manner in which both women prisoners and their families perform as political subjects. It also seeks to understand how prison, a place of repression and silencing, can also become a space enabling women to articulate a political identity. How do reformulated political identities function, and how are they performed? When surrounded by containment and brute force, how does resistance, resilience, and sumud reformulate and manifest? It is also important to understand how the lives of political prisoners inside Israeli colonial prisons are connected to politics on the outside. In my research, I ask how outside politics influence prisoners' decisions, social relations, and daily life. This leads me to consider how the community still watches women inside prison, creating what

I call a *silent censorship* over women's decisions, identities, and social practices. In the context of the limitations imposed very differently by the prison and the outside community, I examine how individuality can be performed inside prison, how women negotiate the restrictions of carceral space, and the tactics they use to survive.

This paper is based on interviews that were collected between 2012 and 2015 as part of my doctoral studies. I interviewed twenty-seven Palestinian women who served time in various Israeli prisons and who come from different locations across the West Bank.* My own experience of living under occupation was a fundamental part of my social interaction with the participants. This was true, for example, when, in our interviews, women spoke about events that all Palestinians have lived through, such as the First Intifada, the constant invasions of the cities, the death of innocents, and the Second Intifada. Thus, my interviews also became a space for me to think about my own experience under occupation. I felt I was part of the collective Palestinian community, and I thought about the meaning of being "we Palestinians." However, at times when participants spoke about their personal experiences, which are completely different from mine, I was positioned as an outsider who had never been in such situations. Unlike the participants in these interviews, I have not been incarcerated in an Israeli colonial prison.

These interviews provide a close examination of their narratives and experiences before, during, and after imprisonment. They explore how these experiences have influenced their lives, social positioning, and performance of political struggle. I have used a methodology that allows me to uplift voices that have been rendered silent and highlight experiences that have never been deeply discussed. Using semistructured conversational format interviews, I gave my interlocutors the opportunity to reflect on their personal experiences and share them in their own way and on their own terms. The participants in this

---

*   Women who participated in the research were from the West Bank. As a Palestinian researcher living in the West Bank, it is impossible for me to access the Gaza Strip because of the restrictions the Israeli occupation imposes on our mobility between the two areas.

research belong to different political movements, offering insight into how the different Palestinian political parties deal with the imprisonment of women, though all have been in service of the broader struggle to free Palestine from colonial occupation. Participants were in prison during different periods between the 1970s and the present; here, I focus more on personal experiences than historical sequences. I have used anonymous names for some participants, in respect of their wishes and to protect them from the occupation, especially when they were discussing the details of their arrest or sensitive issues connected to their political activities. But in other cases, women have asked me to use their real names, and I have respected their wishes when I felt that doing so would not put them or me at risk.

WHAT IS AN ISRAELI COLONIAL PRISON?

Ahlam is a Christian woman who lived in Ramallah and had been imprisoned in the early 1980s, convicted to serve five years of a life sentence. Ahlam was then exiled from Palestine in a prisoner exchange in the eighties, followed by a return to Palestine at the establishment of the Palestinian Authority in 1995. Ahlam started our conversation by describing prison. She used evocative metaphors to illustrate the experiences of isolation, restriction, and control, "Prison is doors and keys, like a big box with four doors, with another box inside, and another box. This is prison . . . I left prison with breathing problems because everywhere is closed." This statement is a reflection of how closed and isolated space inside prison is. To live in a box is to be disconnected from the outside world, with innumerable boundaries imposed upon a person's thinking, behavior, mobility, and actions. In response, the person starts to create a world of her own inside these boxes, solitary and disconnected from the things going on outside the box. Incarceration begins with disengagement with the outside world, a withdrawal from the day-to-day mobility and sociality one takes for granted. Just as imprisonment inaugurates a total isolation and disconnection with the outside world, it simultaneously produces the possibility for both a lack of a sense of personal autonomy and for selfhood to arise through resistance. Indeed, Ahlam experienced a form of social death. Her arrest was a shock for her family and those in the surrounding community, who never knew about her involvement in politics or military activity. She was cut off from her family, who disavowed her after her military action and condemned her relationship with a Muslim man. Ahlam was also cut off from her community. She was left alone during the time of her imprisonment.

Ahlam describes how this concatenation of boxes constructing prison creates multiple layers of isolation for the prisoner, namely the isolation from the outside world, and especially from her own family and community. In her account, women are thus severed from their most critical ties of social belonging through the organization of space. In this regiment of isolation, women lose their own space, privacy, and autonomy, including agency over what might be deemed the simplest decisions in life. Though severely isolated, the imprisoned women are always aware of being under the constant surveillance of the prison guards and also of the indirect social monitoring from the outside world. We learn from Ahlam how people become something other than "autonomous" in such conditions. And yet, paradoxically, it is in prison that some women start to think about who they are and seek to represent themselves as political subjects, having not understood themselves in this way prior. Women prisoners are bound by both the Israeli prison authority's control over them and the surveillance outside, but women nevertheless attempt to resist and become more autonomous.

Israeli prisons for Palestinian women are places that constitute a space of direct encounter with the Israeli soldiers. The guards and the prison administration have control over prisoners' daily life while also setting the rules of the prison. The guard's keys are physically the only means by which women can move through the different doors and corridors of the prison and access life essentials, including family visits, medication, reading material, and open space. But, as these keys are worn round their necks, the guards are the ones who have the power and wield control over the space, producing a relation of power between the prisoner and her captor. The authorities are an ever-present feature of the women's life in prison. As one of the women in the film *Inside Israel's Jails* put it, "The administration is watching us all the time. If it is not the officer, then it is the guards."[11] The social life and relationship between Palestinian women political prisoners thus becomes subjected to a form of disciplinary power. The women's constant awareness of being watched shapes their actions, both physically and psychologically. Bearing this surveillance becomes part of their daily lives in prison; it becomes *instinctual*, or as Anton Oleinik describes it, a "natural strategy."[12] This daily practice is an important component of performing their sumud and of surviving the social death that imprisonment confirms. Women in prison live in a suffocatingly limited space, a series of boxes, as Ahlam vividly describes it, reducing the space allocated to the body under surveillance. But such constrained space directly contributes to molding the subject's agency of resistance. Allen Feldman argues that the "shrinkage of the space of political enactment" corresponds to the expansion of personhood.[13] I argue further that it also entails an expansion of the ways in which women resist the Israeli prison authority's control and surveillance.

When Palestinian women create their own strategies to survive prisons' limitation and restriction, they form modalities and practices of sumud. Women in prison are in a constant confrontation with the Israeli occupation. They perform strength and enact everyday life activities through their own terms: this is resistance in their encounter with the Israeli authorities. Most women in prison believe in the injustice of their imprisonment and the Israeli control over the Palestinian prisoners, disavowing the psychological imperatives of the captor's objective to have them internalize their subjugation, repent for their beliefs and actions, or concede on their commitment to freedom. In their perception, the Israeli authorities enjoy this control as a form of revenge, a notion reflected by Itaf, who was imprisoned for four years several times in the early nineties, and then, in the Second Intifada two times for more than five years. Itaf described prison as "the gloating of enemies." But this sense of the Israelis's pleasure in their incarceration rather encourages women to resist by acting strong and creating their own lives inside prison. This is what Palestinian women in prison call sumud, the sustenance of *life*.

POLITICAL LIFE INSIDE

Politics become the center of women prisoners' daily practice, despite political activity being banned by the Israeli prison authority. Women prisoners organize themselves as collectives, dividing into different committees. Itaf talked at length about these committees and the ways in which they shaped life inside. "The life inside prison is somehow very organized, there is collective work and committees, which are the security committee, the financial committee, the educational committee, and cultural committee, under the supervision of the representatives." Itaf described how, through these committees, some individuals are responsible for formal education, others for organizing political discussions, and others for consciousness-raising sessions. Each wing chose their own representative, whose role I will return to. Important here is noting how each wing also assigned women to lead these committees and liaise with the representatives as well as with the other women in the wing. Though each wing has their own programs that they organize according to their political views, there is still a unified structure across the wings in that each has a representative as well as different committees. The organization and participation in these committees despite technically being disallowed demonstrates how the women prisoners still find ways to be politically active in resistance of the Israeli Prison authority; to strengthen their sumud. Here, we see how women inside of prison replicate the popular committee formation, cooperation, and coordination models that exist as part of Palestinian political life on the outside that maintains the grassroots infrastructure of popular struggle.

Locked in a restricted space, the women feel that creating a system to manage their collective relations and decisions is a necessity, lest the individualism of imprisonment's psychological effects succeed. Palestinian political prisoners have an internal system, developed over years, that has been adopted by new generations of prisoners. This system organizes and structures incarcerated people's lives inside prison. Toward this end, each wing chooses a representative who is responsible for maintaining daily activities, including collective reading and political discussions as well as prisoners' finances. They are the only people who have the right to communicate with the prison administration. They organize the women's meetings with their lawyers and account for the problems and needs of the women in their wings, taking responsibility for everything connected to the well-being of prisoners. The representatives are also charged with presenting the prisoners' interests and transmitting their complaints to both the prison authority and visiting officials as well as to the Red Cross and other human rights organizations.[14]

The election day is one of the big celebrations for women in prison. Any woman can nominate herself to be the representative by presenting her agenda and stating what she can achieve for the prisoners. In my analysis of the election day, I draw upon the film *Inside Israel's Jails*, aired by the BBC in 2005, as it provides an in-depth account of the politics of these elections. Women consider the elections to be lessons in democracy. Ameneh, the representative of the Fateh wing, comments, "Throughout the historic struggle for Palestinian people, democracy has always started in prison . . . In a small way, we as prisoners are setting an example, which is what our people need right now."[15] The community of Palestinian women prisoners tries to be an ideal society and to reflect on how they can organize themselves within a very restricted and controlled space in direct confrontation with the Israelis. By showing that they still can practice democracy under such circumstances, they feel they can teach the Palestinians on the outside the value of collective struggle even under difficult circumstances while simultaneously maintaining a collective front against the Israeli prison authority.

Usually, the representative is a person with strong character, able to negotiate with both the prisoners and also the prison authority. She should be able to build relations with the people around her, to speak on behalf of prisoners and advocate for their rights, and to negotiate ways to improve their life conditions. In addition, she is responsible for working with the other political parties' representatives to negotiate actions, to make decisions related to the prisoners of her wing, and to make collective decisions related to all prisoners. In her talk with the other women before the election, Ameneh clarifies the role of the representative, "We must all remember that this election is not about who wins; it is about serving you all." Ameneh thus emphasizes to the other women that the role of the representative is to serve the prisoners. It is a role that requires hard work rather than being merely for status or show. In the film, Ameneh again reflects on her role, commenting, "To the girls I am more than a leader. I am a sister. On top of that, I help them in humanitarian social matters."[16] Each representative becomes aware of her duties and how she will occupy a very important place in prisoner life. Responsible for the other women's well-being, the representatives occupy the top of the wing hierarchy.

This representative should, in theory, be approved by the prison authority, as she is the one who has to communicate with them, but prisoners can still elect someone the prison authority doesn't want. In the film, one of the prisoners comments on choosing Ameneh: "I can see from their faces, the look they gave us, they are not happy with the results, and right now no one can control the girls' reactions . . . The basic goal is to control us. They won't succeed as long as we stick together." Women use the election to challenge the control the Israeli prison authority tries to impose on their decision making and self-determination. The tension between the prison authority and prisoners is clear in the film, as both sides try to challenge the other. It is apparent, for example, when the officer of Hasharon Prison comments, "The representative is chosen by the prisoners, but I have the final say."[17] This struggle for power creates some violent confrontations in which the elected representative is placed in isolation after facing violence and torture. Nevertheless, the women find ways to communicate with her and follow her directives as a way to continue to challenge the prison authority and resist their decisions.

INSIDE-OUTSIDE POLITICS

In addition to the representatives the incarcerated women elect from among themselves to communicate between different political parties, another representative is chosen to act as the spokesperson representing them to the outside world. Each political movement in the prison thus has a representative responsible not only for reporting what is happening inside to the political leaders of her movement on the outside but also for liaising with the prison leaders in the men's prison. Representatives use different methods to communicate their reports. It can be accomplished through lawyers, family visits, or smuggling letters. The leaders outside use the same methods and additionally communicate orders through radio programs that the women listen to. Rania described this network of communication:

> We had the national meeting. Each group chose their representative. We meet and discuss what we are doing, then each representative has to communicate with the leaders of her political party, and report what was going on. The representative has some space to make decisions, and if things got complicated and difficult, we have the national committee in the prison that usually agrees about the things not to vote about, and so we represent the women there.

Rania's description illustrates that the women do not independently make decisions about strategies connected to collective action, like going on hunger strike or asking for changes in the prison system. This reflects how the politics inside the prison are highly dependent on the politics outside and the broader political infrastructure that governs the Palestinian liberation struggle. The political movement outside prison supervises their prisoners, following their needs, problems, arguments, and their relations with the other political parties. Most of the time, women prisoners must follow what the leadership on the outside decides for them, even regarding the daily practices of life inside. In addition, these representatives are responsible for updating their own political movement about each woman's attitudes and loyalty. Therefore, the role of the representative is not just to coordinate and guide prisoners, but it is also one of a monitor, verifying that everyone does what she has clearly been told is required of her.

Women try to avoid raising any complaints to the prison authority that might diminish their unity against the Israelis and normalize the fractures the colonial regime attempts to stoke within the Palestinian collective body politic. If any woman attempted to make an individual complaint to the authority, the other Palestinian women would consider her a traitor for breaching the collective consensus methods they rely on to persevere and remain steadfast. In this collective modality, internal conflict must be dealt with among prisoners without ever requesting the interference of prison authorities. They are aware that this tension serves the prison authority's interests and can be exploited to further interfere in the women's lives and decisions. Therefore, a woman suffering in these conflicts will prefer to remain silent or to try to use her own tactics to deal with the situation by communicating complaints to outside leaders and family.

Tensions between political parties affect the women's relationships with each other, as some women become more rigidly entrenched in their political ideologies while in prison. By restricting and isolating women into small cells and areas according to their ideologies, the architecture of the prison can also work to intensify prejudices. Salma, who was imprisoned in 2008 for six months, allocated to the Hamas wing, was surprised when she recognized one of her best friends in prison. She was eager to talk to her and tried to be close, but the other woman, who was in the Islamic Jihad wing, was cold and didn't welcome her as Salma expected: "I am sad about this. We were in Hamas and the Islamic Jihad, but each one had their programs and agenda. They never visited each other. They had real problems. There were ten rooms for Islamic Jihad, and five for Hamas. We have a system for visiting each other's rooms, but we never exchanged visits with the Islamic Jihad." This conflict among the different political parties is stronger and clearer than it is outside of prison. As Colvin argues, prisons are "a mirror and a microcosm of society," and inside these societies there are power inequalities and people who can dominate the lives of others.[18] In 2006 the political division between Hamas and Fatah* illustrated and influenced political prisoners' relations with each other and, as many of the participants who were imprisoned after that period have discussed, also increased the conflict among them.

---

*   The Fatah–Hamas conflict, also referred to as the Palestinian Civil War, is the conflict between the two main Palestinian political parties, Fatah and Hamas, resulting in the split of the Palestinian Authority in 2007.

A network of communication exists between the women inside prison and political leaders and families on the outside, which allows the women to ask for assistance easing problems and conflicts with other women. Women can complain about these problems and ask for intervention from the leaders outside prison. Such complaints can be passed through lawyers or family visits, and in return, the leaders communicate directives to the women through special radio programs. As they are organizational decisions, all women follow these orders. Salma described her experience with the Fateh representative: "Ameneh stopped her girls being violent with me because I went to my brother, who is the representative and leader of the PFLP in the men's prison. He threatened her family that if anything happened to me, something really bad will happen to them. She was worried about losing everything, so she stopped . . . The lawyer came specially to tell us to stop this." The relationships and power dynamics among the different Palestinian political parties thus greatly influence the relationships among prisoners and is also a reflection of these relations.

THE POLITICIZATION OF SPACE

"I know the architecture of the room was very small, but it is wide with the things you gain. It was a space to learn. I managed to use this space for three years." Khawla was aware of the limitations and deprivation of prison space. As her comment above suggests, this awareness, however, was the starting point for managing its confines and finding different tactics to subvert its restrictions. Being aware of the space, and its politics, allows Palestinian women to manipulate it and to generate profound instincts, survival tactics, political lessons, and emotional and political growth. Women are conscious that this space is the site of a direct and unrelenting battle with the Israeli occupation. For Palestinian prisoners, Israeli prison is a site of confrontation with the enemy. Palestinian women try to resist the power of the Israeli prison administration by refusing cooperation, creating different political activities, and producing Palestinian political themes through their handcrafts and writing. Such resistance is the foundation of everyday life for Palestinian prisoners. Khawla, and other women, emphasized how busy they were during their imprisonment and how they wanted to use their incarceration to gain knowledge to help them after their release. They also intended to show the Israeli occupation that imprisonment would not stop them from learning or hinder their empowerment or preparation for release and that prison was a space for them to maintain their sumud. Most of the prisoners considered prison a preparation stage for the outside world.

Palestinian women's understanding of the prisons as a direct battle with the Israeli occupation influenced the way in which they perceive space and time. Khawla commented on how she spent her time, saying, "I don't remember I had time. I was so busy. I used to read nine hours a day, and then we had group discussions. I used to teach women who couldn't read or write. We did not have time." Most of the imprisoned women created their own world. They dealt with space and time differently, but all of them had to act as political prisoners, which meant that their activities, as individuals or collectives, had to reflect their politics and steadfastness. Prison is not an empty receptacle, independent of its contents. Its space is shaped by the ways prisoners perceive and utilize it. Khawla repeatedly reiterated how busy she was and that she never had time; she was using her time to educate herself or to educate other women.

Mariam asserted that every prisoner has access to both internal and external resources that can be used to challenge the limitations of the space. She said: "You own your brain, and you have books, and the other people around you, Israelis or Palestinian. These people will extend your circle. However, you have the walls of the prisons, but with this you start to move out of it. This is not an easy story at all. When you live it, you go through stages . . . These stages help you to lead this space. You use your imagination. It should work because it is connected to a partly forgotten reality." She explained how the passage of time was a very important element in enabling prisoners to understand the nature of the space. She describes them going through stages connected to the time they had spent in prison. But time is not the only factor. Their interaction with the other prisoners and the prison administration is another element that constructs the space for them. Mariam also focused on how subjects themselves determine their experience of prison. She asserted that incarcerated people should use their minds, read, and communicate with others to build their own world. Imprisonment does not just entail the subjection of the person. Prisoners also interact with and relate to the objects around them. Imprisonment is shaped by the kind of objects and the possible kinds of relations any subject has to those objects. The understanding of space creates different kinds of relations but also transforms according to the subject's affective and instrumental relation with the space of incarceration.

The geography and management of the space and the limitation on movement overdetermine women's daily life in prison. The women's day-to-day activities are organized collectively in each wing, usually consisting of group readings, discussion groups, social and recreational activities as well as some individual activities such as reading, writing, socializing, practicing handcrafts, embroidery, and other hobbies. These activities and interactions help women to create their own secure social relations, as they become close to others who have similar interests. Additionally, the activities enable women to understand and talk to each other without worries or fear. Some of the activities must be serious and political in nature. Below I discuss some of these activities in more detail and consider how they influence women's subjectivities and relations. This shows how these activities become their tools to resist and continue their journey in the resistance movements inside prisons.

"PRISON IS A SCHOOL"

For Palestinian prisoners, educational activities are a form of resistance against the prison's restrictions and isolation; therefore, prisoners attempt to educate themselves by reading as much as they can. In the Palestinian culture, the Israeli prison is often regarded as a school. Ahlam described it in the following terms: "You can say that prison is a school, another life. It is a university to learn a lot from . . . It is a zoo . . . Do you want me to tell you why? Sometimes they have this sudden search, they come to the cage and start looking at you, it's hard and humiliates you." It is clear that Ahlam was deeply impacted by the limitations, restrictions, and forms of discipline she was subjected to in prison. It was a dehumanizing space, one she related to the experience of animals in the zoo: watched, caged, and guarded. Ahlam's comments illustrate the contradictions within prisoners' experience of the space and how they challenge and resist the dehumanization through educational and political activities.

Reading and writing are the primary activities prisoners try to focus on during their imprisonment. Ismail Nashif argues that reading and writing are ritual practices. These are the main activities practiced by political prisoners in order to establish themselves as a social group; they are signs of political subjectivity that Palestinian prisoners use to mark themselves as political prisoners and differentiate themselves from Israeli civil prisoners. Most women I interviewed expressed that prison provided an opportunity for them to read and learn as much as they could. The Palestinian political prisoners understood the meaning of *thaqafa*, or culture, as seeking to reinstall, reconstitute, and reaffirm Palestinian-ness as a national identity. The context of thaqafa delimits a site of liberation from prison conditions that frees the captive.[19] They read Marx, communist literature, Chinese literature, Islamic literature, and many other political, social, and educational books. Salma said, "It was a golden chance to read. In the prison there was a small, nice library. I used to take out and exchange books." Each prison has a library, like Salma's, where prisoners can borrow books. These libraries contain books donated through the Red Cross and other organizations, sometimes in response to the prisoners' requests. However, the women's library is underresourced, and it is hard for them to request books from the outside.

Their *time* in prison teaches women how to lead their own life, organized and constantly occupied with educational and political activities. This is a means of steadfastness, through which women are not only able to challenge all the restrictions and deprivations of prison life but also the power of the Israelis to disable their development. Khawla, like many other women, used her time inside to learn and read as much as she could. She said, "I told you I never had time. I wanted to use every minute. I was in confrontation with the time. I was worried the time would finish without learning." Palestinian prisoners try to challenge the Israeli colonial prison practice of isolation by making the space one of production on their own terms. As Nashif argues, "the reading/writing sign, site and space of actions, practices and rituals are the main activities practiced by the political captives in order to establish themselves as a social group."[20]

SIMPLE THINGS

Embroidery is a popular craft among women in prison. They often feel that it helps them to release their emotions around the isolation and the hardship of prison. As most Palestinian women learn embroidery in schools as part of the effort to preserve Palestinian identity, women in prison can spend a great deal of time practicing this hobby, producing pieces they can give to their families or even keep for their future homes after release. They teach each other different patterns and exchange different designs and colors. Women try to always reflect political beliefs in their work. Rania commented, "We did pieces that had intifada themes. Others represent Palestine. Others were connected to national figures like Handthala. We used to write poetry from Mahmoud Darwish that we copied from magazines. We made portraits for walls, bags, pillows."

The practice of embroidery and handcrafts creates a social environment for women. They can chat about personal topics, discussing their dreams or sharing their sorrow and loss with their close friends. It also becomes a means of building trust, when, for example, a woman asks another prisoner to show her how to make something, or to help her to choose colors, or to draw some patterns for her to make something special. Women produce very original pieces that reflect their own individual identity within the political themes. Embroidery here is not just the craft of sewing; more fundamentally, it is about the construction of relationships. It creates a time and space for the women to open up and become closer to their emotions, and, importantly, to be people with complex lives and histories. Through these activities, women are able to talk about their memories and share their private lives and experiences with the other women. Palestinian women prisoners exercise their agency under the cover of these socially accepted "female activities."

In prison, the environment is built to diminish agency and individuality. Women are generalized into political subjects—political prisoners, political movement activists, freedom fighters, resisters, and so on. There are, however, moments in which they can not only express their individuality but also exist as full persons. During the day, prisoners are granted a short time of release from their cells for forty-five minutes. They spend the time outside of their rooms in a small communal hall, usually an open space. Prisoners have the opportunity to meet with the women from different cells. They gather to chat, eat, and drink coffee together, and to exchange books and ideas. Sabreen felt that this was her time to build relationships and meet with her close friends. She said, "I used to have strong relationships with all the women. We used to have nice gatherings, inviting each other for lunch in the release time, or to have coffee. We use to do a lot of simple things but it made us feel really happy." Sabreen and her friends tried to create their own world, in which they could normalize, and cope with, the prison structure.

Incarcerated women learn indirectly how to live in this space and also to create their own social life. Through their social practices, like drinking coffee and chatting, women make prison resemble a feminine space. In these periods of socializing, women perform as women, momentarily released from the pressure of performing a masculinist politic in service of an established understanding of what constitutes the political domain. They cook, eat, laugh, sew, gossip, and share secrets. Rania described her interaction with the other women in this time of release, "You share with the other women simple dreams and secrets." The women become close to each other, developing trust and confidence among their small circle.

In this circle of friends, women create a liberatory space in which they can talk about their experiences, emotions, and secrets without surveillance or expectations. Khawla shared her romance with the group leader of her political organization, who was also imprisoned during the same period, with her cellmates. All of them read his letters to her. She said, "We loved each other before prison. He used to write me letters. He was a poet, and he used to write nice words for me. All our wing used to read them. I wasn't shy at all. These letters used to change the prison environment." For Khawla, sharing her private letters with her close friends was a way of strengthening solidarity with them. Sharing her dream world, a world of the love and emotion they were deprived of inside prison, made women feel happy and created something new to talk about.

Over time, women become familiar enough with each other to talk about many personal topics. Khawla described the discussions she took part in within this small circle of friends, "We used to talk about everything and nothing. We talked about politics. We talked about our secret loves, about our dreams, our ambitions. We talked about our losses, but it was clear they were hiding a lot of their stories and emotions." Despite their closeness, the women try to avoid expressing some of their emotions and feelings. They remained worried about the conservative culture and still felt restrictions around issues connected to their feelings, emotions, and private lives. In addition, women fear the judgments of others or that someone will find out something about them that will influence other people's perception of them as a political prisoner.

Women can't talk about everything openly. They try to keep their secrets and feelings among those women who they trust, but still, they have some limitations on their expression and the subjects they feel they can discuss. For example, women avoid talking about their losses and fears of the future because this kind of talk is often judged as distorting the reputation and the experience of prisoners. After her initial comment that the women in her circle talked about "everything," Khawla clarified that, in fact, not everything could be freely spoken about. She said: "You can face some aggressive reactions from some women when we were talking about some issues. This reaction can be part of the feeling of need and deprivations . . . I don't know, but you are forbidden to talk about such issues because you have to be strong and you are a freedom fighter . . . So your personal loss and issues are not important, and you have to focus on national and political issues." As Khawla suggests, the main areas women try to avoid talking about are those connected to their sense of loss. Many women felt profound worry about aging in prison or that, because they were getting older, they may remain single and childless all their lives. For some women there was a sense of loss around their desires and sexuality that they were discouraged from expressing. All of these deprivations are consequences of their imprisonment, so to articulate emotion over them would impact their performance as political prisoners. It would make them appear more concerned about their own personal problems rather than national and political issues, which is deemed to be the central concern for political prisoners.

Though the prison space is not free from the control of cultural, gendered expectations, in creating their own world inside prison, women are often able to talk and act in more open ways than in the outside world. This environment recalls the space of "the harem," in which women gather and socialize to evade the restrictions they normally face from conservative cultures. In *Dreams of Trespass: Tale of a Harem Girlhood*, Fatema Mernissi, a Moroccan Islamic feminist, examines Islam and women's roles within it. She gives her own account of such spaces, describing her youth in a Moroccan harem during the 1940s, and considering topics such as Islamic feminism, Arab nationalism, French colonialism, and the clash between the traditional and the modern. Like the women in the harem that Mernissi describes, women in prison constantly negotiate between what is allowed and what is not, between how they are expected to perform and the need to find their own world within all these restrictions, between living under surveillance and trying to find a space with other women where they can open up without any restriction or fear.

CONCLUSION

Because prison is a space that works to diminish political prisoners' agency, Palestinian women try to be part of a collective prisoner body with the common goal to resist the Israeli prison administration by performing political agency all the time. This means they try to talk, work, and act politically in every small detail of their lives. Palestinian women find their own ways to create their space of negotiation as they try to negotiate constant restrictions to find spaces of liberation. In such spaces, in often-gendered activities, they can express personal needs and individualism, providing respite from the selfless, impersonal performance expected of political prisoners. The relationships they build inside prison, based on familiarity, similarity, and also the shared experiences of bodily exposure, facilitate the building of secure social networks. Within these bonds of understanding, trust, and solidarity, women create a space of shared sumud: this is the politics of everyday life. In this space, women socialize, cook, eat, and sew together. These gatherings offer opportunities for women to share their hidden desires and to escape from the political pressures of the space. As the women become closer, they start sharing their secrets and can sometimes talk about topics that are usually forbidden, both inside and outside prison in the conservative culture they belong to. However, some women feel that it is inappropriate for Palestinian women prisoners to discuss their feelings of loss or desire in such an environment. Those women who have rigidly internalized this conservative culture refuse such discussion, which they consider an aberration from the appropriate performance of political prisoners. It is organized both upon notions of resistance and sumud and upon individuals' experiences. Any analysis of prison life can only be partial because behind the walls of any prison there is another world. We can't fully perceive all of its details or access all of its secrets and relations without becoming part of the prisoners' body.

Israeli colonial prisons are the sites of immediate confrontation with the Israeli prison authority who represents the Israeli occupation. For many Palestinian women, their incarceration is the first time they will have prolonged interaction with individual Israeli soldiers. Palestinian women feel they must present their political beliefs all the time, in all their daily activities, such as reading, writing, embroidery, and handcrafts. Palestinian women try to show that they are using the time of their imprisonment as a means of resistance and that the experience of prison is not breaking them but can be utilized prepare for the outside world. Outside politics also influence, and often determine, the relations inside prison, so that prisons cannot be thought of as independent spaces but as intricately connected to the outside. For women in prison there is a constant rhythm in the repetition of habits in the everyday routines of women. For them, politics is something they experience in the details and practices of everyday life: it is in their conversations and social activities. The repetitive, routine activities of everyday life are saturated with national themes. Through this routine Palestinians perform their sumud and it becomes the motivation of their everyday life under the occupation. Sumud then, is not merely a political act of defiance but a practice of collective surviving, coping, and thriving in conditions of extreme duress as a process of maintaining and reformulating life.

NOTES

1. Lena Mhammad Meari, *Sumud: A Philosophy Of Confronting Interrogation* (Davis: University of California, 2011), 4.

2. Nadera Shalhoub-Kevorkian, *Militarization and Violence against Women in Conflict Zones in the Middle East: A Palestinian Case-study* (Cambridge: Cambridge University Press, 2009); Julie Peteet, "Women and Conflict in Israel: *Israel: The Embattled Land, Jewish and Palestinian Women Talk about Their Lives* by Beata Lipman," *Journal of Palestine Studies* 19, no.4 (July 1990): 127–28, doi:10.2307/2537401; Simona Sharoni, "Rethinking Women's Struggles in Israel-Palestine and in the North of Ireland," in *Victims, Perpetrators or Actors: Gender, Armed Conflict and Political Violence*, ed. Caroline O. M. Moser and Fiona C. Clark (London and New York: Zed Books, 2001), 85–98; Samira Haj, "Palestinian Women and Patriarchal Relations," *Signs*, 17, no. 4 (Summer 1992): 761–78.

3. Haj, "Palestinian Women and Patriarchal Relations," 773.

4. Penny Johnson and Eileen Kuttab, "Where Have All the Women (and Men) Gone? Reflections on Gender and the Second Palestinian Intifada," *Feminist Review* 69, no. 1 (2001): 21, doi.org/10.1080/014177800110070102.

5. Shalhoub-Kevorkian, *Militarization and Violence*, 14.

6. Claudia García-Moreno and Anita Riecher-Rössler, "Violence against Women and Mental Health," in *Violence against Women and Mental Health* vol. 178 (Basel: Karger Publishers, 2013), 18, doi.org/10.1159/000345276.

7. Addameer Prisoner Support and Human Rights Association, "Palestinian Women Political Prisoners Systematic Forms of Political and Gender-Based

State Violence," (Jereusalem: Addameer Prisoner Support and Human Rights Association, December 2010) retrieved November 19, 2015, http://www.addameer.org/sites/default/files/publications/palestinian-women-political-prisoners-december-2010.pdf.

8. Ismail Nashif, *Palestinian Political Prisoners: Identity and Community* (London: Routledge, 2008), 17–18.

9. Cited in Sharlene Nagy Hesse-Biber, "Feminist Research: Exploring the Interconnections of Epistemology, Methodology, and Method," in *Handbook of Feminist Research: Theory and Praxis*, ed. Sharlene Nagy Hesse-Biber (Los Angeles and London: Sage Publications, Inc., 2007).

10. Sahar Khalifeh, *The Wild Thorns*, trans. Trevor LeGassick and Elizabeth Ferna (New York: Interlink Books, 1985, 149.

11. *Inside Israel's Jails*, directed by Nick Read, written by Israel Goldvicht, aired March 22, 2005 by the BBC (London: Raw TV).

12. Cited in Dominique Moran, Judith Pallot, and Laura Piacentini, "Privacy in Penal Space: Women's Imprisonment in Russia," *Geoforum* 47 (June 2013): 138–46, doi.org/10.1016/j.geoforum.2013.01.002.

13. Allen Feldman, *Formations of Violence: The Narrative of the Body and Political Terror in Northern Ireland* (Chicago: University of Chicago Press, 1991) cited in Nashif, *Palestinian Political Prisoners*, 75.

14. Nahla Abdo, *Captive Revolution: Palestinian Women's Anti-Colonial Struggle within the Israeli Prison System* (London: Pluto Press, 2014).

15. *Inside Israel's Jails*

16. *Inside Israel's Jails*

17. *Inside Israel's Jails*

18. Sarah Colvin, "Voices from the Borderlands, *Eurostudia* 7, no. 1–2 (2011): 10, doi.org/10.7202/1015007ar.

19. Nashif, *Palestinian Political Prisoners*, 74.

20. Nashif, *Palestinian Political Prisoners*, 78.

فاطين

Jana Traboulsi, "Houses," 2021

PART THREE
OTHERWORLDS

Fig. 1. Instagram post by @thoughty_organizer, June 29, 2018. Image courtesy of #DefendTheCriminalized Collective.

"IMA MAKE IT LOOK FLY!"

ABOLITIONIST FEMINIST AESTHETIC CODING IN FASHION AND ADORNMENT

Gloria A. Negrete-Lopez

As an abolitionist, fat, Xicana femme, I navigate social media with attention to images that conjure femme-centered futures big enough to deconstruct the state's inherent settler-colonial anti-Blackness, xenophobia, and misogyny. The first time I saw @thoughty_organizer's #DefendTheCriminalized bodysuit on Instagram, I was taken aback by the unapologetically abolitionist stance and style of this piece of clothing.[1] The Instagram post featured the one-piece bodysuit laid over a floral desk calendar that reads June 2018. The tight-fit lines of the garment are framed by a stapler and tape dispenser on one side and a pen on the opposite side. The sexiness of the bodysuit is counterbalanced by elements of work, craft, and collective organization included in the photograph. The more I looked at the post, the more I realized the importance of the garment and its form as a bodysuit. The square neckline is formfitting to the chest and torso with thin, fixed straps. Lettering across the bodysuit powerfully links the carceral state to racial capitalism along with the conceptual binaries that organize these violent institutions and the urgent need for abolition in order to imagine radical forms of freedom.[*] Together, the message and

---

[*]   The implicit links between the carceral state and racial capitalism are bound up in the physical, political, and sensorial lives of those crushed by anti-Black cisheteronormative US law.

aesthetic choice (which are inseparable) name the urgency of abolition to imagine radical forms of freedom. When I think about wearing this bodysuit, I feel a sense of radicalness and femme fierceness. Bodysuits, as a form of clothing, convey femme-ness, femininity, fashioning, and sensuality all wrapped up in a single article of clothing.* Without reducing to the "binaries" of man/woman, male/female—which are central to statecraft—this bodysuit is a gesture to queer femininities that challenge gender and sex and, accordingly, challenge the larger carceral state. Among other things, the #DefendtheCriminalized bodysuit is a poetic call to action that references the body, making express the connection between the politics of the body and freedom work.

This article examines the abolitionist feminist work of two Instagram accounts, @thoughty_organizer and @emotionalgangzter, with the hope of understanding how each platform utilizes abolitionist aesthetics as a catalyst for organizing against the state. The #DefendThe-Criminalized Collective (which operates under the username @thoughty_organizer) uses their Instagram account to form a rigorous and playful relationship with abolitionist language; they use sartorial and embodied aesthetics as a vehicle to address the complexities of dismantling prison systems. Similarly, writer, organizer, and abolitionist Alejandra Pablos (who operates under the Instagram username @emotionalgangzter) joins them in using her profile as a popular education site that, among other things, critiques the most pervasive narratives used by those in the immigrant justice movement. These two accounts are in conversation with each other, in real time, and have organized collaboratively in the past. Unlike other prison abolition social media campaigns, the two accounts I discuss here are striking because they have created an online abolitionist feminist aesthetic code. This code is transmitted through the fashion and adornment of femme and gender nonconforming people.

---

* For this essay, femme is defined as a radical form of femininity that seeks to challenge sexist, racist, and homophobic diatribes. Femme acts in defiance to the patriarchal world and invites us to reimagine femme through an abolitionist framework. This definition is inspired by a genealogy influenced by the works of Kara Keeling, Natasha Omise'eke Tinsley, Julia Serrano, Lisa Duggan, and Kathleen McHugh.

This article seeks to make an intervention into abolition feminism by closely examining online communities that center the many connected calls for state abolition. With attention to the critical importance of aesthetics, style, self-artistry, and the fashion choices of women, femmes, and gender nonconforming Black, Indigenous, and People of Color, I argue that the abolitionist feminist aesthetics inherent in the expressive choices of these online communities are based in a poetics of visuality, embodied sensuality, and femme labor that challenge masculinist—and more generally sex/gender normative—perceptions of anti-prison activism while also deepening analysis about the meaning and practice of abolition.

INSTAGRAM AND THE POLITICS/ POETICS OF VISUALITY

The photographic archive that I focus on in this essay is rooted in a poetics of visuality and sensuality that illuminate the role of aesthetics in abolitionist feminist thought. Gloria Anzaldúa's poetic approach to visual theory understands images to be theory-made; images are allowed to speak for themselves and offer theoretical engagement through composition, form, and medium.[2] The Instagram photographs representing imagery like the bodysuit not only think for themselves, they also cocreate theoretical and active communities centered around mutual aid, consciousness raising, and abolition. More than that though, they put forward theory of (and *through*) the transformatively beautiful and sensual.

Beyond the notion of image-as-theory, I also draw on the work of transdisciplinary scholar Jillian Hernandez to read Instagram as a photographic archive.[3] I also read it as a repository of creative works and as a uniquely positioned social media platform that utilizes photography as a means to draw in viewers' attention, which also makes it an important addition to online community and university activism. With Instagram, photographic and visual information is foregrounded, amplifying the aesthetic dimensions of political messaging and taking seriously the abolitionist message transferred onto the bodysuits as a living text. Through this medium, abolitionist organizers and believers attend to the hypervisible bodies and invisible labor of Black, Indigenous, undocumented, women, femmes, and queer people.[4]

As Hernandez points out, visual archives cannot possibly hold all information, because these digital spaces are also made up of anti-Black, anti-Brown algorithms designed by corporate capitalism. They are also heavily regulated and emphasize individualism. Yet, with Instagram as a stage, activists produce their own resistance code in which users advocate for and organize the abolishment of capitalism, including through the anti-capitalist practice of cocreation and corroboration in the form of reposts, comments, or "likes." While this digital archive of feminist abolition depends heavily on the combined use of photographs and text to resist the state violence deployed through political and deputized actors against Black, Indigenous, Latinx, and (im)migrant communities, it's striking that the violence being resisted often manifests on a visual register (not only via surveillance but also through destructive projections). Traveling alongside Anzaldúa's thinking about images and Hernandez's insight into the communal, unruly, and (thus) abolitionist potential of digital media, we may be able to see how women and femmes of color popularize abolitionist aesthetics through these online platforms and communities.

ABOLITION AESTHETICS, EMBODIMENT, AND THE MASCULINIST "UNIFORM" OF ANTI-PRISON ORGANIZING

To contextualize the importance of visuality, sensuality, and adornment to abolition aesthetics, I point readers to some of the sartorial logics of anti-prison organizing. As a queer femme, I have spent the last decade of my life in graduate school studying prison abolition. There have been many times when I have felt isolated in prison-abolitionist spaces and was read as suspect because of my stylish, fat femme-ness. Anti-prison and anti-police organizing is often embodied by an anti-femme fashion and bodily aesthetic hewn out of masculinist anarchist politics. Those who deviate from this aesthetic—or who see the very potential of aesthetic as important in imagining radical futures organized around freedom—are read as insincere, as problematic consumer capitalists, or as frivolous and unfocused on the cause. To be clear, the spectrum of aesthetics to which I am attentive does not position abolitionist masculine and femme fashion as existing on two polar extremes. Instead, I view these categories as multiple, dialogical, and in dynamic conversation with one another because they share an abolitionist ideal; however, in the context of anti-prison organizing culture, they often operate according to different expressions and codes of adornment. However, the traditional cismasculinism of some radical organizing movements may inform the way adornment is considered in the work of freedom.

In anti-prison and anti-police organizing spaces, I have experienced individuals wearing the "all black uniform" and other types of recognized anarchist color combinations (black and red) as preferred by people often read as "authorial."[5] But in the abolitionist activist spaces I visited, the black-blocking uniform was rarely body conscious. Instead, it was aimed at erasing bodies and the differences that inform the lived experience of those bodies. As a fat, queer femme, I came to feel as though abolition was something that had to be separated from my body and my personal fashion and style choices. Abolition and radical freedom spaces seemed to be strictly rooted in a disembodied, disaffected, academic or intellectual disposition. As a result, these spaces can be seen as masculinized and anti-aestheticized. I make a distinction between the #DefendTheCriminalized bodysuit and the respectable activist uniform to further reveal the bodysuit as a mode of fashioned aesthetics that can help us imagine queer femme abolitionist futures.

The use of the #DefendtheCriminalized bodysuit, a historically fraught article of clothing, enriches the sartorial landscape and the very analysis of anti-prison organizing by implicitly challenging the policing of women's bodies. The bodysuit was originally created by French gymnast Jules Leotard to wear during evaluated performances on the trapeze.[6] In the 1940s, designers Claire McCardell and Mildred Orrick created their own versions of the suit inspired by elements of dance in their one-piece stretchy leotard. These early iterations of the bodysuit created controversy, which led to censorship and policing of women's bodies in the public sphere, similar to the policing of bathing suits. Eventually, in 1985, Donna Karen utilized the bodysuit as a foundational piece for her Seven Easy Pieces collection, launching a minimalistic version made from jersey. Understanding the bodysuit means understanding the activated history of policing bodies.

Beyond this, the term "bodysuit" explicitly references the "body," and the policing of it functions according to a weaponizable politics of respectability that polices the body *by* policing clothing, style, and embodied aesthetics. This weaponization occurs even among those who would claim to embrace a radical politics. For example, when the #DefendTheCriminalized Collective became a portal for me and for other women, femmes, and genderqueer abolitionists to come together and curate conversations about fashion(ing), aesthetics, adornment, embodiment, style, and sensuality,[7] our work garnered a number of negative online comments. Many of the negative comments were more aggressively pitched toward those wearing the #DefendtheCriminalized bodysuit, revealing an ongoing commitment to the "binaries" that undergird the logics of prisons and policing. Following this punitive understanding of the controlled/controllable body, the commenters particularly antagonized and criticized the fat bodies, femme bodies, and gender nonconforming bodies seen working the bodysuit. However, through styling and repurposing aesthetic items, the #DefendtheCriminalized Collective draws on the traditions of gender and body nonconforming communities* in order to interrogate and ultimately blur and dismantle binaristic laws and damaging stereotypes

---

*   The followers featured throughout the digital archive are in many instances abolishing the gender binary by taking up the important work started decades before by elders such as Sylvia Rivera, Miss Major Griffin-Gracy, Marsha P. Johnson, and countless others. As a result, in this essay I strictly focus on reading the photographs of the screen-printed clothing, ephemera, and adornment techniques. This critical decision is due to safety concerns and privacy measures for those featured wearing the clothing. Many of the community members and supporters are Black, Indigenous, gender nonconforming, undocumented, formerly incarcerated individuals whose lives are always/already precarious.

about gender and the body. In so doing, they provide brief instances of abolitionist imaginaries.

The assumed masculinity of activist labor and street protest reveals the ways in which embodied expressions of femininity go unseen, unacknowledged, dismissed, and always doubted. But the bodysuit centers attention on those who do not embody masculinity only. More importantly, the bodysuit refuses an essentialist, reductive account of the body and allows us to envision the importance of desire in political discourse (which are not antithetical, as anarchists have historically suggested regarding the role of pleasure in work). In her own radical thinking, Audre Lorde insisted upon the power of the erotic (of desire) and the relationship our bodily and experiential differences have in the erotic.[8] Where the wording on the bodysuit (and perhaps the bodysuit itself) issues demands like "Abolish Binaries," the negative reactions to it (even among fellow abolitionists) draw us to ask questions like: How might our ideas of the body reflect legacies of racial, gender, and carceral violence that are anti-difference? How might we queer the importance of bodily difference? Could femme of color aesthetics and embodied adornment allow us to really see and celebrate bodily difference without categorizing or punishing it, which is central to the abolition project? Beyond aesthetic and erotic matters, the bodysuit makes possible an acknowledgment of who exactly is doing abolitionist labor and how widely varied and invisible those laborers, and the bodily impact of their labors, can be. After the bodysuits were created, the collective also screen printed shorts—referred to as "booty shorts"—with the phrase ABOLISH ICE on the backside. Shortly thereafter we began to see different color bodysuits (black and gray), "unisex" shirts, hoodies, crew neck sweaters, and baby onesies. In wearing the consciousness-raising clothing, abolitionist action is happening, but it has been turned into something personal, something integrated with the body and the bodies of comrades rather than an abstracted or deaestheticized, disembodied practice. The ways in which these collectives co-create within their communities and alongside others teach us how online activism is being translated into personal action by incorporating visual elements that can be worn and carried on the individual's body. The clothes show that we have a stake in this political movement and, when shared on Instagram, it gets translated into a whole aesthetic activism.

FASHIONING AESTHETICS AS ABOLITIONIST PROPAGANDA

"The femme aesthetics of the garments worn and shared by the #DefendTheCriminalized Collective also function as abolitionist propaganda.[9] The use of "propaganda" is similar to the work done by prison abolitionist organization Critical Resistance (CR), which collaborates with visual artists to create visual campaigns, images, and other forms of propaganda. In addition to the aesthetic function of the bodysuit, this propaganda actively shifts the narratives surrounding abolition within (im)migrant justice narratives, particularly in the way that messages like "Abolish Binaries" might be utilized to not only undermine gender categories but also binaristic categories like "good immigrant" and "criminal immigrant." Furthermore, the message on the bodysuit and subsequent garments work to express the meaning of prison abolition, which, according to Angela Davis, seeks to end policing and the use of the prison system as the primary solution to address larger social, political, and economic problems.[10] This also means an eradication of the prison system and any other sites of forced imprisonment such as immigrant and juvenile detention centers. As such, another screenprint shirt created by the collective states "ABOLISH ICE &/ ABOLISH DHS &/ ABOLISH Prisons &/ ABOLISH the Police &/ ABOLISH Binaries &/ ABOLISH Landlords &/ ABOLISH the Nation State &/ #DefendTheCriminalized." The block-lettered words state the collective demands of the "#DefendTheCriminalized Call to Action." Later reprints of the screen added phrases like ABOLISH Poverty" and "ABOLISH Landlords." Here, aesthetic choices are made into propaganda through certain rhetorical strategies like printing the word ABOLISH in all capital letters, repeated eight times, multiplying one right after the other for emphasis.

These abolitionist aesthetic choices also work to undermine binaries and highlight exactly *who* is at the heart of abolitionist by training its focus on fashion as an inside-outside collective practice of resistance. According to their Instagram profile, "the design was created by a collective of illegals, immigrant, and border crossers in Los Angeles" with the understanding that their "affinity *lies with criminalized communities across the nation*: poor, queer, black, refugee folks whose existence and survival is criminalized every single day."[11] To that end, any discussion about abolitionist aesthetic choices must also recognize the reality that incarcerated people have little to no choice about clothing. The bodies and actions of incarcerated people are so heavily surveilled and controlled that it makes it almost impossible to wear anything other than "prison approved uniforms." Yet, it is important to remember that despite the constant surveillance, incarcerated people still find ways to incorporate personal style.[12] As much as the state wants to regulate bodies deemed criminal, these same bodies still find a way to resist. The stylistic and aesthetic resistance by incarcerated people is not lost on the Instagram organizers mentioned in this essay. For them, abolition also must mean that the voices and experiences of those currently or formerly incarcerated people with clothing must be centered. The work created by @thoughty_organizer and @emotionalgangzter utilizes narratives created and shaped by formerly incarcerated people. For example, Pablos (@emotionalgangzter) is open about her experiences as a formerly incarcerated person, and the organizing work that she does on her social media pages is geared toward abolitionist work in Arizona. She is also in constant contact with incarcerated people and actively listens to their needs. For instance, she has organized fundraisers to send commissary money to women inside the Arizona State Prison Complex-Perryville.

The propaganda and resistive function of style for organizers outside *and* inside shows how abolition is ultimately an invitation to imagine the social world in radically different terms. It is an invitation to ask what freedom is or might mean. It is in this spirit that I see abolition aesthetics as central to the project of imagining.

COLLECTIVE DAYDREAMING ON- AND OFFLINE: MAKING ABOLITIONIST FUTURES WITH @THOUGHTY_ORGANIZER AND @EMOTIONALGANGZTER

This article argues that the aesthetic co-creations and collective daydreaming of the Instagram profiles @thoughty_organizer and @emotionalgangzter put into motion abolitionist futures. According to Lena Palacios, Black, Indigenous, and other non-Black women of color "engage in a politics that calls for collective self-recognition and a 'turning away' from the carceral state, every time they daydream about the Americas disappearing into a singular landmass and sacred place called Turtle Island, these collectives engage in ceremony."[13] This collective daydreaming and plotting for the sake of our futures function as world making ceremony, and I would add that the #DefendThe-Criminalized Collective and Pablos both offer a glimpse into this abolitionist world-making that centers aesthetics as a way of initiating, activating, and vitalizing the imagination. Daydreaming, like online activism, creates a connection between the online world space and everyday lived space, and the point of imaginative connection is the aestheticized body. Daydreaming and connection are femme-centered organizing principles that expand the type of aesthetic coding I am tracking. In thinking alongside Palacios's description of women coming together, I am interested in how dreams of freedom are envisioned by the #DefendTheCriminalized Collective and produced through online activism that is being transmitted and materialized into actual fashion and bodily objects that make one feel connected to something in the world and online. I also want to invoke the Critical Resistance (CR) and INCITE! Women of Color Against Violence statement: "We seek to build movements that not only end violence, but that create a society based on radical freedom, mutual accountability, and passionate reciprocity. In this society, safety and security will not be premised on violence or the threat of violence; it will be based on a collective commitment to guaranteeing the survival and care of all people."[14] #DefendTheCriminalized Collective and Pablos deploy similar tactics committed to building up movements centered on imagining radical freedom and providing care to those most vulnerable. For example, Pablos and the #DefendTheCriminalized Collective have co-created work with artists and other creatives that vary in scope and in size. These social media accounts do not just exist in the digital space, the organizers have also created events centered on community building such as teach-ins, fundraisers, and parties fostering acts of ceremonies that bring forth a glimpse of abolitionist futures.

The events created by #DefendTheCriminalized Collective are a strong component of their community-building and mutual-aid work. Early on in the group's history, they sold their bodysuit and other articles of screen-printed clothing as a way to fundraise direct assistance to Central American migrants stuck in Tijuana, Mexico. The collective also co-organized with other groups in the Los Angeles, Orange County, and Inland Empire regions to fundraise bail money for people in immigrant detention and direct support for migrants deserted by the California Border Patrol in isolated locations.[15] Additionally, the collective organized events that involved community building such as the "Future Femmes" event. According to the group, the space was imagined for "hood femmes, womxn, and girls" in order to lead with anti-capitalist values that celebrate, dialogue, and build with others.[16] This event, moderated by Pablos, was organized as both a "teach-in" and a "pop-up" event. The organizers associated with both Instagram accounts work to center community, material conditions, and the *situatedness* of differences foregrounded by abolitionist aesthetics, and mutual aid has always been at the heart of their work. For #DefendTheCriminalized, mutual aid includes efforts to gather supplies needed for those in migrant caravans, getting people out of detention, helping community members pay legal fees, and information regarding rent strikes. Mutual aid has been an essential part of the group's objective since its inception, and it continues to fuel the organizing they do online and in real life. All of the work that they do is methodical and discussed in great detail by those participating. In fact, #DefendTheCriminalized Collective's very story begins with an action that sought to bring attention to the way that migration is tied to incarceration. The collective began by staging an act of civil disobedience, standing and sitting on top of jail beds positioned in one of the busiest intersections in Los Angeles to draw attention to the links between criminalization of migrants and jails/prisons. To be sure, the collective has a deep history of utilizing what is known as "carceral aesthetics." Theorized by scholar Nicole R. Fleetwood, "carceral aesthetics is the production of art under conditions of unfreedom."[17] Abolitionist aesthetics, then, may propose something similar: sensory pleasure in the context of freedom work. This is just a small example of the events organized by the group in order to cultivate digital spaces and in-person spaces that centered abolitionist work and theory. Placing community and collectivism at the core of their work is arguably in the Black radical feminist tradition of adornment and everyday style, to bring attention to the co-optation of #AbolishICE.

The online community that is being built and fortified through the Instagram profiles of @thoughty_organizer and @emotionalgangzter is attentive to the historical legacies of abolition and follows familiar lineages of critique and activism, but they also translate the conceptual work of abolition into a visual vernacular of activism, using textual cues, printed on clothing and through the use of hashtags, in their daily posts to circulate conversations around abolition beyond just the academy. In a world where undocumented (im)migrant people and children are captured, disappeared, and are incarcerated for an indefinite amount of time on a daily basis, abolitionist feminist, inexpressible. This work draws heavily from the writings of Gloria Anzaldúa, who teaches us that "the artist uses the imagination to impose order on chaos . . . provides language to distressed and confused people—a language that expresses previously inexpressible."[18]

The #DefendTheCriminalized Collective's focus on making copies, through screen printing and in using Instagram as a mode of circulation of online activism, highlights the importance of the multiple in the work of the femme-centered group. Screen printing is an analogue of the constant posting of the Instagram story. Circulation of reports, petitions, events, news, and other forms of online engagement are currents of involvement and solidarity that are translated directly into material/textual form through the screen-printed garments worn in "real life." In this way, the fashions become a continuation of the work happening through a different medium, producing yet another sense of shared commitment. This labor of making copies follows the conversation happening between fashion activism and online activism and helps us to understand something about the visuals and fashions that emerge in response to the prison industrial complex.

In the T-shirt project, the repetition of the word "abolish" reminds viewers of the way that communities, especially those criminalized, such as Black, Indigenous, (im)migrant, are unfree. The group was frustrated with the co-opting of the #ABOLISHICE by many in politics and decided to reclaim the term and to explain what it meant for them. For the collective, abolition means "#Defendthecriminalized and is an ongoing CALL TO ACTION / We are unapologetic / Uncompromising / We want liberation for ALL oppressed and criminalized people of the world / Nothing short of that." Stating the goals of the collective and translating them to their followers/audience further advocates how abolition is not only a theoretical framework in which to organize but also a theory in practice. The feminist abolitionist framework that #DefendTheCriminalized utilizes takes into account how femme fashioning and adornment challenge normative logics of white supremacy that aim to obliterate difference through distortion.

PINK SWEATERS ON THE LINE: VISUALIZING INVISIBLE FEMME LABOR AND AESTHETIC RESISTANCE

Although all of the garment styles deployed by @thoughty_organizer and @emotionalgangzter are not pictured in this article, I want to focus briefly on a collection of crew neck sweaters to illustrate the organizers' visual analysis of the labor needed to screen print and ultimately *enact* the call and demand for abolition. The staging of the Instagram photograph of pink hanging sweaters (figure 2) is an intervention into the invisibilized labor of this community. The clothesline in the photograph offers the viewer a brief glimpse of the type of labor needed in order to create abolitionist feminist aesthetic materials. Part of the collective's abolitionist ethos is a do-it-yourself (DIY) aesthetic practice, an everydayness and attitude regarding the creative work that they produce and redistribute. The act of screen printing is an embodied technique that involves the artist's attention to reproduction and transfer of the abolitionist message. Utilizing elements normally considered an integral part of household labor such as the clothesline is a mirror of the feminized labor and materials that are often obscured within political and social movements. The movement for abolition is no different. #DefendTheCriminalized Collective understands that labor deemed "feminine/household" is hardly ever made visible and not valued because it happens within the home. Screen printing for the collective is part of the invisibilized domestic and feminized labor that is often the foundation for hundreds of mutual aid networks in poor and criminalized communities. For them, attending to the aesthetic does not require a turning away or abstraction of labor or material conditions.

Fig. 2. Instagram post by @thoughty_organizer, February 1, 2019. Image courtesy of #DefendTheCriminalized Collective.

The post's appropriation of the term "PINK ARMY"[19] also works as a signifier and reference to the mutual aid work and activism done by the 1980s group the AIDS Coalition to Unleash Power (ACT UP).[*] They juxtapose the color pink, which is a symbol of domesticity, femininity (and femme-ness), and queerness alongside the word "army," which is defined by the Oxford English Dictionary (OED) as "an organized body of soldiers trained and equipped to fight on land; a land force."[**] The photograph of various sweaters appearing in the post acts as a metaphor demonstrating the "pink army" ready to organize in the name of dismantling the carceral system. Similarly, the caption and image also mobilize an organic, community-centered and community-facing site of organizing, which challenges the co-optation of the terms abolish/abolition within movement spaces, even amongst the collective's own followers. #DefendTheCriminalized challenges performances of "allyship," including by members of their Instagram following, and instead call for their followers to be respectful "accomplices" in dismantling prisons, detention, borders, and other systems of the carceral state.[***] They ask: How are their social media followers

---

[*] Firstly, ACT UP formed in 1987 in New York, NY. During this emergence, ACT UP utilized and transformed modes of resistance, such direct action, videography, and screen printing in response to the AIDS crisis. For example, the appropriation and critical transformation of the pink triangle, historically used to identify gay male prisoners in Nazi concentration camps, is rendered in the collective's 1987 Silence=Death campaign. This references queer resistance within times of political repression and state violence. Secondly, this mode of appropriation in queer codes of resistance by ACT UP can also be seen in the work of @thoughty_organizer in their continuation of this legacy of street protest, DIY aesthetic, and art action. Finally, it is also important to note that the Stonewall rebellion, another important moment in LGBTQIA history, created a link between the criminalization and harassment of LGBTQIA people and prison abolition. Understanding these two historical points in LGBTQIA resistance have also greatly influenced the work of the collective.

[**] It should be noted that this play with militarism, though, is not without dilemma. As scholars like Julian Go, Amina Mama, and many others have noted, military maneuvers of imperialism, conquest, and border enforcement form the root of modern US policing and are connected to notions of "defense" of the domestic in ways that enable logics of gender violence.

[***] The term "accomplice" used by the collective is directly tied to the 2014 zine and statement called "Accomplices not Allies: An Indigenous Perspective

willing to corroborate? In the sale of items and other forms of support, the collective notes that accomplices are "engaging in "MATERIAL SOLIDARITY!" as the money exchanged for these articles of clothing is a form of material solidarity that allows for mutual aid and continues efforts to #DefendTheCriminalized by economically supporting the needs of the community. Being accomplices to abolition is also about defying internalized binaries that surround identity formations such as gender, sexuality, race, disability, and citizenship.

Fig. 3. Instagram post by @thoughty_organizer, December 27, 2018. Image courtesy of #DefendTheCriminalized Collective.

The 2019 post featuring the #DefendTheCriminalized pink sweat-shirt is not the first time the collective has worked to visibilize invis-ible, "domestic," or femme labor in their work. The Melt ICE. Burn Prisons. screen print was first printed on a tube top (later also uti-lized on turtleneck crop tops) and featured in a post, hanging across clotheslines and Christmas lights (figure 3). Beyond its work to make the invisible visible, this article of clothing echoes the emphasis on femme aesthetics and embodiment, as it is meant to fit tight on the chest and does not have any sleeves or straps, held up, instead, by

---

Abolishing the Ally Industrial Complex" created by Indigenous Action.

tight stitching and/or elastic. What's more, this is one of the designs that demonstrates how the #DefendTheCriminalized Collective has evolved their message into a more succinct abolitionist feminist stance. This position is a direct result of the ongoing contributions, lived experiences, and institutional knowledges of trans people that are an integral part of the collective body and organizing principles. In addition to what I call "#DefendTheCriminalized call to action," the Collective has five other screen prints. The second is ABOLISH ICE, the third is FUCK ICE (infinity sign), the fourth is ABOLISH POL-I.C.E., and the fifth is Melt ICE. Burn Prisons. This last screen print is also one of the most used screen prints by the collective and featured on several different items like totes, sweaters, and shirts. On the tube top, the words "melt" and "ICE" are inside a black rectangle making the lettering direct and minimalist as compared to some of the other screen prints discussed above. The collective is playing on the words melt and ice (as in frozen water). Here ICE is presented as the acronym for the Immigration and Customs Enforcement. Although one cannot simply melt an institution like ICE, it can be slowly chipped away at. It is important to note the period at the end of the phrase "Melt ICE.," as it signifies a definitive statement that ICE must be dismantled "period." The letters are not created by the paint but through negative space within the black rectangle. The black rectangle can be read as a minimalist representation of a prison, and the text becomes the pathway to freedom. The phrasing on this tube top illustrates the kind of rhetorical/aesthetic play with language that brings intellectual pleasure to the political demand and makes it accessible to the community. Too, the symbolic accomplishment of the black-rectangle-as-prison uses visuals to express what is inexpressible, as Anzaldúa says. The screen-printed design in the photograph uses text and symbols to provide an alternative abolitionist understanding that seeks to inform, educate, and organize the community to see themselves as participating in abolitionist world building.

Finally, a playful but important aesthetic and discursive element of the tube top message is the period at the end of the phrase "Melt ICE," as in ICE must be dismantled "period." While female hip-hop artists like

City Girls and Megan Thee Stallion have widened use of the vernacular term "period," it has been a long-standing expression of definitive discursive force among young Black and Brown femme and queer culture.

The abolitionist feminist discourse utilized by the #DefendThe-Criminalized uses femme aesthetics to critique an immigrant rights discourse that refuses to acknowledge the relationship between abolishing ICE and a larger movement for prison abolition. The second phrase on the tube top screen print states "Burn Prisons" in black lettering without any background. It is necessary to pause and examine both phrases in conversation with one another. The collective created "a quick history" documenting the early actions and they state, "In *summer 2018* some of us came together again bc [*sic*] we saw how *politicians, candidates* and mainstream immigrant rights orgs were *coopting and watering down the #AbolishICE* movement . . . Together we created this design ("the call to action" screen-print) to explain what abolishing ICE means to us."[20] This brief look into the history of the collective reminds us that abolishing ICE is not the end but merely an extension of the work already being done to abolish prisons. One cannot exist without the other. They are mirrored movements that must be thought of as connected to one another. The tube top is a reminder of the necessary work that must happen alongside each other. Understanding the #DefendTheCriminalized history reminds us, as the viewer, of the importance of having both of these phrases alongside one another to remind those in the immigrant rights movements of the necessity to also demand for the abolition of prisons.

The phrase "Burn Prisons." acts similarly to "melt" in that they are both actions concentrated around heat and fire. Again, if one institution is going to be "melted away," then the other must also have the same fate which is "burning it down." "ICE" and "Prisons" one alongside the other demonstrate the similarities that exist between the two. As much as government and ICE officials want to say that ICE detention centers are not prisons, the collective reminds us that they are one and the same. Both function as institutions of captivity that together serve as mechanisms of control for communities of color. For this collective, femme clothing and adornment is one of the many tools they are utilizing to engage in abolitionist organizing with their immediate community in Los Angeles along with their online virtual communities.

BEYOND THE GARMENT: ABOLITIONIST BODILY ADORNMENT

In addition to photographs from followers wearing the abolitionist propaganda, tweets, memes, screenshots of articles, and quotes with themes that range from abolition to anti-capitalism, the Instagram account of the #DefendTheCriminalized Collective includes photographs of other abolitionist feminist aesthetics that include other forms of femme adornment. According to the OED, adornment is "(t)he action or an act of adorning or embellishing something; the result of this; embellishment, ornamentation." From this definition one can assume that adornment is "an act" which I would characterize as a deliberate choice or a series of choices to embellish "an object" or maybe an ornamentation on an object. I would also propose that adornment is an invitation into self-styling and self-artistry that allows bodily difference and experiential knowledge to be presented as a direct affront to the logic of normativity that is predicated on sameness and distortion of difference.

Fig. 4. Instagram post by @thoughty_organizer, July 31, 2018. Image courtesy of #DefendTheCriminalized Collective.

One photograph of femme adornment, highly stylized nail art (see figure 4), demonstrates what Jillian Hernandez calls a "femme Latinx beauty practice(s)." According to Hernandez, this specific beauty practice is a type of poetic and refers to ways cis/trans/queer women and femmes relate to and recognize each other.[21] I also look at the beauty practice of "nail art" and "getting nails done" to examine closely the intimate labor and relationality that this work allows. I highlight the relational aspect of this nail art as being interconnected to larger critiques that seek to destroy the violence enacted against criminalized, undocumented communities.

Nail art is an element of abolitionist femme aesthetics that centers histories of working-class Black, Latinx, and Asian communities. The race/gendered spaces of hair salons and/or nail salons are spaces of community building, intimacy, and sharing. Furthermore, they are built on a poetics of sensuality and visuality. When this image appeared on my Instagram feed, I was immediately drawn to this photograph of someone's hands, specifically moved by the Old English calligraphy design on the nails of the index, middle, and ring finger of both hands, calligraphy that calls up Black and Latinx vernacular style. The focus on the hands also reminds me of the labor that is done with hands and how the hands can be a site of exploitation and intense work especially for the gendered bodies of women, femmes, and gender nonconforming people. This photograph also demonstrates the social media–based labor as well as the embodied labor behind the nails. In the photo, the points of each nail appears as if it is sharp enough to inflict injury or pain—femininity, here, is not a docile accompaniment to masculine codes. With these nails, femininity becomes femme-ininity, which breaks with the sex/gender binary that supports white supremacy. I want to linger on the way that abolitionist femme adornment can be utilized as a weapon instead of being seen as "weak" and/or other gendered assumptions. These nails are a reminder of the way that fashioning and adornment can be utilized as protection. It is also important to note the hashtag #MilitantFemininity used in the caption. For the collective, this is a hashtag that is utilized throughout their social media page and functions as a challenge to the gendered idea of femininity as weak and self-absorbed. Adornment of the nails is just as important as the style and shape of the nail, and it is the place where the nail technician shows their skills.

The photograph documents a femme aesthetic practice that externalizes abolitionist feminist thought as a response to the invisibilized labor of women, femmes, and gender nonconforming people of color. Nail art is not something new or unique; it is an aesthetic choice that has made its way into popular, mainstream "high fashion" publications and the repertoire of designers. For many working-class women and femmes who have expressed themselves using nail art, their aesthetic choices were often ridiculed as a caricature rooted in misogynoir. For example, the white nail color acts as a blank canvas for the nail technician to receive some guidance and/or a request from the customer. In this instance, asking a nail technician to write out the phrase "FCK ICE" in calligraphy might prompt them to ask about the meaning behind the phrase, which, in turn, would result in a moment of community building and sharing between both people. Notably, the caption for the photograph says " 💅🏽FCK 💅🏽 ICE 💅🏽 All day, everyday [sic]. #HastaLaVictoria #Venceremos! #MilitantFemininity."[22] This caption is similar to what is written on the nails on the hands featured in the photograph. The design on the nails says "FCK ICE," an abbreviation of Fuck the US Immigration and Customs Enforcement. Although the use of the expletive might offend some, it is important to closely examine the way in which it is mobilized as a crucial element of femme aesthetic adornment. If one examines the phrase "FCK ICE," the first part of that statement, "FCK," I argue is utilized by the person in the photograph to mean "destroy" and "put an end to" ICE and all of its actions. ICE, as an agency, is responsible for executing deportation orders such as kidnapping people from their homes or taking people away during routine immigration check-ins; it is also responsible for caging families, including children, for an indeterminate amount of time. The real profanity occurring on these nails is the violent acts committed by ICE and its officials. Putting the phrase "FCK ICE" on your nails is an abolitionist feminist act of femme adornment that utilizes nail art as tool for abolitionist organizing.

FEMME AESTHETIC ABOLITION:
A PATTERN OF PRACTICE

Prison abolition is a pattern for everyday living that is manifested not only through the community building happening online via social media but also in daily activity and life. Alejandra Pablos's personal account catalyzes feminist abolition discourse while crossing it with other aesthetic actions. Pablos is an Arizona-based abolitionist writer and organizer who is actively fighting against her own deportation order. She has been featured many times on the #DefendTheCriminalized social media page and considers herself part of the collective. Her social media account is an insightful critique on criminalization, immigrant rights movement discourse (specifically deserving vs. undeserving), detention/incarceration, sexism, and reproductive health. Through her social media account, Pablos has also utilized abolitionist feminist aesthetics to convey critiques on the detention-industrial complex that further reinforces the necessity to continue saying #AbolishICE. The photograph and social media posts included below (figure 5) were taken at the 2019 Coachella Music and Arts Festival.

The caption on the post reads:

> DHS (department of homeland "security") is the largest police force in the US and is under complete control of the Trump administration. They have shown that they have no respect for anyone's human rights and that they are completely unaccountable. As a movement abolish ICE means:
>
> 1. Defunding ICE so they can no longer surveil, detain, and deport, our communities and reinvest that money into the basic education, health services and infrastructure for our community. It isn't enough to simply move ICE from one agency to another. We need to disinvest from policing at every level in this country, and that includes ICE.
>
> 2. Defund detention: There are [a] record number of people in immigration detention right now, and over 70% are in private detention centers. Most of the people currently behind bars right now could easily be released by ICE if they just paroled them in [*sic*]

or gave them bonds. This should be done immediately and DHS should close down all detention centers.

3. Decriminalize Migration: That means changing the laws that are criminalizing people at the border. Before the [1930s] migrating wasn't a crime. This changed when racist lawmakers wanted to create a way to lock up migrants and deal with [the] "mexican" problem. Last summer, through his Zero Tolerance policy, the DOJ weaponized these laws to create the family separation crisis. These laws are used in my home town of Tucson to prosecute thousands of people through Operation Streamline. We should immediately repeal 1325 and 1326 that make crossing the border a crime, and also take away the '96 immigration laws that make it easier to deport immigrants like myself. #chingalamigra @conmijente 📷: @laqulonaconcausa[23]

Fig. 5. Instagram post by @emotionalgangzter, April 21, 2019. Image courtesy of Alejandra Pablos.

Pablos succinctly and eloquently describes what abolishing ICE means; it is not just as a call to action that gained popularity in the summer of 2018 when it became widely known that children and families were held in detention centers alongside the Trump regime's "Zero

Tolerance" (im)migration policy. The hashtag #AbolishICE made its rounds, not only trending on social media sites such as Twitter but also within the news cycle and the political sphere as many politicians began using it on their social media platforms. It is important to note how Pablos utilizes a photograph of herself wearing a skirt emblazoned with the words "Abolish ICE" to call in her followers and others to incorporate feminist abolitionist analysis that works to end ICE and other governmental agencies that prey on criminalized people. The photograph activates the viewers and the caption, then provides them with an opportunity to think through the function of ICE and the Department of Homeland Security (DHS) in a critical way.

The femme aesthetics of fashioning within abolitionist feminist discourses that I argue for in this essay are what draws the viewers into Pablos's post. Making an abolitionist feminist call to action through the use of her wardrobe, Pablos takes the opportunity of attending Coachella to make a statement about the need to abolish Immigration and Customs Enforcement. The photograph includes elements of color, lighting, and sensuality that draws the audience's attention to the photograph of Pablos posing in front of a colorful, geometric, large-scale Saguaro statue. Abolitionist feminist aesthetics of femme fashioning and adornment are key elements for Pablos and her organizing. The adornment of, alteration to, and expansiveness of her skirt is what makes Pablos such an important figure when discussing abolitionist feminist aesthetics. The skirt is an example of the creative labor that organizers like as Pablos engage in. The garment was designed by Pablos and executed by a community of like-minded kin; in the photograph we see her arms extended out and with her hands holding onto a portion of her long skirt, unfolded and spread out, perfectly displaying the words "ABOLISH ICE" sewed on the bottom. This skirt is reminiscent of those utilized by ballet folklorico performers who are a key staple in Mexican culture, practice, and tradition. It is designed to be worn by different body shapes, refusing the shaming logic of sizing that defines mainstream fatphobic fashion. It is also necessary to note that the skirt features the words "abolish" and "ICE" in all capital letters as if the statement was being yelled out. The space between each word allows the viewer to read the phrase accurately so that there is no mistake about what the skirt and Pablos are saying. Pablos is defiant in her stance, with her head tilted up slightly as her gaze remains steadfast, looking down toward the camera. In 2018 her story received national attention when she was singled out by ICE after participating in an act of civil disobedience and was detained for forty-three days.[24] As a result, on December 11, 2018, she was given a deportation order by an immigration judge and, at the time of writing, is actively appealing that decision. She was granted bond and brought home after a nationwide, organized community effort advocating for her release. Her defiance in the photograph is not only directed toward the camera, it is also directed at the violent detention and removal that the US nation-state wants to enact on Pablos. Despite her criminalization, Pablos is steadfast in her commitment to abolition and expanding the critique of abolition within (im)migrant rights spaces.

The creativity and resilience of the work created by Pablos and the #DefendTheCriminalized Collective is manifested through the femme aesthetic choices of both online accounts. These two accounts understand the importance of embodying an everyday practice of prison abolition and the necessity of externalizing that politic through fashion. Early writings about abolition and radical feminism describe two important elements of abolitionist organizing; for example, writer Fay Honey Knopp discusses two elements of activism: consciousness raising and creativity.[25] These two elements are enacted throughout Pablos's social media page. For example, Pablos swiftly and deliberately engages in political education work as consciousness raising that elevates issues of criminalization, detention, and incarceration within Black, Latinx, Indigenous, and other non-Black people of color communities. This online activist labor is parallel to the reworking of the skirt so that it contains not only a political statement but also a call to action, similar to the work done by the #DefendTheCriminalized Collective. The statement created by Pablos is rooted in an abolitionist feminist discourse that uses something as simple as a skirt to make a statement about the larger structural issues and the need to dismantle the institution that is enacting so much violence to the immigrant community. Using a skirt, a piece of clothing synonymous with femininity—especially something rooted in Mexican cultural traditions—to bring forth a conversation centered on abolition is abolitionist feminist aesthetics in practice. Abolition is not just some abstract idea. Through the work of Pablos and her social media page, one can see how hers is a daily practice of embodiment. In turn, the act of wearing this skirt at the event that takes place about 114 miles away from Adelanto Processing Center, where people are detained in inhumane conditions, has the power to familiarize people with an understanding of abolition feminism (figure 5). Pablos is utilizing a femme aesthetic fashioning and adornment approach to convey an abolitionist feminist discourse as to why it is necessary to dismantle ICE along with the DHS as communicated in her caption. Despite the fact that Coachella draws people in from all over the country and stages musical acts from all over the world, including Latin American countries, the disconnect of inviting musicians from countries like Mexico while ICE continuously criminalizes the migration of people from Central America and Mexico makes one wonder exactly how culture is welcomed and valued while the people who carry that culture are not.

I argue that the #DefendTheCriminalized Collective and Pablos's skirt used an abolitionist feminist discourse that mobilizes femme aesthetic coding in fashion and adornment to convey aesthetics rooted in prison abolition. The various screen prints created by the collective, especially their "Call to Action," is a cartography for abolitionist everyday practice. The screen print is a study of the various maps of abolitionist everyday practices and strategies that moves a theoretical concept into the aesthetic sphere of fashion and adornment. I imagine the #DefendTheCriminalized "Call to Action" printed on everyday objects of life from books to buildings to on the street and, ultimately, inside the hearts and minds of the community. That said, I argue for the importance of this abolitionist feminist practice that was manifested through online fashion and adornment. This femme aesthetic coding I named throughout this article was an external manifestation of an internal theory that responded to institutionalized oppression and violence at the hands of the US nation-state. The posts featured throughout this text are also examples of coded images that were posted and then circulated throughout social media and now have a life of their own through publishing. In crafting a careful analysis of a handful of Instagram posts, I was able to conduct a close reading of the fashion photographs in order to unpack their meanings. More importantly, the photographs document the community building taking place on social media centered around prison abolition. This work is important because it seeks to make visible that which is often invisibilized. It draws attention to the importance of shifting culture and culture making, which includes fashion and adornment, within abolitionist theory and practice that moves beyond the academy. The garments featured in the photographs speak to an abolitionist feminist poetics of visuality and sensuality that give the body power and force.

Embodying the collective's call to action, I decided to post a photograph of myself wearing the bodysuit, which accentuated every curve and carefully outlined my protruding stomach with the hashtags #abolitionist and #FemmeOfColorVisibility.[26] I tagged the collective, and they responded immediately with "OMG FRIEND?! Can we PLEASE SHARE!??? Like PORFAS." This online exchange further reinscribed the importance of community building and how a bodysuit on a fat Xicana femme is an act of resistance that centers women, femmes, and other gender nonconforming Black, Indigenous, and people of color. Similar to the translation of a screen print, my photograph was reposted and circulated amongst the community of followers that #DefendTheCriminalized has cultivated. I am proud to be part of such a community of abolitionists committed to challenging narratives of "deserving" and "undeserving" within (im)migrant justice discourses. Following and contributing to these accounts committed to popular and critical education about abolition constantly move and challenge me to rethink my own learned understanding of abolition. Through this writing and the online activist work at the center of it all, I, similar to Pablos, consider myself a member of the #DefendTheCriminalized squad, a network of women, femmes, and gender nonconforming folks who believe in and organize around abolition as an everyday practice and future. In owning one of the #DefendTheCriminalized "Call to

Action" bodysuits, I feel energized and compelled to show how the body creates new forms of shared engagement and solidarity that happen through visual codes, signs, and elements, and that using these codes can make one feel like they belong. I am committed to abolishing the many abstract and visual boundaries that alienate femme, woman, gender nonconforming sensuality and activism and that seek to keep our communities apart. In the spirit of abolitionist feminist aesthetic coding, I close this article with a collage poem that I was inspired to write based on the visions of the #DefendTheCriminalized Collective.

The Squad

ABOLISH ICE &
ABOLISH DHS &
ABOLISH Prisons &
ABOLISH The Police &
ABOLISH Binaries &
ABOLISH Landlords &
ABOLISH The Nation
State &
#DefendTheCriminalized

ABOLISH ICE &
ABOLISH DHS &
ABOLISH Prisons &
ABOLISH The Police &
ABOLISH Binaries &
ABOLISH Landlords &
ABOLISH Poverty &
ABOLISH The Nation
State &
#DefendTheCriminalized

EACH ITERATION GROWING EXPANDING ADDING
MORE AND MORE
The sum of all the parts equals a mass, a group, a crew
     A SQUAD
Is your squad suited up?!
If we gonna stunt on this hating ass cis-tem
we gonna make it look sexy!
This isn't a trend
 #IssssaaaaMOVEMENT!
MILITANT FEMMES TO THE FRONT
This isn't just a cute bodysuit with a message it's
A 🗣CALL🗣TO 🗣ACTION

ABOLISH ICE &
ABOLISH DHS &
ABOLISH Prisons &
ABOLISH The Police &
ABOLISH Binaries &
ABOLISH Landlords &
ABOLISH Poverty &
ABOLISH The Nation
State &
#OrganizeTheCriminalized

#FreeThemAll from ICE &
#FreeThemAll from DHS &
#FreeThemAll from Prisons &
#FreeThemAll from The Police &
#FreeThemAll from Binaries &
#FreeThemAll from Landlords &
#FreeThemAll from The Nation
State
#OrganizeTheCriminalized.

NOTES

1. #DefendTheCriminalized Collective (@Thoughty_Organizer), "Tag @ thoughty_organizer and @uniondevecinos if you share," Instagram, June 30, 2018, https://www.instagram.com/p/Bko6VYhFlpk/.

2. Gloria E. Anzaldúa, *Light in the Dark/Luz en lo Oscuro: Rewriting Identity, Spirituality, Reality*, ed. Analouise Keating (Durham, NC: Duke University Press, 2015).

3. Jillian Hernandez, "Beauty Marks: The Latinx Surfaces of Loving, Becoming, and Mourning," *Women & Performance* 28, no. 1 (2018): 67–84.

4. Here, I am thinking about the hypervisibility of Black women's bodies as theorized by Nicole Fleetwood's idea of "excess flesh." See Nicole Fleetwood, *Troubling Vision: Performance, Visuality, and Blackness* (Chicago: University of Chicago Press, 2011).

5. Terry Lee Stone with Sean Adams and Noreen Morioka, *Color Design Workbook: A Real World Guide to Using Color in Graphic Design* (Beverly, MA: Rockport Publishers, 2008).

6. Nancy MacDonell, "Still Risqué, the Formfitting Bodysuit Rises Again," *Wall Street Journal*, November 27, 2019, https://www.wsj.com/articles/still-risque-the-formfitting-bodysuit-rises-again-11574857951.

7. Arundhati Roy, "Arundhati Roy: 'The pandemic is a portal,'" *Financial Times*, April 3, 2020, https://www.ft.com/content/10d8f5e8-74eb-11ea-95fe-fcd274e920ca.

8. Audre Lorde, "Uses of the Erotic" in *Sister Outsider: Essays and Speeches by Audre Lorde* (New York: Crossing Press, 1984).

9. @thoughty_organizer, "#DefendTheCriminalized Mutual Aid in Praxis Workshop," presentation at "#FreeThemAll: Abolition Beyond Detention Virtual Teach-In, May 5, 2020.

10. Angela Davis, *Are Prisons Obsolete?* (New York: Seven Stories Press, 2003), 16.

11. Thoughty_Organizer, "Our Story," Instagram story, 2019.

12. Juliet Ash, *Dress behind Bars: Prison Clothing as Criminality* (London and New York: I. B. Tauris & Co. Ltd., 2010); John J. Lennon, "'You Haven't Given Up': How Prisoners Are Finding a Place for Personal Style on the Inside," *Esquire*, February 25, 2020, https://www.esquire.com/style/mens-fashion/a31083835/prison-personal-style-fashion/.

13. Lena Palacios, "With Immediate Cause: Intense Dreaming as World-Making," *Abolition: A Journal of Insurgent Politics*, no. 1 (2018): 57–67.

14. Critical Resistance and INCITE! Women of Color Against Violence, "Gender Violence and the Prison-Industrial Complex," in *Color of Violence The Incite! Anthology*, ed. INCITE! Women of Color Against Violence (Cambridge, MA: South End Press, 2006), 226.

15. #DefendTheCriminalized Collective (@Thoughty_Organizer), "DO NOT SCROLL! Share! Donate! We are our communities' LIFELINE! Show UPPPPP!!! #MurderPatrol," Instagram, May 22, 2019, https://www.instagram.com/p/BxyI9Qug-sE/.

16. #DefendTheCriminalized Collective (@Thoughty_Organizer), "S U N D A Y ! TEACH IN + POP UP with and FOR hood femmes, womxn and girls!" Instagram, May 14, 2019, https://www.instagram.com/thoughty_organizer/p/BxcwarmgCFa/.

17. Nicole R. Fleetwood, *Marking Time: Art in the Age of Mass Incarceration* (Cambridge, MA: Harvard University Press, 2020).

18. Anzaldúa, *Light in the Dark*, 39.

19. #DefendTheCriminalized Collective (@Thoughty_Organizer), "PINK ARMY: if wearing 'radical' gear is the extent of your 'activism' then CHECK YOURSELF & proceed to unfollow," Instagram, February 1, 2019, https://www.instagram.com/thoughty_organizer/p/BtXZeaDBtVO/.

20. #DefendTheCriminalized Collective (@Thoughty_Organizer), "Our Story" Instagram story, 2018. The words italicized appeared in red font on the Instagram story. In order to keep the integrity of the words I have decided to italicize it to keep at close to the original writing as possible.

21. Hernandez, "Beauty Marks," 68.

22. #DefendTheCriminalized Collective (@Thoughty_Organizer), "FCK ICE All day, everyday. #HastaLaVictoria #Venceremos! #MilitantFemininity" Instagram, July 31, 2018, https://www.instagram.com/p/Bl6otI2B4eE/.

23. Alejandra Pablos (@emotionalgangzter), "DHS (department of homeland 'security') is the largest police force in the US and is under compete control of the Trump administration," Instagram, April 21, 2019, https://www.instagram.com/p/BwhjQJcAXic/.

24. Danielle Campoamor, "ICE Detained This Outspoken Activist. Here's What She Had to Say the Day Before a Judge Ordered Her Deportation," *TeenVogue*, December 12, 2018, https://www.teenvogue.com/story/ice-detained-outspoken-activist-alejandra-pablos-interview-judge-ordered-deportation.

25. Fay Honey Knopp, "On Radical Feminism and Abolition" *Peace Review* 6, no. 2 (1994): 206.

26. @LAFemmesofColorCollective, Instagram, January 19, 2015. Available via Instagram.com. Creators of #femmeofcolorvisibility a Southern California–based collective of local Black femmes and femmes of color "building community and solidarity with one another."

GHOSTLY CARE: BOARDING SCHOOLS, PRISONS, AND DEBT IN *RHYMES FOR YOUNG GHOULS*

Christine Finley

We hurt from the before and it makes us hurt so bad right now.
— Ian Fern Campeau, Timothy Craig Hill, and
Ehren Thomas, *A Tribe Called Red*

Inasmuch as colonization consists of damaging ruptures, decolonization relies on the attempts of the broken to love, care, tend, and heal relationships with our ancestors, land bases, and other people. This essay is neither meant to lament the brokenness of our communities nor is it an expression of hope for the settler state to save us from our pain and suffering; despite all the promises, acts, treaties, and apologies, such salvation has never occurred. As Dian Million argues, the heteropatriarchal settler state cannot work on healing in Native nations because the harm of settler colonialism extends itself through institutionalized and sometimes punitive forms of therapy, treatment, or the promotion of "self-care."[1] As a counter-analysis to these distorted and damaging forms of settler "care," Leanne Simpson reconfigures care in a way that allows us think carefully and critically about caring relationships among land, Native peoples, two-spirit queers (2SQ), and other people of color as the central component of decolonization. Instead of chasing after elusive concepts of humanity, justice, truth, or transparency, a different formation of caring relations could emerge from the queer Indigenous abolitionist theoretical framework that is *decolonial love.*[2] Decolonial love constitutes care, sociality, and relationality among, within, and across the breaks and the broken. The care embodied in decolonial love necessarily refuses heteropaternalist settler care that is only expressed through violence, murder, incarceration, and dispossession, particularly in an anti–Black and colonial situation.

One element of decolonial love and its formations of care, sociality, and relationality is that it extends beyond temporal and terrestrial realms, calling instead for restorative and wildly reparative "otherwise" visions and relations from and among ancestors, ghosts, and those who live in the ghastly thresholds of social life—the criminalized, the marginalized, and the disappeared.

Whereas settler colonialism needs the recognition of the colonized to be fully empowered, decolonial love must not allow settler participation into the center of decolonial healing. Documentation of our suffering has not only not worked, it has contributed to practices of officialism that locate authority of experience within institutions instead of within ourselves.[3] Relatedly, decolonial love must draw from radical frameworks that resist the ableist, normative, racist, sexist, Enlightenment-defined ideal of individual "wholeness."[*] Our work, instead, is to take responsibility for each other and recognize that our survival depends on collective wholeness—interdependence and community caring for each other.

A decolonial practice of care and attention is crucial given that Native people face a high rate of incarceration and are targets of police violence, yet we are rarely considered in conversations around the prison industrial complex. Andrea Ritchie's amazing book *Invisible No More: Police Violence Against Black Women and Women of Color* (2017) and Kelly Lytle Hernández's *City of Inmates: Conquest, Rebellion, and the Rise of Human Caging in Los Angeles, 1771–1965* (2017) are notable and substantial exceptions here. As a result of genocide, Native peoples

---

[*] In Denise Ferreira da Silva's *Toward a Global Idea of Race* (Minneapolis: University of Minnesota Press, 2007), one of the most important contributions to the field of ethnic studies, Silva argues that within Enlightenment thinking, the striving for full subjectivity (reason and self-determination) or what she refers to as the "transparency thesis" can only be achieved by white people. Importantly, people of color can never obtain the position of the "transparent I" because the transparent subject requires an unreasonable, instinct-driven "affectable" subject (people of color) that stands in contrast and opposition to the "transparent I."

make up less than 1 percent of the population in the United States. Just because the genocide of Indigenous peoples was almost successful does not mean we have disappeared. This genocide continues when Indigenous politics are not part of conversations around incarceration. I do not only mean the simple inclusion of Indigenous people as prisoners as the solution here but, as Lytle Hernández suggests, we must think of settler colonialism as part of the driving political forces around incarceration along with the logics of slavery, heteropatriarchy, and anti-immigration. Incarceration, as in many communities of color, is only *one* of the major crises Indigenous communities face living in a white supremacist, heteropatriarchal settler state. As Lytle Hernández argues, incarceration is a major part of the settler colonial project of clearing the land of Native peoples, turning land into property that can be owned and then caging poor whites and people of color for a profit.[4] Further, Native peoples are such threats to the settler colonial state that the settler state took and continue to take generations of Native children from their homes and put them in boarding schools to be captured and attempted to strip them of their culture and tried to assimilate them into settler colonialism. When Native parents refused to comply, they were incarcerated.[5]

In order to take care of Native lands and build caring relationships for a different kind of future, incarceration, and with it the destruction of relationships and care among Native people and all people, must end. Incarceration and captivity are intimate apparatuses of settler colonialism and settler care. According to the Bureau of Justice statistics, Native people have a 38 percent higher rate of incarceration than the national average, and Native women are six times more likely to be incarcerated in comparison to white women.[6] Parents who are locked up can't take care of their children or be a part of their communities. These children are sent into foster care, and as other Native feminists have argued, the foster care system is a continuation of the Indian boarding school project of removing Native children from their parents and communities.[7] Currently, migrant, Black, incarcerated, or working-class mothers have had their children violently removed from them (dispossession) to put in the "care" of the settler state as a means of controlling families of color who have been in the US for minutes or for centuries.

Indigenous film and art offer radical new visions of decolonial care, visions of Indigenous people living, surviving, and spiritually seeking to be another way with each other in an active settler colonial situation. Art offers what some scholars refer to as "elsewhere"[8] and takes Indigenous imaginings seriously as texts of hope, fugitivity, and freedom. In this article, I use Jeff Barnaby's 2013 film *Rhymes for Young Ghouls* to glimpse another way of approaching incarceration, colonialism, and decolonial care in Indigenous communities.

Ideas of abolition and freedom[9] are growing in Native America because Native peoples, like many other communities of color, are struggling to live in an active settler colonial situation built on punitivity, borders, and other sites of discipline, state violence, and control. In other words, it is difficult to think about freedom in captivity. However, the lead character in *Rhymes*, Alia,* is a two-spirit First Nation youth who is a survivor of gender violence and resists incarceration in a residential school. Alia's father was unable to escape the violence of residential school and prison. Throughout the film, Alia's father struggles, and while they could have easily blamed their father's brokenness on being incarcerated for years, they don't. In *Rhymes*, it is clear that healing potential lies in the hands of the community, including the community of ancestors, and not in the hands of the settler state that does not take responsibility for the violences inflicted within regimes of captivity. Instead, we are reminded of the ways that Indigenous governance and relationality rely on responsibility and kinship obligations—the opposite of settler cultural practices.

As the film illuminates, this responsibility and caring kinship relation is a crucial element of abolitionist decolonial love that also takes place in the caring relationships between ancestors and the living. What forms is a kind of ghostly anti-carceral care that manifests itself through relationships between beings, the spirit worlds, and the land.

---

*   I will use they/them pronouns to honor Alia's two-spirit identity.

In this way, I argue that Indian ghosts or "ghouls" do a better job of care and protecting life than the settler state.

Jeff Barnaby, a Mi'kmaq First Nations person, wrote and directed *Rhymes for Young Ghouls* (2013). This film, in centering Native characters, history, culture, fugitivity, and survival, works to lay bare the foundation of colonization by offering a context of land and cultural dispossession, chemical warfare through strategic alcohol and drug trafficking on reserves, prisons, the violence of Indian agents, and the effects these collective colonial violences have on First Nations peoples. This film is an Indigenous coming-of-age story of a young gender nonconforming First Nations person set in 1976 on the Mi'kmaq Crow Reserve. This is not a typical coming-of-age story because the main character is not white or gender conforming. Alia does not fall in love, figure out their sexuality, or get happy; they aren't saved by a kind white lady or Jesus; they don't get a heteronormative family; nor do they neatly heal from the violences of colonialism.

In the first ten minutes of the film, Alia's mom, who is intoxicated, accidently backs over her son in a car and then kills herself. Alia wakes up the next morning and finds their mom hanging on the front porch and their dad being arrested and taken away by the police for the death of Alia's brother. At age eight, Alia lost their family existing in this earthly dimension in less than twelve hours. Although this might seem like a damage-based text,[10] this is the beginning of the film and not the end. As Michelle Raheja might say, this is reservation reelism.[11] The film centers on how Alia practices fugitivity and evades residential school, starvation, and sexual abuse with the help of their ghost brother and mother. The ghosts, stories, and dreams give Alia solace and protection *from* the settler state. The violence in their life comes from laws, agents, and institutions of the settler state that are meant to protect First Nations peoples. *Rhymes* is not about land dispossession, but importantly, it is a critique of the next stage of colonial relations with Indigenous peoples, which is the commodification and institutionalization of paternalistic colonial care.

Throughout the film, the teenaged Alia takes care of their family financially in the only way they can: by selling pot. Because this work keeps Alia out of residential school, they have to pay a large fee to the Indian agent to avoid incarceration or placement in the "care" of the residential school.

As a financial and emotional caretaker in their family, Alia is often placed in situations where they are worried about the welfare of their father, who was incarcerated upon their brother and mother's death and is, predictably, broken. But unlike the settler forms of "care" that are based on surveillance and punitivity, Alia's care is pitched toward anti-carcerality. In one scene, Alia's father wants to go fishing after he is released from prison. However, for Native peoples, access to our traditional foods is always limited by the state. It is illegal for Indians to be on the water at that time of the year, and Alia is concerned that their dad will get arrested again. While Alia and their uncle stand on the shore and look helplessly around for their father, Alia's uncle states that "prison broke him." Alia immediately disagrees with their uncle and says in Mi'kmac: "They didn't break him. We did." *We broke him.* This is profound and is a huge shift in decolonial thinking. In some ways, I wanted to hear Alia blame colonialism, heteropaternalism and structural inequalities for the punishment and pain of Alia's father being absent in their life. Barnaby, the writer-director, challenges Native and non-Native audiences to reconceptualize the grief and rage of having a family member captured by the settler state by taking the settler state out of the equation of healing and change. This is not a means of absolving the settler state but of moving us all into a different stage of grief and potential action. Recognizing and accepting a Native man broken by incarceration into the family and Native nation is the first step of anti-carceral care because it is a great responsibility for all involved. Being incarcerated affects everyone and their absence is a loss that must be mourned by the community. This is not just an individual or family responsibility and the pain, rage, and loss belongs to all of them just as much as healing belongs to all of them. I hear and see "We did [break him]" as a radical new way of Indigenous people living, surviving, and spiritually seeking to be another way in an active settler colonial situation. We need to start taking responsibility for each other and recognize that our survival, and more importantly, our living, depends on caring for each other. The only way the state can care for Natives and everyone else is through the threat and horizon of carcerality. Paternalistic care can only be punishing and extractive. Alia could have easily blamed their father's brokenness on being incarcerated for years and colonialism. Obviously, this is true, but Alia is putting responsibility in the hands of their community instead of in hope the settler will take responsibility.

Since ghosts and death are part of Native stories and communities, theorizing the care, love, and caution ghosts provide is also a necessary part of a framing of decolonial love. As Eve Tuck and C. Ree argue, haunting can be productive, and sometimes that is all the power communities of color can access.[12] Natives pay attention to ghosts and hauntings because Indigenous stories are an important part of life, family, and community. Recognizing Indigenous ghosts honors our past and provides hope for a future beyond colonialism. Jeff Barnaby uses ghosts in *Rhymes* as pivotal characters and cautionary tales. Even though Alia's brother dies at the beginning of the film, he plays an important role throughout the movie, and ultimately, haunting extends the characters' expressions of decolonial love and sense of responsibility.

Tyler, Alia's ghost brother, only appears when Alia is alone or with other people he feels safe with. Only some characters can see Tyler. Tyler has an ashy white face; he isn't transparent or represented as a Hollywood ghost. It is unsettling to have a child be a ghost, especially as they navigate the punishing violence of the residential school, which is paternalistically positioned as a site of settler "care." Although *Rhymes* is a movie about residential schools, little screen time is spent on the horrors or visual tropes of the boarding schools. Alia's experience with residential school is mostly fugitive and a meditation on how to escape incarceration. They avoid the residential school for years but gets captured after Alia and their father have a standoff with Indian agents over food sovereignty. Alia and their father get beaten up and arrested. Alia is sent to boarding school, where two nuns forcibly remove their masculine clothes and cut their hair; they are violently scrubbed down, forced to wear a dress of coarse fabric, and then is locked in a prison cell with no furniture. Normalization and settler correction of a two-spirit person's body is a violent process. Alia, for the first time in the film, breaks down and mourns over the things they have seen throughout their short life and the hopeless situation they find themselves in. They fall asleep and dream of their brother being at the residential school with them. In their dream, Alia follows Tyler through the woods surrounding the boarding school. They walk further into the woods when Tyler points and makes Alia see a huge pile of hundreds of Indian children's bodies in a mound resembling pictures from the Jewish Holocaust. For Indian children, the only escape from residential school was often death. In order to be free, Alia must recognize the loss of those who have gone before them. Alia wakes up crying and hears a key click in the cell door. When I first watched this, I thought Alia was about to get sexually assaulted by one of the adults of the school; however, instead of the usual fate of incarcerated Indian children, Alia is rescued by Tyler. They run off and Alia goes home to plot breaking into the school, getting revenge, and freeing their father, who is also is locked up in the school. Alia does not even spend one night in this awful situation. Usually, for Native peoples, we only get to be tragic or dead in popular culture. Possibilities for fugitivity are limited because this is almost beyond our imaginations as a result of what Million calls "learned helplessness."[13] So, having a ghost come to the rescue opens up different possibilities for critical hope and thriving. One of the most difficult things about care and responsibility for broken people is that most of us do not have the capacity for this. We are barely making it ourselves and people around us are struggling too. We need ghosts and ancestral help here! No one else is coming to rescue us from the settler state.

The climax of the film is when Popper, the Indian agent Alia escapes from with the help of their brother, finds Alia and their father in the garage. He beats Alia and their father into unconsciousness, and then pulls down Alia's pants. The camera gives us a side view of the garage and the violence unfolding. The audience anticipates what is coming next because we have seen it so many times before. In the next second, Popper turns around quickly because he hears a gun being cocked.

A gun barrel is pointed at him and the camera pans another foot to reveal that Tyler is holding the gun. Popper, defenseless with pants undone, tries to talk Tyler out of shooting him. From the side angle, we see Popper's head being blown off. He slowly falls to his knees, dead before his whole body hits the ground. Tyler falls back, drops the shotgun, and runs away. Then there is a close-up of Alia with bloody saliva dripping out of their mouth and smiling triumphantly at the death of Popper. Alia's dad accepts responsibility for killing Popper and is hauled off to prison yet again. Thus the movie ends as it begins with Alia's dad taking on the debt, in the form of incarceration, for deaths he did not commit but did not want to explain to the settler state. In a settler context, this is his way of protecting, caring, and being responsible for his family. He does not want to have the settler state document his wife as a drunk Indian mother who accidentally drove over her child who she loved more than herself or try to explain that his ghost son killed an agent of the settler state in defense of his sibling. He knew the state could not protect Native peoples or care for them or them, so, once again, he let them take him away from everything he loved. As a survivor of boarding school, this is the only way Alia's father could imagine how to care for his family and nation. In so many ways, Alia's father is also a ghost. Like the ghosts in this film, he is loved even though he can't physically be with his family and in his Native nation. Alia's father's care is reflected in the debt he takes in the form of being incarcerated instead of another member of his family.

Alia fights back against the Indian agents, against getting trafficked into the foster care system, and does not get incarcerated in the residential school where Indian kids are sexually assaulted, beaten, murdered, and damaged by the settler state with impunity. Alia's strength comes from the memories of their dead mother, the ghost of their little brother Tyler, and the sacrifices Alia's dad makes for the family. The debt Alia and their father owe to ancestors cannot be repaid, but it can passed on, and through, the family. Ghosts give them strength and provide opportunities for fugitivity from incarceration. Incarceration produces ghosts of all sorts even though the intention is to produce subjects who are lost and forgotten. Ghosts haunt the landscape, ancestors, and lead us to wander into the somewhere else. Wherever that may be, it is away from the here and now of settler care. Ghostly care is not an individualistic endeavor. Care is about building relationships, which also means establishing trust and having boundaries respected. This takes time, and it has not been most women of color's experience of life under the settler colonial regime in the US. What if we stopped trying to work on our shit all on our own as individuals and put our healing work into taking care of each other? Fred Moten says: "Fuck self-care! I don't want to take care of myself, I want someone to take care of me." This is a brave, vulnerable call to action for all of us. Who can you ask to care for you? Again, it goes back to the undercommons and general antagonism to struggle to find not just the who are we against but, most importantly, the who we are with?[14] It's time to take a chance on care that does not punish and capture. Let's dream of a world that does not rely on the future of a settler carceral horizon. This ends as it begins: A call, or at this time, a desperate scream to ancestors and ghosts to help, love, and guide us beings to a future of care and responsibilities to one another instead of rights. Ghosts, we honor you and have debt with you. Teach us how to be again because we have forgotten, and we need so much to remember.

NOTES

1. Dian Million, *Therapeutic Nations: Healing in an Age of Indigenous Human Rights* (Tucson: University of Arizona Press, 2013).

2. Leanne Betasamosake Simpson, *Islands of Decolonial Love: Stories and Songs* (Winnipeg, Canada: Arbeiter Ring Publishing, 2013).

3. Eve Tuck, "Suspending Damage: A Letter to Communities," *Harvard Educational Review* 79, no. 3 (Fall 2009): 409–28.

4. Kelly Lytle Hernández, *City of Inmates: Conquest, Rebellion, and the Rise of Human Caging in Los Angeles* (Chapel Hill: North Carolina Press, 2017).

5. Eve Tuck and K. Wayne Yang, eds., *Youth Resistance Research and Theories of Change* (New York: Routledge, 2014).

6. Lawrence A. Greenfeld and Steven K. Smith, *American Indians and Crime* (Washington, DC: U.S. Department of Justice, 1999).

7. Andrea Smith, *Conquest: Sexual Violence and American Indian Genocide* (Durham, NC: Duke University Press, 2015).

8. Marquis Bey, "The Song Required of My Captivity: *Just Above My Head* and the *Trans*-ness of James Baldwin," *Palimpsest: A Journal on Women, Gender, and the Black International* 5, no. 1 (2016): 42–58.

9. Leanne Simpson, *As We Have Always Done: Indigenous Freedom Through Radical Resistance*, (Minneapolis: University of Minnesota Press, 2013).

10. Tuck, "Suspending Damage."

11. Michelle H. Raheja, *Reservation Reelism: Redfacing, Visual Sovereignty, and Representations of Native Americans in Film* (Norman: University of Nebraska Press, 2011).

12. Eve Tuck and C. Ree, "A Glossary of Haunting," in *The Handbook of Autoethnography*, ed. Stacey Holmes Jones, Tony E. Adams, and Carolyn Ellis (London and New York: Routledge, 2016).

13. Million, *Therapeutic Nations*.

14. Stephano Harney and Fred Moten, *The Undercommons: Fugitive Planning & Black Study* (New York: Minor Compositions, 2013).

WHAT I THINK OF WHEN I HEAR THE WORD RECONCILIATION IS DIFFICULT TO EXPLAIN BECAUSE WHEREAS COLONIALISM HAS A LONG AND CONTINUING HISTORY WITH TANGIBLE EVIDENCE, RECONCILIATION IS AN ABSTRACTION OF A FUTURE I WILL FIGHT FOR BUT NOT EXPECT TO BE IN.

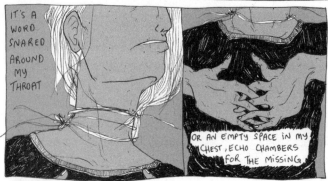

IT'S A WORD SNARED AROUND MY THROAT

OR AN EMPTY SPACE IN MY CHEST, ECHO CHAMBERS FOR THE MISSING

MISSING: PIECES
WOMEN
GIRLS
2 SPIRITS
INDIGIQUEERS
ELDERS
FAMILY
FUTURES
WORDS
HISTORIES
MEMORIES
LANDS

THE COLONIAL STATE IS STILL WORKING TO ELIMINATE AND CRIMINALIZE INDIGENOUS LIFE.

SOME OF US DON'T ACCEPT APOLOGIES ANYMORE. NOT WHEN STATE-SANCTIONED MURDER CONTINUES. WE WILL STILL ORGANIZE EVEN WHEN IN OUR HEARTS WE CAN NO LONGER BEAR TO SEE CROWD-FUNDED FUNERALS.

SOME OF US BELIEVE THAT THERE CAN BE NO RECONCILIATION WHILE THERE ARE STILL FRONT LINES.

Whess Harman, "snaring," 2020

MAPPING THE NETWORKS

AN OPENING ROUNDTABLE ON TRANSNATIONAL TRANSFORMATIVE JUSTICE

Edited and introduced by Melanie Brazzell and Erica R. Meiners

Contributors:
molly ackhurst, Anne-lise Ah-fat, Melanie Brazzell, Lauren Caulfield, Shirley Leslie, Mimi Kim, Meenakshi Mannoe, Kelsey Mohamed, Vanessa Eileen Thompson

OPENINGS

From storefronts in Chicago to church basements in Shoreditch, feminists are at the forefront of abolition. Uprisings for Black lives in the early summer of 2020 breathed a spark into a global fire, a whirlwind of accelerated change that has put abolition center stage in mainstream venues where it was once unthinkable. What is often obscured, however, are local, feminist histories of abolitionist practice. As 2020 marked the twentieth anniversary of the founding of INCITE! Women of Color Against Violence and Communities Against Rape and Abuse (CARA), key practitioners and thought leaders of transformative justice and community accountability in the United States, we are reminded of the importance of tracking how this movement has moved, deepened, and diffused geographically across water, continents, and borders.

This political moment also raises the question of what gets authorized as "abolition" and "transformative justice" (TJ) and who draws the contours around a movement or movements. From our US context, these terms are the products of social movements grounded in radical Black and Indigenous traditions, developed at the intersection of anti-racist and queer-feminist anti-violence organizing, and led by Black and Brown femmes, trans people, gender nonconforming folks, and women. While the terms "abolition" and "transformative justice" emerged from US-based activism, they describe age-old practices that have always been global and often Indigenous, even when communities do not use these labels or when their work is not recognized by dominant and normative institutions as "political."

Fueled by a desire to share stories, trace insurgent internationalist linkages, and grapple collectively shared framework TJ, Melanie—with help from Erica—convened a roundtable at the 2019 National Women's Studies Association conference. That conversation serves as the basis for this written roundtable among ten activists/scholars from five different national contexts in the global north: two colonial metropoles in Europe (the United Kingdom and Germany) and three settler colonies (Australia, Canada, and the US). The roundtable was written and edited before COVID-19 and the Black Lives Matter uprisings of 2020, realities we briefly address in our conclusion.

One of our goals was to continue decentering the US experience in abolitionist organizing. This roundtable, like many analyses of social movements, struggles to combat what our comrade and coauthor Vanessa Eileen Thompson describes in her contribution as "methodological nationalism and imperialism." This asks us to question the centrality of the US in our narration of TJ's genealogy and to contextualize both the US carceral settler state and abolitionist resistance within a global frame. Just as TJ links intimate partner violence and state violence, so too must our transnational analysis link racialized US state violence at home and abroad. Here we twin the term "domestic" to signal both the feminized, heteronormative private sphere and the nationalist security regime.

Abolitionist organizing in the States has occasionally centered a global lens. In 2019 the Stop Urban Shield Coalition in Oakland, California, won its long campaign to get an international weapons expo and SWAT training out of its community, aware that the US was serving as a hub for and exporter of militarized policing. (An anchor member of the coalition was Critical Resistance [CR], represented in this roundtable by Shirley Leslie). Recent campaigns against the growth of e-carceration have targeted G4S, the largest security firm on the planet, and highlighted its global role in profiting from imprisonment and surveillance. Abolition feminists, including INCITE!, supported the fight against US-Palestinian activist Rasmea Odeh's deportation. Transnational analyses like these interrupt the narrative that US "mass incarceration" and racism are statistical outliers in a neutral global order. Such nationalist logics of exceptionalism also mask transnational histories of settler colonialism and slavery—legacies that European countries like to pawn off on the Americas to deny their own responsibility. In turn, these erasures allow contemporary US reformers to uncritically lift up European models of criminal justice as ideals.

We hope to continue this decentering work by amplifying collectives outside the US that are developing analyses of carceral power and seeding transformative practices that grow collective liberation. Methodologically, the roundtable connects and compares TJ projects and abolitionist campaigns at both the level of the "community" (bottom-up) and the "state" (top-down). Top-down because comparative analysis of our movements' political conditions and opportunities requires us to examine our nation-state contexts and the shape of our respective carceral and welfare regimes. We also look bottom-up at cross-pollinations between grassroots movements and instances of transnational solidarity. We use this roundtable to connect community to community, bypassing borders and trying to heed our comrades' call for methodological *trans-* and *anti*-nationalism. Storytelling has often been the genre through which TJ knowledge has circulated, from kitchen tables to INCITE! conferences to frustrated late-night phone calls, so a method of story sharing helps us bridge our different contexts.

The following roundtable is structured by four questions posed to our contributors in 2019: First, briefly describe the carceral state and abolitionist resistance in your national context. Secondly, how are carceral feminisms showing up in your context and communities? Third, discuss examples of TJ and community accountability organizing; what models are being used, and for which harms? And lastly, we offer a back-and-forth between contributors about challenges and debates within and across TJ movements, particularly around limitations and scale. Responses from the panel were transcribed and edited.

What's the current status of the carceral state in your context? What can you tell us about abolitionist campaigns of resistance?

Vanessa Eileen Thompson (VET; Germany): Thank you so much for organizing this transnational conversation, which is crucial because it's very difficult to have horizontal transnational conversations, across time zones and possibilities to travel, language spectrums, citizenship regulations, and related questions of accessibility. Transnational abolitionist conversations, in a way, already challenge various centrisms related to methodological nationalism and imperialism.

I am involved in Copwatch_ffm [Frankfurt am Main], a grassroots organization that struggles against policing (in its various forms) by engaging with people on how to intervene when they see racist, gendered profiling happening, support people who are violated and terrorized by police, as well as engage with communities to keep us safe and free from policing. We work with anti-police and anti-prison abolitionist organisations, Black and of color groups, transformative justice initiatives, anti-racist and decolonial-feminist collectives, self-organized refugee movements, migrant sex worker collectives, and many more groups who struggle for intersectional abolitionist justice within and beyond Germany (for example, in France and Switzerland). The organization grew out of the Initiative in Remembrance of Christy Schwundeck. Christy was a Black woman shot by police in an unemployment office in Frankfurt am Main on May 19, 2011.

In the German context, as well as in other contexts in Europe, racist policing is hegemonically considered to be a "US problem." It is ignored and actively concealed, though the criminalization of Black and brown lives is pervasive, and communities are resisting. This criminalization and premature death through policing and carcerality (mainly in the form of camps) is constitutive for post-colonial and post–National Socialist Germany as well as other parts of Europe. This goes back to the policing and regulation of Black and brown bodies as part of colonial governance. In Germany, several states have passed police laws [that] are the most visibly repressive since 1945. This buoying of police powers, combined with gentrification, the strengthening of racist deportation regulations, and the abandonment of asylum laws, are some of the internal articulations of the carceral state. Externally, Germany has militarized its murderous migration regime at the European borders, outsourcing the criminalization of racialized surplus populations.

But fighting back, creating support networks, and imagining abolitionist futures are part of the archives of Black and brown communities in Europe, too. There have been various urban Black, brown, and migrant youth movements in Germany, from the Black Souls to the Turkish Power Boys in the area around Frankfurt, for instance, who struggled against policing and punitive conditions.

When I think about abolitionist genealogies in post-colonial Europe, refugee activism against the *Lager* system, a regime of detention centers, refugee camps, and deportation, is crucial. Some of the first self-organized refugee groups, The Voice and The Karawane, were led by Black refugees who organized campaigns against isolation in Lagers and against the Lager system itself. This is abolitionism, though the movements don't always use this term to describe their work. People come up against carceral conditions that render their lives unlivable and struggle for their lives; they create alternatives in the making without drawing explicitly on abolition as a political movement and theory of practice. I think abolition is a commitment to create livable futures; people do it all around the globe. It is thus not really the label that matters but what people actually do to get free, to free themselves, and to create new worlds. Being attentive to local and situated contexts enables us to engage with radical forms of abolitionism and how they travel and are connected.

Multi-marginalized feminist and queer communities have led the way in building organizations—there is the refugee women's group

Women in Exile and queer migrant/POC/black groups such as LesMigraS in Germany and Collectif Cases Rebelles in France. These initiatives struggle against interpersonal harm within communities as well as state violence, carcerality, and criminalization, and have developed forms of abolitionist care. They have called upon anti-police, anti-Lager, and anti-prison abolitionist initiatives to leave no one behind, as in the case of Rita Awour Ojunge, and struggle against state violence without overlooking violence within various communities. I think there's still much to do in terms of engaging these abolitionist and TJ archives and presences in the context of Europe and to learn from them as they link abolitionist struggles with the abolition of borders, both those in our minds as well as material border regimes.

Kelsey Mohamed (KM; UK): We are in the midst of one of the biggest prison expansion projects in UK history. In 2016 the government announced plans to build 10,000 new beds in six "mega-prisons" as well as five so-called residential centers/community units for women. They also want to open "secure schools," which are prisons for children 12 to 17 years old, as well as a mega detention center for immigrants. We're also seeing an increase in police powers around stop-and-search (similar to stop-and-frisk in the US) as well as tagging (electronic monitoring) and community policing. We're in the middle of this massive expansion of the carceral state at the moment, which is also facing pushback—for instance, community organizers in Port Talbot, South Wales, were able to stop the building of a mega-prison there. Our group, Community Action on Prison Expansion, is focused on disrupting the others, including a very immature but fun meme campaign against one prison construction company, Kier.

Almost a fifth of our prisoners are held in private prisons, and our public prisons are also, for the most part, privately run, so it is still private companies that get contracts around facilities management, catering, and security in addition to exploited labor and services provided by incarcerated people for profitable industry outside. As abolitionists we believe all prisons should be abolished whether private or state-run. But at the moment, our biggest priority is to block current expansion before we can even gun for more abolitionist, non-reformist reforms.

This means we have to challenge overall public safety narratives around prisons and policing, as there isn't much mainstream critique of the idea of policing. The towns where they are building these prisons have been hit massively by austerity and deindustrialization, and the media coverage there is focused on knife crime and youth crime to fuel people's fear. Austerity has also cut police funding, but this stokes a narrative that police and prisons are what need to get refunded, rather than investing in our communities.

In response, we're delivering prison abolition and community accountability workshops, supporting local campaigns resisting new prison construction, and helping campaigners develop skills. We're very inspired by US work from Critical Resistance and Fight Toxic Prisons, including protesting prisons on environmental grounds, tactics of contesting planning permissions, etc. I also work with Sisters Uncut, a grassroots feminist direct action group of prison abolitionists looking at the intersections of domestic violence, criminal justice, and the impacts of government austerity. They occupied a former women's prison in London and liberated it as a women's space as well as empty council (or public) housing to protest how the housing crisis limits the ability of domestic violence survivors to leave their abusive partners.

Shirley Leslie (SL; US): Critical Resistance (CR) is a grassroots abolitionist organization in the US seeking to build an international movement to end the prison industrial complex by challenging the belief that caging and controlling people makes us safe. As abolitionists, we face similar challenges to many of the other groups represented here today: the prevalence of non-abolitionist reformist visions and a massive uphill battle toward reimagination of community safety and liberation.

For example, in our current San Francisco jail fight, the No New SF Jail Coalition (of which CR is part) has been pushing the city to close a seismically unsafe county jail (County Jail #4 at 850 Bryant Street) that has been slated for demolition for over twenty years. As much as we've pushed for the jail to close with no carceral offshoots, and for an investment in community-based programs and facilities instead, we constantly have to push against the narrative that the city crafts to promote carceral options. When prompted to come up with alternatives to keeping the jail open, we have been repeatedly presented with the option of transferring imprisoned folks to another jail, renovating 850 Bryant, or more recently, the creation of a "justice campus" that would couple mental and behavioral health services with policing. The narrative that renovating 850 Bryant or creating a carceral building with community services in-house is the "just" or "humane" course of action is prevalent with city officials. This conveniently overlooks the discriminatory and interlocked systemic issues throughout [San Francisco (SF)], while additionally emphasizing the lack of imagination or willingness to create a community without criminalization. In the SF county jail system, over 80 percent of those inside are being held pretrial, over 40 percent were unhoused upon being imprisoned, over 30 percent were/are in need of mental and behavioral health services, and almost 60 percent are African American, despite being 3 percent of the SF population.

But there has been a swell of resistance to the existence of the jail and the non-abolitionist reforms proposed. Community organizations, people held inside the SF county jail system, and loved ones of those being held in 850 all understand that jails only serve to harm community members. Thankfully, after lots of strong community organizing, an official ordinance has finally been passed to close the jail for good in November 2020! All of us did work and will continue to work together to shift the idea that cages are promoting community safety and that putting prettier faces on these systems does nothing to address the true harmful and systemic barriers we face every day.

Meenakshi Mannoe (MM; Canada): As a prison abolitionist, living as an uninvited guest on the unceded territories of the Musqueam, Squamish, and Tsleil-Waututh Nations in so-called Vancouver, transformative justice is a deeply fraught term. Before even hypothesizing what justice and accountability could look like, within my own communities, I am met with the question of who am I to determine justice when I directly benefit from the theft and dispossession of Indigenous land and sovereignty.

2020 started with a militarized raid on sovereign Wet'suwet'en territory and the arrest of matriarchs outside the Unist'ot'en Healing Centre. For me this moment was my first, far-too-late, reckoning with the police state that operates under the guise of politeness in Canada. For Indigenous people across Turtle Island, this was the latest invasion. Within prison walls, foster homes, or social service caseloads is very real, devastating impact that Canada continues to have on Indigenous peoples. So, for me as a settler—even a racialized, queer one—I must tread very carefully as I dream a different future.

Any approach to TJ must uphold the inherent and inalienable rights of Indigenous peoples to steward their lands and care for their communities. As an abolitionist, this is complicated by the reality of intergenerational trauma, imposed poverty, and a violent diaspora that has been legislated by racist laws. On a large scale, abolition means land return and redress, as well as decarceration and cancellation of colonial courts, cops, and corrections. In an everyday way, this means resourcing Indigenous folks—from these territories, and folks who have been forced off their territory and into urban centers—so that they can make decisions about everyday (including activist) life in the city.

Many folks are doing this good work and thinking through the nuances, including the tremendous work done by Robyn Maynard,[1] the analysis and interventions offered by poet and abolitionist El Jones, and the mutual aid undertaken by groups like Join Effort, No One Is Illegal, Anti-Police Power Surrey, and Red Braid Alliance. The abolitionist work I am thinking of weaves together Indigenous sovereignty, anti-poverty work, anti-racism, and unapologetic inclusion of trans women and sex workers.

How are carceral feminisms showing up in your context and communities?

Lauren Caulfield (LC; Australia): I mainly work at the nexus of intimate partner and state-sanctioned violence—where the harms of family violence intersect with and are amplified by the harms of policing.

After decades of feminist-led campaigning against gender violence, in 2015–16 the state of so-called Victoria implemented a Royal

Commission into Family Violence. While that public inquiry "heard stories of inconsistent and harmful police responses to family violence"[2] and observed harmful gender stereotypes and (hyper)masculine cultures of victim blaming among police, it received a huge number of submissions—including from family violence agencies—that accepted the centering of police as first responders in violent situations. Where critique and acknowledgement of some of the harms and impacts of this policing were made, the calls were for reforms such as police training and procedural review. The commission recommendations and their implementation by government in turn authorized and extended the role of police as central to the family violence service system. This has entrenched a policy context founded on the idea that police responses to family violence equate to safety. Notably, there have been no corresponding accountability measures enacted to track the impacts of this policing on people experiencing violence or to address harm related to police responses.

When policing receives sweeping authorization as a response to family violence, this justifies and drives police expansion and propels increased criminalization, in turn targeting First Nations people and communities of color. Now we're working in the context of this wave of expanded policing, which continues to be both gendered and racially targeted, with a massive increase in the number of family violence survivors, especially women of color, being listed by police as "primary aggressors" and often charged, and the highest prison population since 1895. Aboriginal women are being criminalised at staggeringly high rates, are the fastest growing population of people in prison in Victoria, and are again bearing the brunt of intersecting state and interpersonal gendered violence[3] while continuing to lead the work to resist it. In this way, the current trajectory of family violence policing is core to the police-to-prison section of the prison pipeline here.

This carceral creep has significant impacts for the people who access family violence services and the services themselves. Feminist anti-violence movements in so-called Australia were historically grassroots led, fiercely independent, and often highly critical of police responses.

However, over time carceral approaches to anti-violence work, under-pinned by whiteness and middle class–centered politics and the pressure to build relationships with police in the name of safety, have contrib-uted to ongoing mainstreaming of family violence services and led to closer and closer connections with police. More recently, this has led to changes like the increasing colocation of family violence services and police, or the training of prison guards to engage in family violence risk assessment. These arrangements risk drawing family violence ser-vices closer into a shared carceral culture, excluding or increasing risk for the many people for whom police do not represent safety, and leaving workers and agencies enmeshed with policing and less and less able to speak out for fear of damaging relationships or causing reper-cussions for the people they support. Reckoning with these impacts, interrupting the whiteness of carceral feminism, disputing ideas of police responses as equating to safety for everyone, and regaining ter-rain against co-option of our radical histories is the current context of our work and the challenges of community accountability organizing in response to gender violence.

In terms of resistance, it is a challenge to speak back to what feels like a juggernaut of carceral responses to violence and their impunity from critique. When police self-evaluate their "progress" on family violence, how do we meaningfully intervene as communities and describe the lived experiences of that policing and its impacts? As always, we have challenges of capacity and time, and it can be hard to get any time out from the urgency of crisis responses and ongoing harm to reflect and build our capacity for transformative responses. But there are significant opportunities at this moment as well. As policing impacts those people most targeted by both gendered and state violence, and the pain and scale of its impact is felt and seen by communities, there's an increasing imperative to build alternatives. This is a very important solidarity moment, a moment to radicalize or reradicalize. One part is to recapture some of that political and organ-izing terrain—to build/rebuild the connections between feminist anti-violence campaigns, prison abolitionist organizing, and move-ments responding to state violence and deaths in custody. Another is to resist co-option by building skills for accountable communities and developing community-based strategies.

SL: Over the past couple decades, Critical Resistance has participated in coalitions against a number of jail expansion proposals, several of which have been touted under the guise of meeting the needs of women and queer people. There was a 2006 proposal for women's prison expansion for 4,500 imprisoned women, which would have increased women's prison beds in California up to 40 percent. This was all under the pretense of addressing the specific needs of cis and trans women in prison. Many of those women suffer from severe and often life-threatening mental and physical illnesses that reflect the lack of access to preventive care for low-income communities and communities of color. There are no ways in a carceral environment to address those health conditions, and often, being imprisoned either causes or exacerbates those existing conditions. Prisons are rife with gendered and sexualized human rights abuses, such as sexual abuse, medical neglect, or brutal physical violence. Time and again, we've fought against similar proposals knowing very well that, in a carceral environment, you can never and will never address the systemic societal needs of women and queer people. That mode of inclusion and recognition within a carceral system is an exploitative way to extend the scope of the prison industrial complex. We advocate for those jail funds to be reallocated to community resources that women, girls, transgender, and gender nonconforming people actually need, such as housing, health care, education, employment, and community-based responses to interpersonal harm.

VET: In Germany, the debates around the cases of sexual and gendered violence in Cologne on New Year's Eve 2015/16, as well as the expansive racial profiling the year afterwards, strongly point to the workings of carceral feminism. Media and police created a profile of the perpetrators as "Nafri" (North African), a figure that is a historical sibling to the racist constructions of the black rioter, repeat perpetrator (*Intensivtäter*), and rapist (the so-called *Schwarze Schmach am Rhein* was a racist response to the post-war occupation of the Rheinland by French West African soldiers who developed relationships and had children with white German women).

Liberal and white feminisms played a huge part in these debates and in the construction of masculinities of color as hypersexist as well as homo- and queerphobic. The result was a liberal but murderous interpellation of state security and the criminal legal system, as Germany made both feminist reforms to its law governing sexual offences while also implementing stricter deportation laws. I think the intertwined temporality of these reforms after the incidents in Cologne, and the racist, anti-immigrant discourses and practices in which they were embedded, demonstrates again how liberal feminist approaches often go hand in hand with racist laws.

Another case is the reform of the so-called Prostitutes Protection Act, which came into force in July 2017. Protection here is framed as surveillance and results in criminalization particularly targeting illegalized and migrant sex workers, rendering multimarginalized groups especially vulnerable. These cases show that carceral feminism is not only complicit with but also prepares the way for the expansion of the punitive, militarized state.

molly ackhurst (ma; UK): It is possible to argue that carceral feminism exists in abundance within the UK. Rampant professionalization of services, similar to in the US, alongside a decade of austerity, has resulted in competition for funding or "competitive tendering" and a reliance on "simple solutions" to violence. These often rely on single-axis understandings of harm; focusing in on locking away those who cause sexual harm, as opposed to the structural aspects of why the harm happens. Despite increasing evidence that the criminal legal system in the UK does not work, the consistent demand from mainstream support services and academics is for more reform and more laws. An example of this can be found in the widespread support for the Domestic Violence and Abuse Bill, a piece of legislation very similar to the US Violence Against Women Act, which increases police powers and also harshens sentencing guidelines. We are also seeing more obvious complicity with carceral politics: many services publicly espouse racist, anti–sex work, and anti-trans views. Some organizations went as far as embedding immigration officers into their services in 2018, with the intention of targeting perpetrators of harm without considering the impact on survivors with tenuous immigration status. Furthermore, despite devastating funding cuts for sexual violence services across the UK, services within sexual violence organizations focus on reducing attrition in sexual violence criminal cases often experience funding increases.[4]

Nonetheless, what unites the majority of those we would typically call "carceral feminists" is a deep awareness that the criminal legal system does not actually work. In fact, interestingly there is increasing recognition within the "sector" and also the academy that there is a need for non-carceral approaches. Yet in spite of this messy in-between place, there's a reluctance to imagine what unequivocal non-carceral support could be (similar to what Shirley described about San Francisco city officials). It is as if workers and academics are trapped on a merry-go-round: round and round they go, unable to step off and let go of carceral views, but also unable to imagine and articulate something new. Notably the reasons often given for this holding on to carcerality is that there's not enough time, space, or money to do the work of reimagining. It is as though underfunding, vicarious trauma, and burn-out excuses everything. However, we must question if it is this simple. As Alison Phipps's work illustrates, the notion of the wounded (often white) feminist "has been the justification for community and state violence, both historically and now."[5] Work is needed to interrogate carceral investments and imaginative blocks; for while there are sparks of abolitionism within the movement, these will be crushed without careful attention.

Who is doing transformative justice–community accountability–inspired work in your context? What models are they using to address which harms?

SL: In all of Critical Resistance's work, we recognize how valuable transformative justice (TJ) is as a method of community empowerment and accountability that works in tandem with the systemic changes that we know desperately need to happen. In our literature to the public and key decision makers, we always uplift community organizations implementing transformative justice as examples of where to invest locally, such as generationFIVE, Young Women's Freedom Center, Hospitality House, and the Bay Area Transformative Justice Collective. These groups use TJ either internally in their organizations or externally in their community. The common denominators and desires throughout all of their models are: safety, healing, and agency of everyone involved; accountability and transformation of those who perpetrate the harm; community response and accountability outside of the state and the state's violence; and transformation of the community and the social conditions that create and perpetuate that violence. On that last point, we often demand that funding priorities be fundamentally shifted to provide for people's basic needs: housing, health care, food, water, and community.

Mimi Kim (MK; US): I'm most associated with INCITE!, an organization started in 2000, about two years after Critical Resistance, and after that, the organization Creative Interventions that started in 2004. So I'm in a good position to look historically at the development of what most people now refer to as transformative justice, at least in the United States. I'm very excited to explore this within an international context, something I rarely have the opportunity to do. While I've been in a collaborative space, primarily digital spaces, with people from Canada, Mexico, Germany, Australia, New Zealand, and Spain, to name some other connections, we have not necessarily had opportunities to speak and share in person. We have shared materials and websites but have not had a chance for more generative conversations to compare what has worked and has not—and in what contexts—and to build global movements. We must be vigilant to uplift what some of us call "transformative justice" without using US dominant language and models as some kind of standard or in a way that devalues or even disappears local and Indigenous practices.

I have been involved in a lot of foundational projects as well as floundering "what are we doing?" moments, including the action camp Philly Stands Up organized in 2011 or when a bunch of us said, "Let's just get together" and got a place in Miami to meet. We brought together very local projects to see what we had in common, to make sure we were collaborating, and to uplift each other's work.

Some of these organizations started around 2000, so we're twenty years into the history of TJ; it's our twentieth anniversary. We're a scrappy bunch: most of us did this with little to no money, but we've also been really collaborative and stood in solidarity with one another. The approach has often been: "Wow you do things really different but let's look at what you're doing in your context" without claims to "We are the best, please use our model, it is copyrighted and you have to pay for it," which I see more often in the restorative justice space, which tends to be very white. I hope that is a spirit and a politic that we can keep alive.

We have a lot of organizations that no longer exist, though the people involved are still doing the work in whatever capacity we can, whatever hat we need to wear. I believe that has kept the movement, if you want to call it that, growing. As organizations fall away, they have kept their materials alive, keeping a digital presence. All of us say we need to document this work, and we have managed to, and then Mariame Kaba, who is prolific, makes a giant website with every kind of resource.[6] In the end, everybody has their own contribution and their own genius, each organization.

In a rare international opportunity, we recently met in Mexico with Indigenous communities, formerly incarcerated trans femme people, and other abolitionist or anti-carceral activists to more deeply share what we in the US mean by transformative justice while opening the conversation to what this might mean in the diverse context of Mexico and Central America. What was memorable was that Indigenous women, who said they were rarely even invited to a gathering like the one we joined, were able to reflect upon and elevate their own justice practices—those that were still intact, some that had already disappeared, and others that they were struggling to continue. These legacies and contemporary examples of collective, community-based, anti-colonial, and non-policing practices served as a clear reminder of the Indigenous roots of these practices, those that may not resonate with labels such as "transformative justice" but which serve as living models that many of us strive to achieve. Those hoping to come to hear from US "experts," found expertise from their own Indigenous neighbors.

Anne-lise Ah-fat (AA; Australia): When looking at what is explicitly named transformative justice and community accountability work in so-called Australia, it has largely come out of do-it-yourself punk/activist/queer communities attempting community responses to mainly sexual assault. In my work with Undercurrent Community Education Project and the Transformative Justice Network, we've been informed by some amazing work and thinking locally, from groups like A World Without Sexual Assault Collective and Thunder Collective, as well as internationally, especially Mimi's work with Creative Interventions and the group she mentioned, Philly Stands Up.

Importantly, there is a long history of anti-prison and anti-colonization struggles by Aboriginal peoples working against the phenomenally high rates of Indigenous incarceration and deaths in custody. We see community responses/accountability work in Aboriginal communities as a direct outcome of punitive and carceral responses to Aboriginal peoples by the state. We continue to grapple with TJ here within the context of colonization and on stolen land, and I want to highlight the importance of undertaking solidarity work with Aboriginal people as part of TJ work.

Most transformative justice and community accountability work I have been a part of and witnessed sits outside of and/or alongside the community service sector, with a lot of crossover, in that many of us engaging in community accountability work also do paid work within the service sector. From my perspective, this crossover came about as a way for us to deepen, develop, and bridge skills that we could then use within our communities. As an example, a few years ago I began to practice as a men's behavior practitioner in an anti-violence agency, undertaking individual and group work with men who use family violence. I continue to learn and transfer skills from this work into community-based responses and vice versa.[7]

The projects I am involved in engage in both capacity and community building for violence prevention as well as responses after violence has happened. I currently coordinate the Transformative Justice Network, which focuses on capacity building and supporting groups/communities who want to prevent and respond to violence, and also building meaningful pathways to safety that don't force people experiencing family/intimate partner violence to rely solely on police and prisons. Some of the workshops we have run include, "How we centre survivors within community accountability interventions," "What to do when the person who has caused harm does not want to be involved in a community response," and "Rehearsing community accountability." Further, Undercurrent Community Education Project uses TJ frameworks for our education work with young people in schools, focusing on building respectful relationships and challenging the dominator beliefs/actions/cultures that enable the widespread prevalence of family/intimate partner violence. Undercurrent also has a commitment to provide learning, dialogue, and healing spaces for the public outside of the services sector. In 2019 we focused on healing for people who have experienced harm, facilitating a six-part series of creative workshops for people interested in incorporating art into their healing journeys.

Some of us at the Network are also individually involved in interventions and facilitate community-based responses to family and sexual violence. Personally, I now usually sit within a support role for people undertaking community-based interventions, many of them using the Creative Interventions Toolkit to inform their work. The length of these interventions vary, and similar to molly, I have noticed that people are engaging in once-off conversations with people who have caused harm and naming this TJ work. First and once-off conversations are very important in opening up dialogue for accountability and change, but what we know about family violence is that harmful behavior resulting from entitlement thinking and dominator culture take a long time to shift. When we stop at that first conversation, we fail to take into account the long-term work involved in working towards non-violent and respectful relationships.

A few of us are currently thinking about how we might shift these individual interventions into group work. However, over the years I have seen fewer people wanting to engage in this kind of collective, long-term intervention work, particularly because communities have low capacity and few resources, and reflecting on community responses that have replicated punitive/carceral responses.

LC: One other example of our TJ efforts locally is to build frameworks and trainings focused on decentering police in the context of safety planning and crisis response, to shift the focus away from narrow risk assessment and the current language of safety as shorthand for calling the police that dominates a lot of responses to family violence. We notice the steady presence of knee-jerk assumptions that police are sites of safety for everyone, even when it's abundantly clear they're not—for instance when someone has been criminalized and each contact with police worsens that, or where the person using violence against them is a police officer and they are managing risks around that. Of late we've been approaching this from the perspective of capacity building and "Beyond 000" trainings (000 is our version of a 911 call [in the US]), with a view to getting organized in advance of a crisis and being directed by the person experiencing violence to respond to the coexisting risks or harms they're facing.

For this work, we've drawn on the long ongoing genealogies of Indigenous-led community safety work here, we've been inspired by the work of Rachel Herzing and others, and we also sought to document more of the interventions, tactics, and plans folks are already using. We're running a series of workshops and trainings with communities focused on community-based safety planning, risk management, and asset mapping in response to family or partner violence that focuses on what community assets—skills, networks, resources, relationships, safety strategies—can be leveraged or activated in a crisis to genuinely enhance safety.

KM: When talking about transformative justice and prison abolition in the UK, it often exists in pockets within existing organizations or service providers in the anti-violence sector who say, "I'm an abolitionist but I have to do this for my job," similar to what Anne-lise described. The groups doing this work are pretty small, like a space in the punk scene called DIY Space for London. Many have been inspired by people in the US, and we ask ourselves, what does it look like in a UK context, given our very different culture around activism and movement building? Demographically people of color are such a small part of the population, so you are always such a minority when organizing anti-racist struggles.

In Hollaback! London, molly and I have been delivering bystander intervention trainings as a way to bring abolition and community accountability into people's daily lives, to create an incentive for people to act when they witness violence, particularly in public space, [and] to build community through intervention in places where it feels as if there is no community, like on the Tube. In the UK, there's such a culture of "that's none of my business," and on top of that abusers often isolate survivors, so someone who's being abused is more likely to feel they have no community, and it's often going to be strangers who need to intervene. But how do we expand those trainings, coming out of the feminist sector, to ensure that we are doing properly anti-racist work? When our desire to believe women becomes the dogma that "anything that makes you uncomfortable is wrong," for white women that is not actually the case if their discomfort is racist (f.e., they assume a Black man on the street to be dangerous). Being uncomfortable is not the same thing as being unsafe. So we're trying to broaden and deepen that bystander intervention training to take power dynamics more into account. This has developed into an organization I and a couple friends started called Cradle Community, with the aim of building community capacity to run these trainings and work with communities on issues of safety and accountability.

ma: To expand on what Kelsey was saying, transformative justice exists in silos within the UK, and because of that it's difficult to truly and concretely state what models are being used and what harms are being explored—but what we can say is that there is a lot of beautiful and emergent experimenting happening. From speaking to folks doing the work, it feels as though a variety of TJ principles are being used to respond to all manners of harm, but there's been an increasing shift towards using TJ around sexual violence: the majority of the more formalized TJ processes I've heard about and supported in the last year have been related to sexual violence. While the reasons for this are not truly knowable at the moment, it's possible that the turn towards more transformative methods stems from a combination of (1) the very public recent failures of the criminal legal system here for survivors,* (2) a lack of funding to specialist services, which makes it difficult for survivors to actually get support, and (3) the increasing noise we are hearing in the media about TJ as an "alternative" to the criminal legal system. While there are groups like those mentioned by Kelsey, who take inspiration from US organizations and try to practice everyday TJ while also doing the essential community building work similar to that mentioned by Lauren and Shirley, we also have people turning to TJ in the hopes it can be a one-off process. There's a risk here that TJ may experience a similar dilution to what we've seen happen with restorative justice—so it's something we need to be mindful of as we continue to do the work because there's already evidence that it's starting.[8]

Melanie Brazzell (MB; Germany & US): As Vanessa shared earlier, communities of color have been fighting racism, fascism, and state violence (particularly in relation to migration) in Germany for decades, from Kanak Attak in the '90s to Reach OUT and KOP (Campaign for Victims of Police Violence) in the 2000s to NSU Watch, refugee organizing, and #Migrantifa today. Over the last decade in Berlin in particular, I witnessed the demographics of our communities transform through migrations triggered by the Arab Spring and the Syrian civil war/counterrevolution. Berlin's rising status as an affordable metropole also attracted a more racially (though not always class) diverse wave of migration. This has corresponded with a rise in Black and PoC organizing, particularly from women, trans, and queer folks, with a sense of transnational community across Europe and beyond as well as a strong influence from North American frameworks like TJ. Women, queer, and trans folks of color are leading the charge on intersectional queer-feminist organizing and thought leadership in groups like xart splitta, Center for Intersectional Justice, CuTie.BIPoC Fest, and LesMigraS.

---

* Following on from the very public R v. Allen case, shifting rules around disclosure of evidence in criminal legal cases has had a huge impact on cases. This has resulted in prosecutions around sexual violence falling to their lowest levels in a decade in England and Wales, with some mainstream feminists decrying that rape has been 'decriminalized' as a result.

Similar to molly and Kelsey in the UK, the work I've witnessed in Germany taking the name TJ responds to sexual and partner violence, and, to a lesser extent, sexist and heterosexist behaviors. Social movements, including the anti-violence movement, have by and large not been institutionalized into a nonprofit–industrial complex like in the US. So there remains a strong ethos of mutual aid and self-organization for survivor support with infrastructure (networks, conferences, books) to facilitate that thankless and unpaid but life-giving work. However, when we founded the Transformative Justice Collective in Berlin in 2011, many queer-feminist activists were hostile to the idea of humanizing perpetrators. TJ has become more popular since then and opened up nuance and complexity within that position of rage and resistance. I believe this is because queer- and women of color–organizing has pushed the white German–dominated queer-feminist scene to adopt an intersectional understanding of sexual violence, going beyond gender to incorporate a critique of state violence and punishment. More people are braving a process with communities and/or people who cause harm, and our collective consulted on a number of such processes (witnessing our share of messes) until we formally ended in 2019. The work continues in other self-organized formations, and new groups are forming to do TJ work more sustainably as well as a nationwide network to coordinate exchange.

In 2010 I started something as a branch of the collective that eventually grew into its own tree: the What *really* makes us safe? Project. As our collective received more and more requests to intervene in concrete situations of violence, I reached out to practitioners in the US—in a spirit of "We are improvising this and have no idea what we're doing. Y'all are the mothership, so . . . what's the good word?" As those conversations snowballed into research for a master's, I discovered that we are not alone: everyone is in a place of improvising and experimenting and failing. I brought what I learned back to my Berliners through various events, which culminated in a toolkit with contributions from our collaborators that address the realities of state violence, gender-based violence, their intersections for refugee/migrant women, and TJ alternatives in the German context.

That work is documented on the What *really* makes us safe? website.[9] As I transition towards TJ research rather than practice, documentation is one way I believe researchers can support movement work. Stories of hyperlocal experimentation otherwise get lost in burnout, transitions, or simply not knowing when a process is "over" or who to document for. Storytelling has been the backbone of the movement,[10] so I want to encourage us to continue gifting one another our stories, even when they aren't round or coherent and we don't know where they begin and end.

MM: Canada has mastered the art of an apology without repair—evidenced in national projects such as the Truth & Reconciliation Commission, the National Inquiry [into] Missing and Murdered Indigenous Women and Girls, and official apologies for heinous acts such as the Chinese Head Tax or the Komagata Maru Incident. Inquiries and apologies allow Canada to perform as a nation-state with a moral compass and disguise the realities of a country founded on the theft of land, which continues to carry out the genocide of Indigenous people.

Because of the tremendous interference of the Canadian state, widely used transformative models have been co-opted by state or nonprofit governance. One obvious example is Gladue—a sentencing principle that attempts to instruct judges to consider "all available sanctions other than imprisonment [...] with particular attention to 'the circumstances of Aboriginal offenders.'"[11] While Gladue principles assert that the lived and intergenerational experiences of Indigenous people must be taken into account, these principles only come into effect through interactions with the formal criminal justice system—sentencing or bail hearings.

To understand TJ as it exists outside of formal, colonial institutions, we must look to practices rather than specific terminology. In February 2020 the Wet'suwet'en Hereditary Chiefs asserted their sovereignty over the Yintah and refused to surrender their territory to Canadian invasion. In the weeks and months that followed the Royal Canadian Mounted Police invasion at Unist'ot'en, a movement—led by Indigenous people across Turtle Island—declared Reconciliation Is Dead. In a settler-colonial state, the basis of transformation is Land Back.[12]

When I consider TJ in so-called Canada, I see work that is being done by folks pushed to the margins—even in progressive communities. The folks who take up this work may not espouse themselves as TJ-types, and instead use titles like "peer," "person with lived/living experience," or "experiential worker," but their work is transformative and provocative.

What are the challenges and opportunities with transformative justice and community accountability experiments?

MM: I do see terms like transformative justice and mutual aid being taken up more quickly than prison abolition, and I wonder why. I don't see a hierarchy between any of these approaches to justice and dignity, but the persistent fear of talking about criminals (and in turn, criminalized people) does give me pause. There are groups of criminalized people (deemed homogenous) who are "deserving" of freedom from prison walls, and dismantling this false and static notion is critical to deepening our work. In fact, this is the most challenging work within a TJ framework—[H]ow do we bring in and support the people who have done harm, sometimes repeatedly, and in doing so have evaded accountability? I think of the words of Ericka Hart at the Women's March on Philadelphia (Lenape Territory), "[W]ho is this for?" For if our abolition work is not for the "dangerous" ones, the "evil" ones, the "irredeemable" ones, how can we commit to justice that decenters the colonial state? And for settlers, benefiting from theft and genocide, how can we be the arbiters of abolition? We should be doing this challenging work, with guidance from Indigenous knowledge keepers, and address violence and harm as part of unsettling our occupation of stolen land.

MB: I see the same problems everywhere, including Germany. One is a weaponization of TJ to marginalize survivors and avoid accountability. Another is communities not understanding themselves as such or collapsing rather than cohering to step up when harm happens. Many of us lack the tools to assess if something is conflict or violence, find the appropriate response while recognizing that not everything needs a process, and develop "right-sized"* proportional consequences for harm. Without cis men taking up these skills, TJ continues to fall

---

*   A term I learned from Shannon Perez-Darby.

on the shoulders of trans and nonbinary people, femmes, and women, particularly of color, and becomes emotional labor or service provision for movements.

The German context has some unique challenges, including the question of translation, both literal and figurative. Others in this roundtable work in English-dominated contexts, so Germany is an exception. I notice a disparity between who's doing the work of TJ and who's claiming this term for their work. As a collective, we struggled with how to translate English terms into German. "Race" is a word soaked in Nazi ideology, "survivor" connotes survivors of the Holocaust, and "people of color" has been imported in its original English, although it does not fully map onto Germany's regimes of racialization. We were aware that an English vocabulary did not map one-to-one to our realities and that social capital (like education, language access, and travel) shaped our audience's access to US concepts. While abolition and TJ were developed by working-class communities of color in the US, translation across the Atlantic often occurs through privileged people (like myself) and institutions like academia. When working on the What *really* makes us safe? Toolkit, my closest collaborator, Nadija Samour, insisted we decenter US imperialism and comparisons and focus on groups resisting many kinds of violence intersectionally without necessarily using "abolition" or "transformative justice" as their frame. Unfortunately, TJ can sometimes crop things out of the frame—either local genealogies more resonant for people or aspects of the work that get lost in translation (for example, equating TJ only with interpersonal processes between survivors and persons who cause harm, rather than community or political work with an abolitionist analysis). In response, like Vanessa shared earlier, I orient towards people's practices more than their labels when understanding what TJ in Germany looks like.

If effective models are emerging, can and should we scale up?

MK: This question of "scaling up" is very alive right now. Some people say, "[Y]ou can't scale up," and yet they keep giving trainings, trying to do local skill building, offering curricula, all of which one could consider a form of scaling up. The Bay Area Transformative Justice Collective's concept of the "pod" rather than the "community" has been so helpful. People were already creating pods, whether it's your local bunch of friends or large community, but to actually give it a name and have a practice around it has really helped. I think we're grappling with the scaling up question, but in some ways many of us have already been doing it.

I think that the challenge with the language of scaling up is the neoliberal corporate context in which it is usually raised. "Scaling up" connotes copyrights, trademarks, and standardization. It is tied to franchising or making sure that your model, your organization, or your individual name gets elevated and diffused. It's fed by funders, market strategists, and communications experts who tie scaling up to sustainability and growth—not necessarily of our communities but of our organizational entities or personal reputations.

I, for one, am not opposed to the general notion of scaling up—meaning that we need to figure out how to increase our community-level capacity to nurture and sustain TJ principles and practices—to build the values and underlying infrastructure and practices toward liberation. I think that figuring out how to do that and to continuously do this with integrity and effectiveness is important. I think it is part of our accountability to our politics and our communities. At Creative Interventions, we called this "regeneration," not "scaling up." This language aligns closer to the metaphors of organic life, decentralization and the deep questioning of corporate formations such as nonprofit entities. This thinking as well as imagining and practicing these ways within our daily lives have become more familiar within social justice spaces and have been so beautifully articulated in the work of adrienne maree brown among others.

I think we in the TJ and other movements have actually been doing this work, work that looks something like "scaling up" while rejecting or at least deeply questioning the use of that language. I find these contradictory dynamics and the creative, emergent ways in which we can think about processes and practices particularly fascinating and important. After all, isn't this the work of social movements and the transformation of social conditions? I welcome engagement with the thought of "scaling up" and alternative formulations of what this means in the present moment and emerging future.

SL: One logistical challenge of proposing TJ as a method of community empowerment, specifically in our jail fight, is that we don't want the state to be the arbiter of TJ. So, we have to be very cautious and intentional in our advocacy for TJ facilities and resources so that they don't become state led, but remain community led. One greater challenge is that folks are still working toward a societal and ideological shift in thought so that TJ can be more widely accepted in the mainstream and take root as a more commonplace practice. Thankfully, we constantly see more groups implementing TJ!

ma: Over in the UK, we see similar challenges as those mentioned by Mimi and Shirley in relation to scalability and who "does" TJ, but this is exacerbated by the political climate here and the mainstream silence around abolition. There have always been big tensions within the UK left and also inside the groups doing anti-violence work about what the role of the state should be, and while this isn't an issue specific to the UK, the hopelessness of austerity has only furthered this.

AA: Similarly, in so-called Australia we face challenges regarding the question of scaling up. As the prison industrial complex scales up, how are we supporting and in solidarity with communities facing this expansion? Lauren mentioned the expansion of family violence policing and criminalization in Australia, which was supported by the community services/anti-violence sector. Whilst being tentative and apprehensive about how TJ frameworks will be appropriated by the State, there is a huge need for abolitionist thinking and practice to be brought into these spaces. I see this work mostly done by clients advocating for themselves—or their families, communities, and caseworkers advocating for them—not by organizational leadership. Interestingly, when I have seen TJ frameworks popping up in the anti-violence sector, the grappling seems to be about funding, and/or lack of it, which really speaks to our large reliance on state funding.

We also have practical considerations as we organize in a place which is sparsely populated (related to colonization and strict, racist border policies). However, a range of people continue to do community accountability work, so the question of scale for me is also dependent on whether people are committed to doing this work long-term, which is why so much of my work is now focused on building capacity with people who want to do this work together throughout their lives. Interestingly, at Undercurrent Community Education Project we have attempted to "scale up" over the years and have for the first time chosen to spend this year inwardly focused so that we can become more sustainable. Again, this is so we keep people interested and invested in movement building for a long time!

BUILDING POWER IN A SHIFTING LANDSCAPE

The landscape has continued to shift since this roundtable initially transpired in 2019. The pandemic moved much TJ work online, also flagging the risks of interpersonal violence under lockdown and the need for safe and affordable housing for survivors. Concurrently, the Black Lives Matter (BLM) movement gave new fuel to abolitionist struggles worldwide. The scale is global: In Australia, the banner of BLM was used to protest the deaths of Aboriginal people in police custody. Germany saw arguably the largest BLM protests outside the US, and in the UK, protestors toppled a monument of a slave trader, leading to a reckoning with Britain's public memorials to racists.

BLM's success has increased mainstream interest in abolition, putting pressure on the TJ movement to provide a ready-made set of alternatives to policing that can be scaled up. People clamor: Can TJ organizations provide us with a twenty-four-hour phone number, a home-delivery service, a task force, at least a guidebook? While material is in circulation, the hunger for tools grows, but as participants in this roundtable demonstrate, TJ is a set of varied approaches contextual to each community yet united by feminist abolitionist values. We can, as Mimi Kim shared, scale in the sense of building "our community-level capacity" and "values and underlying infrastructure and practices," but we must refuse the idea of a one-size-fits-all alternative to police. Any generic template or top-down approach risks mimicking the very carceral logic

TJ contests, which quantifies human life as risk-factor algorithms and universalizes situations of harm into minimum mandatory sentencing guidelines. Grassroots organizers in Minneapolis, Minnesota, and other cities who have won defunding invite us to think on the scale of an entire block, neighborhood, or city: What will it look like to scale TJ infrastructure? Can we "scale out" instead of scaling up? Not consolidating into a credentialing institution that concentrates power, but spreading skills rhizomatically, like API Chaya in Seattle has been doing with its Community Solutions Program? And can we have local, community-controlled TJ co-operatives with no-strings-attached government funding?

It is state involvement in TJ, even if just at the level of funding, that raises the hair on our collective necks. Because TJ emerged in response to the anti-violence movement's co-optation, many of our contributors remain wary of the unintended consequences of even the most benign-seeming state resources. Yet while the TJ movement continues to build alternatives outside the system, we can learn from abolitionists are working for change *inside* the system. What could non-reformist reforms of government funding and control of social services look like that might make openings for TJ infrastructure? This is a question for further roundtables and internationalist dialogues.

NOTES

1. Robyn Maynard, *Policing Black Lives: State Violence in Canada from Slavery to the Present* (Nova Scotia: Fernwood Publishing, 2017).

2. Marcia Neave, Patricia Faulkner, and Tony Nicholson, "Royal Commission into Family Violence Volume III Report and Recommendations" (Victoria, Australia: Royal Commission into Family Violence, March 2016), http://rcfv. archive.royalcommission.vic.gov.au/MediaLibraries/RCFamilyViolence/ Reports/Final/RCFV-Vol-III.pdf).

3. For more context, see Tess Allas et al., "Indigenous Femicide and the Killing State," *Deathscapes: Mapping Race and Violence in Settler States*, 2018, https://www.deathscapes.org/case-studies/ indigenous-femicide-and-the-killing-state-in-progress/.

4. See, for instance, statements by Sisters Uncut, "Press Release: Domestic violence protesters crash BAFTA red carpet to call 'Time's Up' on Theresa May," February 28, 2018, http://www.sistersuncut.org/2018/02/18/press-release-domestic-violence-protesters-crash-bafta-red-carpet-to-call-times-up-

on-theresa-may-call-times-up-on-theresa-may/; and Imkaan (https://www.imkaan.org.uk/statement-womens-aid-recent-develop).

5. Alison Phipps, "The Political Whiteness of #MeToo," *Red Pepper*, June 4, 2019, https://www.redpepper.org.uk/the-political-whiteness-of-metoo/.

6. See TransformHarm.org at https://transformharm.org/.

7. For a powerful example of this, see Sarah Wendt et al., "Engaging Men Who Use Violence: Invitational Narrative Approaches" (Sydney: Australia's National Research Organization for Women's Safety, October 2019), https://www.anrows.org.au/publication/engaging-men-who-use-violence-invitational-narrative-approaches/.

8. Bianca Fileborn and F. Vera-Gray, "'I Want to Be Able to Walk the Street Without Fear': Transforming Justice for Street Harassment," *Feminist Legal Studies* 25, no. 2 (July 2017): 203–27.

9. See What Really Makes Us Safe at https://whatreallymakesussafe.com.

10. Ching-In Chen, Jai Dulani, and Leah Lakshmi Piepzna-Samarasinha, eds., *The Revolution Starts at Home: Confronting Intimate Violence within Activist Communities* (Oakland, CA: AK Press, 2016); Leah Lakshmi Piepzna-Samarasinha and Ejeris Dixon, eds., *Beyond Survival: Strategies and Stories from the Transformative Justice Movement* (Oakland, CA: AK Press, 2020).

11. Quoted in the Native Women's Association of Canada's brochure, "What is Gladue?": https://www.nwac.ca/wp-content/uploads/2015/05/What-Is-Gladue.pdf.

12. Shiri Pasternak and Hayden King, "Land Back: A Yellowhead Institute Red Paper" (Toronto: Yellowhead Institute, October 2019, https://redpaper.yellowheadinstitute.org/).

Tori Hong, "Abolitionist Elder"

HOW MUCH DO MY BLACK LIFE MATTER?

A CONVERSATION WITH CECE MCDONALD AND KY PETERSON

Edited and introduced by Ash Stephens

INTRODUCTION

Currently and formerly incarcerated Black trans and gender non-conforming people should be at the center of abolitionist organizing. While the impact of criminalization lives in the intersections of many communities and contexts, an understanding of the experiences of incarceration for Black trans and gender nonconforming people is essential to our struggles for liberation for all.

CeCe McDonald is a Black trans woman from Chicago, Illinois, who fought off a transphobic attack while visiting friends in Minnesota in 2011. One night, CeCe and her friends were walking to the grocery when two men started launching racist and transphobic epithets at them. At some point, their violent words turned into a physically violent attack and CeCe and her friends had to defend themselves and fight for their lives.

Ky Peterson is a Black trans man from Americus, Georgia, who fought off a sexual assault and attempted rape from a man in his community in 2011. Ky and his brothers were walking to a grocery store when a man repeatedly yelled sexually violent language at them. As Ky and his brothers tried to ignore the man and continue on their way home, he physically attacked them and attempted to kidnap Ky. Feeling terrified for his life, Ky defended himself from the man, and as a result of self-defense, the man died.

Far too often, currently and formerly incarcerated Black trans and gender nonconforming people experience parallel clashes with violence from the state and the prison industrial complex (PIC). In the same year, both CeCe McDonald and Ky Peterson faced horrific attacks that forced them to fight for their lives. As a result of the everyday tactics of the PIC to demonize, punish, and incarcerate survivors of violence, they faced over forty years of incarceration between them.

These experiences of attacks and subsequent punishment for self-defense are not rare. Feminist abolitionists have taught us that defending yourself from violence as a Black person who is trans and/or gender nonconforming (TGNC), a woman, a girl, a disabled person, or otherwise marginalized person, is in direct opposition to the forces of oppression that seek to terminate your personhood and to normalize your premature death.

This conversation explores CeCe's and Ky's experiences of criminalization, including their efforts they took to defend themselves on the inside with support from costrugglers on the outside. They also reflect on movements against policing and police violence, including the recent uprisings against the murders of Black people by policing, and where they see Black TGNC formerly incarcerated people fitting into those movements. The conversation concludes with a glance toward their future work and visions for the world they want to see.

As Black trans people from totally different places—CeCe you're from the major city of Chicago and Ky, you're from rural Georgia—how was it and how is it being trans where you're from?

CECE MCDONALD (CM): I came out as trans in about seventh grade, but I didn't really start medically transitioning until I moved to Minnesota. I've always been very aware of who I am and who I was, even if I didn't have the terms to use. At that time, I only had one trans person in my life, and she was the person who even told me this is what it's like from her experience. But the closest other representation was RuPaul, and I would get fucking annoyed when people would call me a drag queen. I'm just not a drag queen.

I came out in the late '90s/early 2000s, which was a different time. And that's why I'm so excited when I get to see kids come out as trans because as a kid I could never say I was trans. I used to get in trouble for saying that I was a girl or putting on my mama's heels. And I basically lived a double life as a kid. And that's fucked up that a kid has to mentally carry that type of weight. There was a time when my mom would let me buy my own clothes, and I used to buy two separate pieces, my girl clothes and my boy clothes. I guess you could say I was "passing" at a young age, so I was always slipping through the cracks. But I would say I wasn't really allowed to be myself until I moved to Minnesota.

As an adult, I've had to break away from the forced and misogynistic ideas of womanhood that have been placed on me. When people say you have to act like this and talk like this, I kind of took my own path into womanhood that led me into experimenting and challenging myself and my womanhood. I actually stopped taking hormones for about a year and half to just understand that I didn't need the hormones to be a woman. And once I finished that journey, which was just for me, I wanted to understand how I value my womanhood and how to even challenge other people's ideas about womanhood and being trans and what it means to be a trans person. The whole purpose of being trans is to move away from society's ideas of conformity. Everyone thinks it's just that you get up and take medicine but being trans is really, deeply embedded in our souls. It's a mental and spiritual transition. It's something that we have to handle with care.

KY PETERSON (KP): I don't see that many trans people where I'm from. And a lot of people that I grew up with will see me online or at the store and say, "Oh my god, you're so different. What happened? Why did you change?" And in my mind, I haven't changed. I have a little bit of facial hair, but I'm still the same person. Even back then, I didn't identify as a girl. When I was younger, I would tell people that I was a boy, and they would tell me to stop saying it, but I wouldn't. I refused to wear certain things. I would say, "I'm just a boy, that's all I know."

Right now, I'm living where I'm from. And since I recently got out from being incarcerated, for me it's about really getting adjusted to living and being more comfortable and knowing that I'm trans. At one point, I wasn't sure what was going on with me, and I didn't know what it was, but I knew I needed to figure it out.

How did your experiences look while you were incarcerated? What are some ways that you and folks who supported you had to fight back against the jail/prison?

KP: I started testosterone while I was inside. I was the first person that I knew of there [who] had to advocate for hormones for people. In thinking about being in prison and when I was trying to get my hormones, I can't remember if it was a warden or someone else who said, "Trans men don't exist." And I'm thinking, So what are you saying about me? That I don't exist? That I'm not a person? I really didn't understand that. And after that, a lot of people started asking me how it worked to get hormones, and I could only tell them how I did it. My organization, Freedom Overground, that works with TGNC survivors of assault and incarceration after their incarceration, is working on a sheet for people to use on the inside so they can advocate for themselves to get hormones. I also had to work to get boxers in, and now they have those and some shaving stuff for people.

I also remember in 2017 when I came back to the prison from court there were ten to fifteen other trans masculine people in there. I was used to being the only one, but I remember I was happy because now I had friends inside. But I also wasn't happy because I wished we could be friends on the outside, and I wished that we didn't have to be in there.

CM: Reflecting back during that time in 2011, I want to be clear that jail and prison are two different situations. While I was still in jail, instead of putting me in the general population they put me in a specific unit for people they labeled as having mental health issues. There were about ten or so people in a unit. I guess that's where they felt I was the "safest." When I got incarcerated (in prison) it was like they were trying to keep me from my hormones and that was the hardest part. Trans people do have withdrawals from their hormones. The longer you keep a trans person from their hormones, they can get really bad pains. I tell people all the time that it's not a joke. I was in not just physical but also mental pain in how much that affected me.

I was lucky to have people advocating on the outside, calling the prison because I was telling one of my friends that they weren't giving me my medicine and that they kept making excuses. Folks just kept calling into the prison like, "Give her her medicine, give her her medicine!" And the warden came to my cell and said, "We're going to give you your medicine, but can you tell your friends to stop calling?" I was like, "Nope! I'm not telling them nothing because I should've already had my medicine."

I'm glad now that it's against the law in some states for them to deny people their medicine even if you didn't identify as trans before being [incarcerated]. And I guess some folks would see that as a win. But if we stopped locking folks up, then we wouldn't have to be begging the state to see our identities.

Can you reflect on the time you were incarcerated until now and what you see in our movements against violence, policing, and incarceration? From 2011 until now, what have you been noticing?

CM: I can remember we would have to get up at about six in the morning, and the first thing on TV is the news. At that time, in 2012, the news was highlighting the Trayvon Martin case. And I would just be fully bawling in jail from the depression I was experiencing from my case and watching this story unfold on TV, thinking that there really wasn't anything for me to do. This was also a time when the visibility of police violence was kind of growing. It felt like Trayvon Martin's story was the kickoff of this fucked-up kind of visibility of police violence that we've been seeing, and it just escalated from there. All I could think about was that my insides were boiling. I was so irritated with everything. And then, there was my own case, which was about self-defense.

KP: When I was incarcerated, I remember hearing about things going on on the outside. A lot of people would write me letters. I got so many letters. And I knew that a lot of people were protesting. And even now, people are talking about the police and so many Black people who have been killed by police. There's also a lot of trans people who have been killed every year. And now, I'm learning as I'm out and I'm seeing how things work. A lot of things don't really focus too much on trans people. You really don't get a lot of support. There's not a lot of support for trans guys. There are maybe a few things for trans women, but there's not a lot for trans guys. I want to work on something to change that.

CM: While I was locked up, I was corresponding with folks, and I learned about a trans girl who was missing in Charlottesville, Virginia, named Sage Smith. And then, there was the case of young women who went missing from the campus of the University of Virginia. And those folks who I was corresponding with were the first folks who said, "Look when you get out of here, we have to do something, we have to make this visible."

It wasn't until I got out of prison that I learned about Ky's case. I was already on the verge of becoming more political and learning about activism and organizing. I was kind of upset that folks didn't tell me about Ky's case way earlier, seeing as how our cases were happening at the same time. Folks did tell me about Marissa Alexander, and I got connected with her, and I was doing some work around Black folks and self-defense more. I had a platform once I got out and I wanted to use that, and I definitely would've been pushing earlier for Ky's case if I had known about it.

There's still a part of me that gets really frustrated because you have these three cases of Black folks who have been incarcerated for defending themselves—myself, Ky, and Marissa—and then you have the person who murdered Trayvon Martin get acquitted. Sometimes I really question what self-defense is. And I question not having folks [who] have your back when I was warned about major LGBTQ organizations that didn't want to have anything to do with my case.

I'm also really glad that I had folks supporting me, because I felt like my case was important, but also Ky's case was just as important. Especially at the time because it felt really important to talk about self-defense. And like Ky said, there isn't the same support for trans men as there is for trans women; which says a lot because there ain't that much support for trans women! I just think that people should really pay attention and listen to us when we're saying things and not just take it [with] a grain of salt because these issues affect everybody else too. And the issues that other folks are fighting for are the ones that we are on the front lines for. It's really important for folks to understand that.

KP: When I was in, I really would've liked to have more people that were not only willing to put my story out but willing to help me make changes to the criminal (in)justice system where I'm from. The same judge that sentenced me is the same judge that has been arrested numerous times for drug issues, driving while under the influence, and for domestic violence. The same guy that is passing out these huge sentences is the same guy that is getting off scot-free. No one took the time to look back at his previous cases to see the major differences in [the] sentencing of Black people versus him sentencing white people. And I realize now that it's going to take time to make the changes that I want to see.

And also, I've done my time in prison, but I still have eleven years on paper, which is pretty much the same thing as being in prison. There are certain things I can and can't do. I have six years of parole and five years of probation. That's a lot. To me, I'm still in prison. I have to report to my parole officer. And after leaving my job because of racism, I have to figure out how I'm going to explain it to him because I refuse to work in a place like that and under those conditions.

CM: That time on parole and probation is a lot because if you had a ten-year-old, that wouldn't be done until that person was twenty-one. It's unnecessary. I don't even know what to say about that amount of time.

This year has been full of uprisings against policing; what are you thinking about most right now? What are you noticing in our movements?

KP: Since I just got out, I've been trying to get used to this new world, I've been trying to get used to this pandemic. I'm really thinking about how I can help my friends on the inside. I'm really noticing that there's a lot of issues to work on and a lot of fighting between people. There are police issues, there's jails and prisons, there's all kinds of issues. I really wish that different organizations and groups would come together better and talk more because I think that would help more. And I wish they would talk to more trans people, more Black trans people specifically.

CM: George Floyd was killed where I live in Minneapolis, on my birthday, a couple of blocks from where I was at that very moment on my birthday. And of course, me being me, I was at the protests and demonstrations. Let's also not forget that Minnesota and Minneapolis have a history of police violence. We remember Philando Castile [who] was killed in Minnesota in 2016, which was also not too far from where I was living at that time. So, this wasn't anything new to us, this wasn't the first time that this had happened here, or any other place for that matter where police are. Because this will happen as long as police continue to exist.

A couple of days after George Floyd's murder, there was a viral video of a Black trans woman named Iyanna Dior, who was mobbed and beaten by a group of men right here in St. Paul, Minnesota. And as soon as I saw the video I was thinking, Where is the energy when trans people get killed? Trans people get killed by cops too. Where is that energy? Where are folks?

I'm working on a project on the invisibility that Black queer, trans, and [gender] nonconforming folks feel in activism. There have been so many accounts of me being in activist spaces, and I was seen as just not being there. I was at a big conference in St. Louis one time with a friend, and we took part in a demonstration that was happening in the city. And we were out there on this hot-ass bridge, damn near about to die, it's hot, all in the name of police violence and #BlackLivesMatter. And I'm always in the front of these lines, but in the back of my head I'm always wondering *How much do my Black life matter?* After we all met to talk and debrief, I remember one of the organizers was passing the mic around. After a cis dude was on the mic, an organizer asked me if I wanted to say something. But after she asked me that, some dude rushed over and grabbed the mic and said, "Nah, nah, nah, let this brother right here talk." So not only are people devaluing femme voices in these movements when we're supposed to be "equal," but why didn't y'all feel like there was leadership in my story or anything that I would've said, or from any other woman or trans person in that moment? I just felt like he really tried to make me feel really small and really silenced. That pissed me off. From that day, I've just been very aware of the misogyny, transphobia, and queerphobia that exists within our movements. Anti-trans violence is anti-Black violence. If you don't value my life as [a] Black person because you see me as trans, then you see me as Other. That's anti-Black violence.

What are your visions for the future?

KP: I want to do something that really highlights all trans people and all gender nonconforming people. We have so much to give. And it's not as if we're trying to take from people or trying to make it seem as if other people are less important, because we're all important and we're all in this together. I want to put in the work to take steps to make change.

I'm currently working with Blue to start going out and speaking at some point. I want to talk to more people, and not just trans men, but all trans people. I feel like if we get out more and talk about ourselves more in places where people really want to hear and really want to make a change, then it would be good. For me, it's going to be about me finding my place in activism and going out and speaking and having a voice and making sure that it's heard. I want to talk about ways to support our people.

I want to help all of my friends that I made when I was inside because a lot of them are doing long sentences. Prisons just take things away from people. They also hurt people's families and friends.

CM: I'm working on the Survived & Punished project. I'm also highlighting the issues of invisibility of queer and trans folks within our own communities. I'm highlighting solutions to combat the -isms that are within our community. I'm also working on some video projects. I'm a nerdy, geeky type of person. I'm into fantasy, sci-fi type of ordeals, in the way that you can question existence through sci-fi tropes like androids and mutants and using our everyday issues to kind of highlight very true and real stories. I want to do a sci-fi retelling of trans and queer existence within Black culture through talking about different deities that often get portrayed as being cishet but aren't.

And I think some of the conversations we're having now are late and passé. We should be moving beyond trying to figure out how to accept trans and queer people in our movements. We've been here. We've led the movements. We've created some of the movements. So, let's not act like we don't get it, honey. I'm going to forever find ways to create and support my community.

Lacey Johnson, *Tower Card*, 2020

Tower Card is a collage of Pamela Coleman Smith's illustration of the Tower Card from her tarot deck drawn in 1909 and the Oakland Police Department's main headquarters, which is also a tower. The Tower Card from the tarot deck symbolizes things falling apart, structural destruction before a rebirth. Feeling into the quality of time in June 2020, I kept thinking about it being Tower Card Time and wanted to create an image to reflect that. Tarot cards can be tools used to read the qualities of time, and recontextualizing Pamela Coleman's Smith's tower made sense to me both as a symbol and a map to the future, on the way to a rebirth.

CONTRIBUTORS

molly ackhurst (Birkbeck College, SurvivorsUK, Act Build Change) has a practice-based background having worked in sexual violence support for nearly a decade. They love to think about how to break imaginative strangleholds, and currently exist as an activist/writer/facilitator specializing in creative and transformative approaches to trauma and justice.

Anne-lise Ah-fat (Undercurrent Vic, Narrm letter writing to people in prison, Radio A and A, Incendium Radical Library, Healing through Arts) is a community organizer and facilitator living on the stolen land of the Wurundjeri & Bunurong peoples. She loves to reflect on and practice transformative justice in communities she is part of. Anne-lise supports people who cause harm in journeys of accountability and change, and she believes that individual and social transformation can only occur collectively.

Alisa Bierria is a Black feminist philosopher and an assistant professor in the Department of Gender Studies at UCLA. Her writing can be found in numerous scholarly journals and public anthologies, including the coedited volume, *Community Accountability: Emerging Movements to Transform Violence*, a special issue of *Social Justice*. She has been an advocate within the feminist anti-violence movement for over twenty-five years, including cofounding Survived & Punished, a national abolitionist organization that advocates for the decriminalization of survivors of domestic and sexual violence.

Melanie Brazzell (What *really* makes us safe? Project, University of California, Santa Barbara) is a transformative justice researcher and practitioner who has worked in both the US and Germany. As a PhD student in sociology, they explore participatory action research as a movement building tool.

Jakeya Caruthers is Assistant Professor of the Program in English and in the Program in Africana Studies at Drexel University. Her research attends to Black political aesthetics within twentieth- and twenty-first-century cultural production as well as race, gender, sexuality, and state discipline. Jakeya is a principal investigator of an inside-outside research initiative with Survived & Punished California that maps pathways between surviving gender violence, incarceration, and radical possibilities for survivor release. She is also collaborating on a digital archive of feminist decriminalization campaigns waged over the last fifty years.

Lauren Caulfield or Loz (Abolitionist & Transformative Justice Centre collective, Ban Spit Hoods campaign) is an immigrant/occupier living on the unceded land of the Wurundjeri People of the Kulin Nation. She is a community organizer and anti-violence worker/researcher working at the intersection of interpersonal and state-sanctioned gender violence, and coordinates the Policing Family Violence: Changing the Story project. She deeply believes in the creative, resistive, and generative power of communities.

Chris Finley is a member of the Colville Confederated Tribes located in what is now called eastern Washington state. She received her PhD in American culture from the University of Michigan and is a coeditor and contributor to *Queer Indigenous Studies: Critical Interventions in Theory, Politics and Literature* (University of Arizona Press, 2011). Currently, she lives on Tongva land and is an assistant professor of American studies and ethnicity at the University of Southern California.

Joseph Hankins is Associate Professor of Anthropology and former director of the Critical Gender Studies program at the University of California, San Diego. He has been a member of the Los Angeles chapter of the California Coalition for Women Prisoners since 2016.

April Harris is a writer who is incarcerated at the California Institution for Women in Chino, California. April has years of experience advocating for the health, well-being, and freedom of incarcerated people. She has been interviewed by *LA Weekly, The Guardian, San Francisco Chronicle, Washington Post,* and *Solitary Watch,* among other outlets. She is also a longtime member of the California Coalition for Women Prisoners.

Mimi Kim (INCITE!, Creative Interventions, California State University, Long Beach) is a longtime advocate and activist working on issues of gender-based violence in communities of color. She is a cofounder of INCITE! and the founder of Creative Interventions, an organization committed to collective, liberatory, and non-criminalizing transformative justice and community accountability strategies. Mimi is an associate professor of social work at California State University, Long Beach.

Victoria Law is a freelance writer and editor focused on the intersections between mass incarceration, gender, and resistance. She is the author of *Resistance Behind Bars: The Struggles of Incarcerated Women* and *"Prisons Make Us Safer": And 20 Other Myths About Mass Incarceration* and coauthor of *Prison By Any Other Name.*

Colby Lenz is a long-term advocate with the California Coalition for Women Prisoners and the Transgender Advocacy Group (TAG) and a cofounder of Survived & Punished, a national organizing project to end the criminalization of survivors of sexual and domestic violence. Colby has twenty years of experience in grassroots organizing, community-engaged research, and policy advocacy addressing the intersections of criminalization, incarceration, and gender-based violence. Colby is the deputy director of policy and community research at the UCLA Center for the Study of Women.

Shirley Leslie (Critical Resistance): I am the national development coordinator at Critical Resistance. After having been radicalized over the past few years, I searched for a political home and, thankfully, found CR. Recent heavy involvement in a local jail campaign was my first direct organizing experience, and it showed me the importance of community political education and involvement, self-determination, and fervent organizing and advocacy for community needs to be met.

Brooke Lober is a teacher, writer, and social movement scholar who is currently researching legacies of anti-racist and anti-Zionist feminisms in the Bay Area. Brooke's writing is published in the scholarly journals *Feminist Formations, Women's Studies*, the *Journal of Lesbian Studies, Meridians: Feminism, Race, Transnationalism*, and on numerous websites of radical culture.

Meenakshi Mannoe (Pivot, Vancouver Prison Justice Day Committee, Defund 604 Network) is a settler of Indian and Surinamese descent living on the unceded territories of the Musqueam, Squamish, and Tsleil-Waututh peoples in so-called Vancouver, BC. She works as the criminalization & policing campaigner at Pivot Legal Society and organizes with local groups to dismantle colonial, carceral violence in its many forms.

CeCe McDonald is an artist, organizer, and activist committed to dismantling the PIC and winning the liberation of all oppressed people. As a Black trans woman and a survivor of white supremacist and transphobic violence and the PIC, these issues are core to CeCe's life. While incarcerated, CeCe's evocative and thoughtful writing inspired an international community of activists to support #FreeCeCe and movements for trans liberation and prison abolition.

Erica R. Meiners (Critical Resistance, Prison Neighborhood Art & Education Project, Northeastern Illinois University) is a writer, educator, and organizer. Her work includes a coedited anthology *The Long Term: Resisting Life Sentences, Working Toward Freedom* (Haymarket Books, 2018) and *The Feminist and the Sex Offender* (Verso Press, 2020) which explores feminist culpability and resistance to the mounting sex offender regime. She is also a coauthor of the book *Abolition. Feminism. Now.* (Haymarket Books, 2022).

Kelsey Mohamed (Cradle Community, Community Action on Prison Expansion) is a London-based feminist abolitionist organizer, facilitator, and transformative justice practitioner, focusing on campaigns against state, domestic, and sexual violence. In 2021 Cradle Community published *Brick by Brick: How We Build a World Without Prisons*, a grassroots organizing manual for abolition in the UK.

Nadine Naber is an award-winning author, public speaker, and activist. She is a professor at the University of Illinois and directs the project Liberate Your Research. She has authored or coedited five books. She cofounded Arab and Muslim American Studies at the University of Michigan; the Arab American Cultural Center at the University of Illinois; and the organizations the Arab Women's Solidarity Association North America and Mamas Activating Movements for Abolition and Solidarity.

Gloria Negrete-Lopez (she/her/ella) is a doctoral candidate in gender and women's studies with a minor in Mexican American studies at the University of Arizona. Her dissertation, "Imagining Freedom: Criminalization, Visuality, and the Circulation of Abolitionist Messages," focuses on the need to abolish the criminalization of migration. Research interests include: gender studies, Latinx studies, visual/cultural studies, migration studies, and critical prison studies.

Ky Peterson is a trans advocate who served nine years in prison for self-defense. During his incarceration, he fought for trans prisoners' rights to medical care. Ky is vibrant, intelligent, and uncommonly kind with a genuinely loving nature, and a passion for promoting human rights and transgender equality. In 2017, Ky cofounded Freedom Overground with Pinky Shear. Today, Ky shares his story of courage and perseverance with TGNC communities across the country.

Minh-Ha T. Pham is a researcher and writer whose work focuses on fashion labor under global and digital capitalism. She has published in a wide range of scholarly and mainstream publications, including the

New Republic, The Nation, New York Times, Jacobin, and *The Atlantic.* She's also the author of *Asians Wear Clothes on the Internet: Race, Gender, and the Work of Personal Style Blogging* (Duke University Press, 2015) and *Why We Can't Have Nice Things: Social Media's Influence on Fashion, Ethics, and Property* (Duke University Press, 2022).

Romarilyn Ralston identifies as a black feminist abolitionist with incarceration experience. She earned a bachelor's degree in gender & feminist studies from Pitzer College and a master's degree in liberal arts from Washington University in St. Louis after twenty-three years of incarceration. She is the program director of Project Rebound at California State University, Fullerton and chaired the CSU Project Rebound Consortium Policy & Advocacy Committee. She is a long-time organizer with the California Coalition for Women Prisoners and serves on the leadership committee. Romarilyn sits on several national boards, including the Alliance for Higher Education in Prison and Freedom Reads. In 2022, she received a full pardon from Governor Gavin Newsom.

Ana Clarissa Rojas Durazo practices transformative mama pedagogies by day while decolonizing chicanx studies by trade. At University of California, Davis, Clarissa is affiliated with cultural studies and gender studies. Clarissa is an internationally published poet who believes the creative spirit ends violence. She cofounded INCITE! and coedited *Color of Violence: The INCITE! Anthology* and *Community Accountability: Emerging Movements to Transform Violence.* Her writing has appeared recently in *Politico, Truthout,* and *Basta Anthology: 100 Latinas Write on Violence Against Women.*

Samah Saleh is an assistant professor in the Department of Social Work and the coordinator for the Women's studies master's degree program at An-Najah National University in Nablus. She is currently researching the development of the social work profession in Palestine, with an emphasis on community development. She is interested in researching gender and politics, social solidarity economy, and women empowerment. She is an activist with many organizations that focus on women, community development, and social solidarity economy.

Tina Shull (she/hers) is an assistant professor of history at University of North Carolina, Charlotte, specializing in race, empire, migrant detention, and climate justice in the modern US and world. Her first book, *Detention Empire: Reagan's Total War on Immigrants and the Seeds of Resistance*, is forthcoming with UNC Press in 2022. Shull directs the digital history project Climate Refugee Stories and was named a Soros Justice Fellow in 2016 for her work in immigration detention storytelling.

Dean Spade has been working to build queer and trans liberation based in racial and economic justice for the past two decades. He's the author of *Normal Life: Administrative Violence, Critical Trans Politics, and the Limits of Law* and the director of the documentary *Pinkwashing Exposed: Seattle Fights Back!* His latest book, *Mutual Aid: Building Solidarity during This Crisis (and the Next)*, was published by Verso Press in October 2020.

Ash Stephens is a Black trans writer and organizer and part of the abolitionist genealogies of the collectives Love and Protect, Chicago Community Bond Fund, and the New York City chapter of Survived and Punished. A decade ago, they became active in campaigns to support women and TGNC people who are criminalized for self-defense. Ash is a postdoctoral scholar at the University of Illinois at Chicago, researching policing and surveillance of TGNC people from an abolitionist framework.

Vanessa E. Thompson (Goethe University Frankfurt, Copwatch_ffm, International Independent Commission on the Death of Oury Jalloh) is a postdoctoral researcher and lecturer at the Department of Social Sciences at Goethe University Frankfurt. Her research and teaching are focused on critical racism studies, Black studies, feminist theories, post- and decolonial feminist theories and methodologies, critiques of policing, and transformative and abolitionist justice. Vanessa is also engaged in these fields as a community activist.

Emily Thuma is Assistant Professor of U.S. Politics and Law at the University of Washington, Tacoma, and Adjunct Assistant Professor of Gender, Women, and Sexuality Studies at the University of Washington, Seattle. She is the author of *All Our Trials: Prisons, Policing, and the Feminist Fight to End Violence*, published by the University of Illinois Press.

ARTISTS

Asantewaa Boykin is a San Diego native, Emergency RN, daughter of Valerie Boykin and granddaughter of Bertha Brandy. Her poetry combines her love of words, storytelling, and resistance, exploring topics like space-travel, Black femme militancy, and motherhood, which describes her first full-length poetry collection, *Love, Lyric and Liberation*. Asantewaa is cofounder of Anti Police-Terror Project, an organization committed to the eradication of police terror in all of its forms. Along with being a dedicated nurse, she is also a founding member of the Capital City Black Nurses Association. Asantewaa, along with a brave group of organizers and medical professionals, developed Mental Health First or MH FIRST, a mobile mental health crisis response team aimed at minimizing police contact with those who are in the midst of a mental health crisis. While her greatest honor is being the mother of her son, Ajani, and bonus daughter, Aryana, and granddaughter Lilith.

Esmat Elhalaby is a historian of West and South Asia. He teaches at the University of Toronto.

Maria Gaspar's *Disappearance Suit* is an ongoing series that examines marginalized identities in contemporary American culture and beyond. Maria Gaspar, a first-generation Mexican American from an immigrant family, stages performances that contend with the relationship between the politicized body and rural, remote, or romantic landscapes. Gaspar creates disappearance suits for specific locations and enacts a series of performative gestures where her camouflaged figure disappears and reappears.

Whess Harman is Carrier Wit'at, a nation amalgamated by the federal government under the Lake Babine Nation. They graduated from the Emily Carr University BFA program in 2014 and are currently living and working on the territories of the Musqueam, Squamish, and Tsleil-Waututh as the curator at grunt gallery. Their multidisciplinary practice includes beading, illustration, text, poetry, and curation. As a mixed-race, trans/nonbinary artist, they work to find their way through a tasty plethora of some kind of undiagnosed attention-deficit disorder, colonial bullshit, and queer melancholy. To the best of their patience, they do this with humor and a carefully mediated cynicism that the galleries go hog wild for.

Tori Hong: I am an emerging 2D visual artist, activist, and arts organizer. Out of my makeshift art studios, I create bold and vibrant paintings, drawings, and acrylic murals conveying complex and reciprocal relationships. I depict what we (wish to) abolish, who we spend time with, and what we make with our hands and hearts. I am, without apologies, a queer Hmong and Korean American cis woman. I am inspired by my interwoven identities and my love for this world. I root myself in my five-plus years as a community organizer and three years as an independent artist. My artistic vision is to strengthen the relationship between art and ancestors. Through my art, I build on my connections to my late grandparents and to the Hmong and Korean people who came before me . . . and to those who will come after me. My art intends to inspire, support, and challenge others to explore their own ancestral present & future ancestral connections. I see this work as contributing to the cultural and artistic legacies of my people. I view the act of creating cultures, homes, histories, and stories as a queer feminist endeavor, and it is a task I am humbled to take on.

Eileen Jimenez: Eileen's mother is Maria Cruz Jimenez, her grandmother is Eloisa Saavedra, and her great grandmother is Isidora Saavedra, matriarchs of the Otomi people. She is an Indigenous, queer artist, currently living in occupied Duwamish Territory (Seattle). In her art you will see her Mexican and Otomi stories—you see the visual representation of her soul and the colors, the culture, the visions, and the dreams that live there. As an Indigenous leader, community member, and as an artist, everything she does and creates is influenced by her many intersecting identities and lived experiences. She creates the art, the structures, the programming, and the educational experiences she wishes she and her community would have seen and had access to as a girl from the 'hood. In her current body of work, you will see her ongoing journey to heal and to share her family's and community's stories. She aims to create pieces that embody Indigenous life, joy, resilience, and relationship to land.

Lacey Johnson's art practice synthesizes the esoteric, Goddexx art, and the collective unconscious. She works with the radical creative potential of transformative justice and translates it into visual art that is part pedagogy, part manifesto, and part Bene Gesserits at a rave.

My name is **Tabitha Lean**, or as my ancestors know me, Budhin Mingaan. I am a First Nations woman of Gunditjmara descent in this land they call Australia, and I have spent two years in prison in this state, two years on home detention. Now I am on parole, or as I call it, open-air prison.

Amanda Priebe is a neurodivergent white settler artist originally from Amiskwaciwâskahikan (Edmonton), Treaty 6 Territory. She is a lifelong gardener, wild swimmer, and perpetual student of the plant kingdom. In her current home of Berlin, she organizes across colonial borders with housing justice movements and other projects of the radical imagination. Her art practice seeks to support many self-organized groups and independent community projects, and her work can be found in radical journals, books, magazines, social movement spaces, and hopefully on the streets near you.

Cristy C. Road is a Cuban American artist and musician who uses illustration, writing, and punk rock music as her preferred mediums. Blending political principles with gender and cultural identity, Road testifies to the beauty of the imperfect. Her career began in 1996, when writing the *Green'zine*, a self-published fanzine. *Green'zine* evolved from a punk rock fanzine with interviews and reviews to a personal manifesto about survival and healing from trauma. She published fourteen Green'zines and has contributed countless illustrations to punk rock, literature, and political organizations. She's since published three graphic novels that tackle gender, sexuality, cultural identity, and healing from trauma: *Indestructible* (2005), *Bad Habits* (2008), and *Spit and Passion* (2013). Her most recent project is the *Next World Tarot* (2017, 2019) a tarot card deck envisioning a world based on radical redefinitions of love and social justice. Aside from creating art, Road is a songwriter and guitarist. She currently fronts Choked Up and fronted the Homewreckers from 2008 to 2016. She lives and works in Brooklyn.

Favianna Rodriguez is an interdisciplinary artist, cultural strategist, and social justice activist based in Oakland, California. Her art and praxis address migration, gender justice, climate change, racial equity, and sexual freedom. Her signature mark-making embodies the perspective of a first-generation American Latinx artist with Afro-Latinx roots who grew up in Oakland during the era of the war on drugs and the birth of hip hop. Favianna's practice includes visual art, public art, writing, cultural organizing, and power building. In addition to her expansive studio practice, she is the cofounder and president of the Center for Cultural Power, a national organization that empowers artists to disrupt the status quo and ignite change at the intersection of culture and social justice.

Jana Traboulsi is a visual artist, graphic designer, and educator. She holds a BFA in graphic design from the American University of Beirut and an MA in media and communication studies from Goldsmiths in London. She is the cofounder and creative director of pan-Arab quarterly *Bidayat* and the artistic director of Snoubar Bayrout publishing house. In 2014, she cofounded Sigil, an art collective based in Beirut and New York. In addition to commissioned and collective projects, her work explores creative methods of research and the relation between text and image as a place for critical thought and commentary, often bridging between the personal and the socio-political. Since 2004, she has been teaching design and illustration studios and lectures in history and theory. She recently joined ESAV–Marrakech as the pedagogical director of the graphic and digital design department.

INDEX

ABOUT HAYMARKET BOOKS

Haymarket Books is a radical, independent, nonprofit book publisher based in Chicago.

Our mission is to publish books that contribute to struggles for social and economic justice. We strive to make our books a vibrant and organic part of social movements and the education and development of a critical, engaged, international left.

We take inspiration and courage from our namesakes, the Haymarket martyrs, who gave their lives fighting for a better world. Their 1886 struggle for the eight-hour day—which gave us May Day, the international workers' holiday—reminds workers around the world that ordinary people can organize and struggle for their own liberation. These struggles continue today across the globe—struggles against oppression, exploitation, poverty, and war.

Since our founding in 2001, Haymarket Books has published more than five hundred titles. Radically independent, we seek to drive a wedge into the risk-averse world of corporate book publishing. Our authors include Noam Chomsky, Arundhati Roy, Rebecca Solnit, Angela Y. Davis, Howard Zinn, Amy Goodman, Wallace Shawn, Mike Davis, Winona LaDuke, Ilan Pappé, Richard Wolff, Dave Zirin, Keeanga-Yamahtta Taylor, Nick Turse, Dahr Jamail, David Barsamian, Elizabeth Laird, Amira Hass, Mark Steel, Avi Lewis, Naomi Klein, and Neil Davidson. We are also the trade publishers of the acclaimed Historical Materialism Book Series and of Dispatch Books.

ALSO AVAILABLE FROM HAYMARKET BOOKS

Abolishing State Violence: A World Beyond Bombs, Borders, and Cages
Ray Acheson

Abolition. Feminism. Now.
Angela Y. Davis, Gina Dent, Erica R. Meiners, and Beth E. Richie

Assata Taught Me
State Violence, Racial Capitalism, and the Movement for Black Lives
by Donna Murch

Community as Rebellion
A Syllabus for Surviving Academia as a Woman of Color
Lorgia García Peña

How We Get Free: Black Feminism and the Combahee River Collective
Edited by Keeanga-Yamahtta Taylor

Freedom Is a Constant Struggle
Ferguson, Palestine, and the Foundations of a Movement
Angela Y. Davis, edited by Frank Barat, preface by Cornel West

Rehearsals for Living
Robyn Maynard and Leanne Betasamosake Simpson

#SayHerName
Black Women's Stories of State Violence and Public Silence
African American Policy Forum, edited by Kimberlé Crenshaw
Foreword by Janelle Monáe

We Do This 'Til We Free Us
Abolitionist Organizing and Transforming Justice
Mariame Kaba, edited by Tamara K. Nopper
Foreword by Naomi Murakawa